Praise for *The Red*

T0032500

"*The Red Planet: Gendered Landscapes and Violent Inequalities* explores the way dominant worldviews shrink our possibilities. Bill explains how our historical and cultural narratives have been shaped by socially constructed binaries of gender and sexuality. This book encourages questions about other ways of thinking and living, ways that are perhaps outside of mainstream ability to imagine because of the stories we have been given."—**Jean Alger**, PhD, Professor of English, Trinidad State College

"*The Red Planet* reminds us that our stories are part of us and that we remake and retell them as tools. We choose whether to use them for power over one another, animals, and Earth, or for peace. Hatcher leads us to the edge of what we "know" to better reflect on our options."—**Kara Davis**, Director of Impact, Unovis Asset Management, contributing author to *Letters to a New Vegan*, and co-editor of *Defiant Daughters*

"*The Red Planet* offers its readers a journey through [the] introspection of self, others, societies, and the narratives that have shaped them. This book provides a pathway of understanding through Bill Hatcher's careful and thoughtful investigation into the stories that have fashioned traditional perceptions of race, gender, sex, and the environment."—**Jennifer Fluri**, PhD, Professor of Geography, University of Colorado, Boulder

"I loved the book! It exposed me to so many new ideas and thought processes that could help save us and our planet!"—**Bridgett Larsen**, Geography student, Pikes Peak State College

"Reading *The Red Planet* is an incredible journey that sparked my imagination! It is filled with both thought-provoking fairy tales and profound scientific insights. It not only shed light on the fascinating connection between geography and human evolution but also challenged and informed my understanding of masculinity and femininity."—**Zhen Li**, Geography student, Colorado Mountain College

"The power of [Andean mound sites] is a specific example of the long view of humanity taken in *The Red Planet*. Using a Gendered Landscapes Theory, Bill Hatcher shows how geography may originally have shaped people's minds and cultures which, in turn, reshaped their geography."—**Kimberly Munro**, PhD, Assistant Instructor of Anthropology, New Mexico Highlands University

"I applaud [Bill's] passion . . . *The Red Planet* gives important background on the origins of patriarchal policy that prioritizes domination and exploitation, as opposed to prioritizing the well-being of the planet and the acknowledgment of the sacred feminine."—**Dominique Naccarato**, Lecturer, Clark School of Environment and Sustainability, Director of the Integrated Public Land Management Track, Western Colorado University

"[*The Red Planet*] is excellent . . . As an anthropologist, I particularly appreciated the emphasis on the cultural construction of gender roles, norms, and stereotypes. The author is skillful at holistically blending the historical . . . and [the] contemporary."—**Jaden Netwig**, PhD, Professor of Anthropology, Arapahoe Community College

"I really enjoyed reading this book! It challenged ideologies from both sides while providing information on why, which I found very interesting and useful. The overarching understanding and detail about each topic made it much easier to comprehend the ideas behind each chapter."—**Avery Paull-McGurran**, Geography student, Colorado Mountain College

"*The Red Planet* connects the history of gendered and violent inequalities to landscapes, physical geographies, practices of food sourcing, valuation of metals, spiritual practices and religiosity to name a few. Breaking from traditional analysis, *The Red Planet* provides an expansive view of gendered inequalities as woven throughout human evolution; adapting through space and place to demonstrate how gendered violence is not natural, but a product of human socialization and culture."—**Heidi Schneider**, PhD, Associate Professor and Chair, Department of Sociology, Inclusive Excellence Liaison, Adams State University

"*The Red Planet* is a meaningful contribution to the social sciences of storytelling. This is an accessible inquiry into the tales that are common to various cultures and thoughtful commentary on the hegemonic nature of these stories. This book is a creative blend of folklore and cultural critique, and it makes a strong argument for Gendered Landscapes Theory. This is a useful text for students, scholars, and intellectuals that take interest in the role of stories in human cultures and societal norms."—**Patrick W. Staib**, PhD, Professor and Chair of Social Sciences, Colorado Mountain College

"This book was very fascinating and helped me remember how much I enjoy social sciences such as sociology and psychology. It reminded me of Jared Diamond's *Guns, Germs, and Steel*, but on an adjacent topic, and more focused and nuanced."—**Parker Stein**, Geography student, Colorado Mountain College

"*The Red Planet* taught me to be proud that I am a woman. No matter how the media, religions or others' opinions say, I am not weak because of my gender, I know that I am strong and I am just as capable as anyone else. I learned so much about myself and other cultures and beliefs. *The Red Planet* made me feel validated and heard. I really enjoyed this book and seriously can't wait for the hard copy to come out. I will definitely be reading this again."—**Andi Stephenson**, Geography student, Pikes Peak State College

"I really enjoyed reading *The Red Planet*. This book doesn't try to change your mind but presents statements of fact as they are in our history. If we are to evoke change and be a better species then this book is a good guide to learning how to get on a path to change a mindset."—**Josephine Trenkler**, Geography student, Pikes Peak State College

Also by Bill Hatcher

The Marble Room
How I Lost God and Found Myself in Africa

Principles of Flight
Flying Bush Planes Through a World of War, Sexism, and Meat
(Finalist in the 2018 National Indie Excellence Awards in Social and
Political Change)

THE RED PLANET

GENDERED
LANDSCAPES
AND
VIOLENT
INEQUALITIES

BILL HATCHER

Lantern Publishing & Media ● Woodstock and Brooklyn, NY

2024
Lantern Publishing & Media
PO Box 1350
Woodstock, NY 12498
www.lanternpm.org

Cover design by Cecilia Magalí Torres

Printed in the United States of America

Library of Congress Cataloging-in-Publication Data

Names: Hatcher, Bill, author.
Title: The red planet : gendered landscapes and violent inequalities / Bill Hatcher.
Description: Woodstock, NY ; Brooklyn, NY : Lantern Publishing & Media, [2024]
    | Includes bibliographical references and index.
Identifiers: LCCN 2023028898 (print) | LCCN 2023028899 (ebook) | ISBN
    9781590567265 (paperback) | ISBN 9781590567272 (epub)
Subjects: LCSH: Human geography. | Storytelling. | Geographical perception. | Sex
    role. | Masculinity. | Femininity (Philosophy) | Intersectionality (Sociology)
    | Nature—Effect of human beings on. | Global environmental change. |
    Environmentalism.
Classification: LCC GF95 .H38 2024 (print) | LCC GF95 (ebook) | DDC 304.2—dc23/
    eng/20240116
LC record available at https://lccn.loc.gov/2023028898
LC ebook record available at https://lccn.loc.gov/2023028899

To Kim
For all the love and light you bring into the world.

And to all those who work for social justice, environmental
ethics, and animal rights.

CONTENTS

Illustrations and Credits xi

Foreword by Jennifer L. Fluri, PhD 1

Questioning Our Stories by Jean Alger, PhD 5

On the Personhood of Place in the Andes by Kimberly Munro, PhD 9

Introduction: *Rapunzel* 13

PART ONE:
Forests and Savannas: >60,000–12,000 BP

Chapter 1. *The Genesis Tree* 27

Chapter 2. *Pangendered Landscapes:*
                 The Deep Backstory 37

Chapter 3. *The Irrational Revolution:*
                 Spirits, Art, and Life 57

PART TWO:
River Valleys and Coastal Plains: 12,000–6,000 BP

Chapter 4. *Pandora's Box* 69

Chapter 5. *Feminine Landscapes* 73

Chapter 6. *The Horticultural Revolution:*
                 Goddesses, Matriarchy, and Birth 83

PART THREE:

Deserts, Plains, and Mountains: 6,000 BP–Present

Chapter 7. *The Smith and the Devil*... 97

Chapter 8. *Masculine Landscapes*... 103

Chapter 9. *The Hyper-Masculine Devolution:*
                     Gods, Patriarchy, and Death...................................... 113

PART FOUR:

Pangaea: It Takes a Planet

Chapter 10. *The Lorax* 129

Chapter 11. *Transformed Landscapes*.. 135

Chapter 12. *The Consciousness Revolution: Rebirth*............................ 151

Resources 163

Acknowledgments...175

Bibliography 179

Notes..197

Glossary 221

Index..225

About the Author
About the Publisher

ILLUSTRATIONS AND CREDITS

Illus. 1.   Approximate area of human (*Homo sapiens*) habitation and population density, 100,000–60,000 BP (Bill Hatcher), p. 25

Illus. 2.   Cave painting created by the San people, Cederberg Cave near Stadsaal, South Africa (Wikimedia Commons, Public Domain, https://commons.wikimedia.org/wiki/File:San_Rock_Art_-_Cederberg.jpg), p. 28

Illus. 3.   Khoisan rock art of tree and humans, Lake Chivero, Zimbabwe (Trust for African Rock Art, https://africanrockart.org/trees-rock-art/), p. 30

Illus. 4.   Blyde River Canyon, South Africa. Pangendered landscape of river valley in subtropical forest with mountains (Paul Tosio, CC BY-SA 3.0, https://commons.wikimedia.org/w/index.php?curid=56609030), p. 41

Illus. 5.   *The Druid Grove*, artist unknown. Sacred Celtic tree, possibly an oak tree, in *Old England: A Pictorial Museum* by Charles Knight, c.1845 (public domain, https://commons.wikimedia.org/wiki/File:The_Druid_Grove.PNG), p. 42

Illus. 6.   Replica of pictograph of horses, aurochs, and rhinoceroses, Lascaux Cave, Chauvet-Pont-d'Arc, c.32,000 BP, in the Anthropos Museum, Brno, Czech Republic (Wikimedia Commons, Public Domain, https://commons.wikimedia.org/wiki/File:Paintings_from_the_Chauvet_cave_%28museum_replica%29.jpg), p. 45

Illus. 7.   "Happy 'Holladays,'" boys get guns during holidays
              (Upbeat   News,   https://upbeatnews.com/spa/these-
              controversial-vintage-ads-would-instantly-be-banned-
              today?utm_source=google&utm_medium=kl&utm_
              content=ga_kl_003&utm_term=www.npr.
              org&utm_campaign=un_ga_vintage_dt_
              us_0520_001_kl&gclid=EAIaIQobChMIqtnN-vrz8AIV
              AoCmBB3JjwDwEAEYASAAEgK9M_D_BwE), p. 47

Illus. 8.   The *Löwenmensch*, or Lion-man of the Hohlenstein-Stadel, an
              ivory figurine, estimated to date from 35,000 to 40,000 BP,
              p. 61

Illus. 9.   Approximate area of human habitation and population
              density, c.12,000 BP (Bill Hatcher), p. 67

Illus. 10.   Feminine landscape: Tropical rainforest with stream
              (Designed by Freepik, Photo tropical jungles of southeast Asia,
              https://www.freepik.com/premium-photo/tropical-jungles-
              southeastasia_15617299.htm#page=3&query=tropical%20
              rainforest&position=23&from_
              view=keyword&track=aisp.), p. 77

Illus. 11.   Masculine landscape: Monument Valley, Arizona (Designed by
              Freepik, Monument Valley, Arizona USA, https://www.freepik.
              com/free-photo/monument-valley-blue-sky-usa_10470189.
              htm?query=desert%20butte#from_view=detail_alsolike), p. 78

Illus. 12.   Goddess on World Mountain, engraved gold, Minoan Crete,
              c.1,400 BCE (Eric Edwards Collected Works, https://ericwed-
              wards.files.wordpress.com/2013/07/image-216.jpg), p. 81

Illus. 13.   Venus of Laussel, Dordogn, France, c.23,000 BCE (Jessica
              Lieu, Creative Commons, https://www.worldhistory.org/
              image/6866/the-venus-of-laussel/), p. 88

Illus. 14.   Artist's depiction of Çatalhöyük (Dan Lewandowski, http://
              www.sci-news.com/archaeology/science-catalhoyuk-map-
              mural-volcanic-eruption-01681.html), p. 90

Illus. 15.　Mother Goddess, Çatalhöyük, seated on lioness/leopard throne while giving birth, c.6,000 BCE (Ankara Museum, Wikimedia Commons, https://commons.wikimedia.org/wiki/File:Ankara_Muzeum_B19-36.jpg), p. 92

Illus. 16.　Approximate area of human habitation and population density, c.6,000 BP (Bill Hatcher), p. 95

Illus. 17.　"Men Are Better Than Women!" (Upbeat News, https://upbeatnews.com/spa/these-controversial-vintage-ads-would-instantly-be-banned-today?utm_source=google&utm_medium=kl&utm_content=ga_kl_003&utm_term=www.npr.org&utm_campaign=un_ga_vintage_dt_us_0520_001_kl&gclid=EAIaIQobChMIqtnN-vrz8AIVAoCmBB3JjwDwEAEYASAAEgK9M_D_BwE), p. 105

Illus. 18.　Köppen World Climate Classification System (Updated world map of the Köppen-Geiger climate classification, by Peel, M. C., Finlayson, B. L., and McMahon, T. A. (University of Melbourne); (Supplement), CC BY-SA 3.0, Wikimedia Commons, https://commons.wikimedia.org/w/index.php?curid=14747893), p. 107

Illus. 19.　Sumerian cuneiform tablet: A Private Letter (Zeray Peter, Gift of Mr. and Mrs. J. J. Klejman, 1966 to the New York Metropolitan Museum of Art, donated to Wikimedia Creative Commons, https://commons.wikimedia.org/wiki/File:Cuneiform_tablet-_private_letter_MET_DP-13441-002.jpg), p. 115

Illus. 20.　"It's Nice to Have a Girl around the House" (Upbeat News, https://upbeatnews.com/spa/these-controversial-vintage-ads-would-instantly-be-banned-today?utm_source=google&utm_medium=kl&utm_content=ga_kl_003&utm_term=www.npr.org&utm_campaign=un_ga_vintage_dt_us_0520_001_kl&gclid=EAIaIQobChMIqtnN-vrz8AIVAoCmBB3JjwDwEAEYASAAEgK9M_D_BwE), p. 126

Illus. 21.   Approximate area of human habitation and population
                density, present day (Bill Hatcher), p. 127

Illus. 22.   *The Lorax* (Pinterest commons, https://www.pinterest.com/
                pin/110338259592975860/), p. 130

Illus. 23.   Percentage share of US wealth per income bracket (created by
                Bill Hatcher, after Wolff, 2017, https://www.nber.org/system/
                files/working_papers/w24085/w24085.pdf), p. 138

Illus. 24.   "Do You Still Beat Your Wife?" (Upbeat News, https://
                upbeatnews.com/spa/these-controversial-vintage-ads-would-
                instantly-be-banned-today?utm_source=google&utm_
                medium=kl&utm_content=ga_kl_003&utm_term=www.
                npr.org&utm_campaign=un_ga_vintage_dt_us_0520_001_
                kl&gclid=EAIaIQobChMIqtnN-vrz8AIVAoCmBB3JjwDwEA
                EYASAAEgK9M_D_BwE), p. 144

Illus. 25.   "Tender, Juicy Beef. What's Your Cut?" (Pinterest commons,
                https://www.pinterest.com/pin/338332990736656641/?d=t
                &mt=login), p. 146

Illus. 26.   Map of US military presence in US and abroad as of 30
                September 2021 (Wikimedia Creative Commons, https://
                commons.wikimedia.org/wiki/File:US_Troops_on_duty_
                as_of_September_30_2021.png), p. 148

Illus. 27.   The expanding concept of rights (after Nash, 1989), p. 155

Illus. 28.   Pangaea: Modern political map (Wikipedia commons,
                https://commons.wikimedia.org/wiki/File:Pangea_political.
                jpg), p. 160

FOREWORD

Jennifer L. Fluri, PhD

Which stories reveal the nature of being? Which narratives have shaped your understanding of gender, race, class, and your place in society? When I pose these questions, most people respond with silence. In reflecting and considering how stories have influenced how we understand people and places, I'm reminded of an old joke recently made famous by novelist David Foster Wallace:

> These two young fish are swimming along, and an older fish swims by and says: "Morning, boys! How's the water?" And the two young fish just kind of look at each other and then keep swimming. And then, after a while, one says to the other, "What the hell is water?"

The water represents the stories that engulf us in ways we cannot see. We often do not recognize how these stories have shaped our lives and societies precisely because we are swimming in them—they are all around us. We are the fish, and the grand or dominant narratives surrounding us are the water, repeated over and over again throughout our lives. They have shaped us and become so ordinary that we do not recognize their influence, power, or control over how we know others, ourselves, and our place in the world. Some stories offer different tales, counter-narratives that challenge the conventional chronicles that we believe are foundational to our existence. These counter-narratives are received

1

by most people initially with skepticism, even viewed as threatening by many in positions of power who benefit from the conventional stories that support or bolster their authority.

As a feminist political geographer, I have studied places much different from my home location. My training as a social scientist includes engaging in the practice of self-reflexivity and positionality. Academic jargon though they may be, these two words simply ask one to reflect on one's place in the world. *Which preconceived notions do I have about diverse places and people? What are my prejudices? Which stereotypes have been foundational to my beliefs or understandings about different people? Which stories have I been told that I consumed or enjoyed, and how have they shaped my understanding? What is my position, privilege, or place in the world?* I learned to challenge the ordinary, the normative, and the everyday by asking these questions. *The Red Planet* takes its readers on a journey through this type of introspection of self, others, and societies, as well as the narratives that have shaped them. This book provides a pathway of understanding through Bill Hatcher's careful and thoughtful investigation into the stories that have fashioned traditional perceptions of race, gender, sex, and the environment.

Most of us live in a world designed and ruled by various levels and forms of patriarchy and hierarchal social and political structures. The stories told to us have helped to form our perceptions of these structures and our place within them. The stories we tell and retell shape our knowledge about ourselves, the nature of our being, and the environment we inhabit. As such, stories and myths are foundational to nearly all nations and all religions. For example, the three largest monotheistic and Abrahamic religions (Judaism, Christianity, and Islam) all rely on foundational texts (the Torah, Bible, and Quran, respectively). Most followers of these religions are taught these texts, however, through various forms of storytelling enacted predominantly by male leadership figures (rabbis, priests/reverends, and imam/mullahs). Of the three Abrahamic religions, Christianity and Islam are proselytizing.

Through conversion, these dominating religions have consumed and incorporated the social and cultural practices of existing religions and spiritual beliefs in conquered territories, in so doing recalibrating past stories to meet the objectives of new forms of storytelling. As discussed in *The Red Planet*, in many places, the patriarchal religions destroyed feminine, gender-fluid, nonviolent, and care-based belief systems, replacing them with a patriarchal social ordering that demanded a strict divide between male and female genders, regularly enforced through a combination of stories, coercion, and even violence.

In contemporary societies, stories are retold through various mediums, from fictional books, films, television, to social media influencers. These mediums also provide a platform for storytelling that refutes the dominant narratives. Fantasy and science fiction are storytelling genres that have pushed and continue to push against the narrative boundaries that rely on gender binaries as well as feminine and masculine ideals, heterosexuality, and racist hierarchies. Academic analyses have also countered staunch stereotypes and beliefs that divide and categorize and that exclude specific individuals or communities: for example, feminist approaches to understanding gender equality, gender fluidity, nonbinary and transgender identities challenge the cornerstone of patriarchal social orders reliant upon gender dichotomies. However, such alternative stories are regularly met with steadfast opposition. As theologians and historians remind us, storytelling has changed over time and across geographic spaces in ways that support the ideologies and satiate the hunger for power of social, political, and religious leaders and elites. Those who benefit from conventional narratives are vested in keeping them intact and therefore in criticizing or condemning alternative ones.

The Red Planet guides us through several foundational stories that have shaped many societies, as well as shows us how to engage with them in new ways. Diving into the waters of new interpretations of old fables, we learn how these stories came to be and how they have organized places, environments, societies, and various human relations.

This book revives ancient stories that reinforce the dominant narratives in contemporary cultures as well as tales that have not been told and repeatedly retold because they provide a reflective window into the alternative. A window that opens us up to reflecting, rethinking, and rearticulating our understanding of ourselves, others, and the diverse environments we inhabit. These replacement stories offer new ways of thinking about gender, race, and sexual norms, along with a reconnection to habitats and environments that require care and thoughtful attention rather than a massive rush to extract resources for profit and riches at the expense of people and the environment.

The Red Planet takes a fresh approach to the stories we tell and those we *should* tell about landscapes and the symbiotic relationship between animals, people, and the environments within which they live. Being attentive to our ecosystems remains essential for addressing current environmental crises such as climate change, land degradation, air pollution, toxic waste, and environmental racism. The many narratives surrounding us, which we take for granted, are like the water that the young fish cannot see. *The Red Planet* provides a guide for reconsidering these stories, much as the older and arguably wiser fish recognizes the same water as something that requires reflection and review.

Jennifer L. Fluri. PhD, Professor of Geography
University of Colorado, Boulder
11/30/2022

QUESTIONING OUR STORIES

Notes on *The Red Planet*

Jean Alger, PhD

I'm not a geographer or an anthropologist. I studied literature and rhetoric for my doctoral program and wrote my dissertation on representations of race and ethnicity in American fiction and nonfiction of the 1920s and 1930s. Prior to that, for my MA, I studied British renaissance literature (particularly women's devotional writings) and connected it to medieval mystics like Julian of Norwich as well as the concept of courtly love. The research and writing I did (and still do) center around exploring apparent "binaries" in the cultural products of the European-and-Christian– influenced culture of the United States.

When I read Bill's book and saw that he started certain chapters with a fairy tale or religious story, I felt right at home. This is the kind of work I do: looking at the cultural interpretations and implications of our stories.

Bill begins with a well-known story—*Rapunzel*—and an analysis of it, explaining how the fairy tale has roots in archetypal traditions much older than the Grimm Brothers' version, with which we are most familiar. It is interesting that the ending we know, in which the prince takes Rapunzel and their children home, is viewed as the "saving" moment in the story, when it is actually Rapunzel who saves the prince. When she hears him calling to her, "overjoyed, she [runs] through the forest to meet him, and as they [embrace], her tears of love [restore] his sight, and she [tells] him her story: After she gave birth to their twins—a girl and a boy—the three of them lived in the forest, in a hut she had built" (13).

We can see in this version that Rapunzel cared for herself and her children in the forest for years, while the prince wandered looking for her. He survived despite his blindness, but her tears and love heal him. He then takes her back to his kingdom. Through a modern lens, the removal from the wilderness is a rescue. But if Rapunzel was well and safe with her children, was rescue required? Civilization and wilderness are often pitted against each other: wilderness the threat, and civilization the safe place. This binary, imposed by Europeans as they settled in and colonized much of the world, created the false story of progress as a move away from the wilderness and into civilization, which became the root justification for and the ongoing reasoning behind various systems of oppression:

- Race theory developed around the same time as the trans-Atlantic slave trade to justify the subjugation of "less civilized" peoples at the hands of the "most civilized." This early race theory placed Nordic peoples at the top and Africans at the bottom of the racial hierarchy.* Another harmful binary we can't seem to escape is that of light versus dark, fear of the dark wilderness versus the embracing of bright, open, and cleared places.
- Women have throughout history been subjected to the same binary of the wild and the domestic and thus controlled: either their wildness

---

* For a good overview of the development of the concept of "race," see "Historical Foundations of Race" from the National Museum of African American History and Culture at the Smithsonian. https://nmaahc.si.edu/learn/talking-about-race/topics/historical-foundations-race

must be reined in and tamed, or their domesticity must be protected by the stronger, more rational, more brutal men.[*]

- The perverse has been associated with anything that fits outside of the socially constructed heteronormative "norm." The myth of the gender binary has been and continues to be enforced at the expense of trans people in all cultures, as well as in justification of patriarchal control.

As Bill writes in Chapter 3, "the symbols contained in our art, religions, stories, and cultures were in the process of evolving from a pangendered matrix to a profusion of gendered binaries" (49). From a matrix of possibilities, human worldview was reduced to binary oppositions that insisted on placing one opposite above the other and disrupted a structure that awarded power to the non-male, the non-civilized. The hyper-masculinity Bill explores shows a competitive, individualistic, and selfish world where we do what we want because we can, not because we should.

The Red Planet: Gendered Landscapes and Violent Inequalities explores the way dominant worldviews shrink our possibilities. Bill explains how our historical and cultural narratives have been shaped by socially constructed binaries of gender and sexuality. This book encourages questions about other ways of thinking and living, ways that are perhaps beyond the mainstream ability to imagine because of the stories we have been given.

---

[*] This concept is ever evolving and shifting. The Victorians believed women to be morally superior but physically weaker, unless they transgressed sexual norms, then they could never be redeemed. This, however, applied only to middle- and upper-class white women. The working class and people of color were almost always viewed as deviant, immoral, and therefore unworthy of the consideration of white women in the middle and upper classes. Women have also typically been cast as intellectually weaker (this goes all the way back to Aristotle).

Bill has written a text that would pair wonderfully with ontologies from non-European cultures, encouraging students and teachers alike to question our received wisdom and to look beyond what we think we know, how we think things have to be—to imagine new and more hopeful futures.

Jean Alger, PhD, Professor of English
Trinidad State College, Alamosa, Colorado
11/28/2022

ON THE PERSONHOOD OF PLACE IN THE ANDES

An essay for *The Red Planet*

Kimberly Munro, PhD

"Which mound do you want?" Rebecca asked me as she gave me a tour of the site. I looked around at the two mounds protruding out of the landscape—a larger, more imposing structure, and a lower one with a rounded top located 100 m directly to the west of it. "That one," I said, pointing to the smaller mound, "where you said you've been finding Recuay ceramics." She stared thoughtfully at me for a moment, a faint smile forming across her face. "Funny," she replied. "All the female crew chiefs who have worked on this project have chosen to work on that mound, while we've only had men working on the larger mound."

The two of us pondered that silently for a minute before getting to work at the site. It was my first field season working in the highland Andes, surrounded by all the majesty of deep blue skies, snowcapped mountain peaks, and green and yellow terraced fields. It is one of the most beautiful places on Earth, and for all its nurturing beauty, there is a hardness to life in the highlands—an ethereal landscape mixed with a toughness, the raw brute strength needed just to survive in the harshness of the climate and altitude. A masculine strength coated with a feminine, calming beauty that surrounded us.

That question about the mound's personhood and specific genders has always flittered in the back of my mind and in my work as an Andean archaeologist. More persistent still, however, were broader questions about deciphering the personhood of these ancient structures, the local landscapes, the personality of places and their unique histories.

The power of these places is a specific example of the long view of humanity taken in *The Red Planet*. Using Gendered Landscapes Theory, Bill Hatcher shows how geography may originally have shaped cultures and people's minds, which in turn reshaped their geography.

Human transactions with landscapes are, of course, dynamic processes. In the Andes, not only are natural landscapes interpreted as masculine or feminine forces, but they are also transformed, reshaped, and reinterpreted over time through acts of creation and emplacement.

Hualcayán, the mound site mentioned above, has a more calming personality, while Cosma, the one where I ended up running my own dissertation project, is more defensible and more aggressive. Why do some landscapes and sites feel aggressive while others are peaceful or more energizing? To understand this, we need to first discuss the ancient Andean peoples' cosmological beliefs, some of which still shape the worldview of modern Indigenous communities.

Quechua groups believe that the earth is a feminine entity, known as *Pachamama* (Mother Earth), while water—specifically running water, the ever flowing "vital life force"—is a masculine energy. This is a twist on the cosmologies of many other indigenous peoples. Still, for Andeans, the act of farming—of plowing—and the construction of irrigation canals penetrate and fertilize the feminine landscape. A masculine taming and seeding of the earth, through activities that modify or alter its natural elements, is done to produce new forms of life.

One way to view this masculine alteration is as a conquering or dominating of the motherly landscape. However, Andean beliefs are centered on dualism, or reciprocal relationships. This concept, referred to as *Ayni*, is the uniting of separate yet interlocking and interdependent parts (Stone, 2017). Ayni is a dualistic balance through creation—life born from the coming together of two distinct yet balanced elements, from what the Quechua peoples refer to as *Camay*, or the act of creating. Creation is an ever-occurring process, a constant maintenance and exchange of energetic forces that in turn animates inanimate objects into living beings. Like the flowing vital waters of rivers and canals, Camay is a dynamic source, infusing created beings with vitality or energy. This energy is specific. The energy of *Camac* (creator) and that of *Camasca* (recipient) are individualized. Because energy is not stagnant, it must constantly be exchanged. Once something is constructed, specifically a mound or a shrine, offerings must continuously be given in the form of music, dance, foods and liquids, and material goods. These gifts ensure a reciprocal exchange of life force between the creator and the created.

In the Andes, acts of emplacement laid the foundation for early landscape alterations by the Late Preceramic Period (3,000–1,800 BCE). Starting around 3,000 BCE, monumental temple complexes and *huacas* (sacred Andean mounds, shrines, standing stones, etc.) were constructed throughout the central Andes, signaling an elaborate effort made by early Andean peoples to intentionally create and bring their landscapes into being by animating the natural world around them. By 5,000 BP, large pyramid complexes could be found all along the Peruvian coast, while smaller mounds created for more exclusive/familial rituals were erected throughout the Andean highlands. Prior to this, the landscape had been mostly wild and unaltered, imbedded with animistic and natural forces. Through the making of mounds, the laying of shrines, the erecting of stone pillars or ancestral tombs, a kinship and consanguineal (blood lineage) bonds were tied to each landscape, with each monument existing as a standalone being, an entity with its own personality, history, and trajectory.

These animated entities had the power to influence, reward, and punish the living and had to exist in their own trajectories. Local landscapes then were imbued with their own life forces, personalities, and genders. Today, each community in the Andes reveres a Catholic patron saint, someone who is annually paraded through the streets and given material offerings and gifts of song, dance, and reverie. These Catholic saints have replaced the original huacas and ancestral protectors, although the latter still have the power to affect and influence the livelihood of each community member.

The Cosma center, as well as Hualcayán, are examples of how each local landscape has a personality of place, which includes birth, backstory, and gender. While much of the meaning may be lost to us, understanding Andean concepts and Indigenous worldviews may help us decipher the landscape as a text.

The more feminine nature ascribed to elements within Hualcayán may have been due to the forced removal and resettlement of the community to a *reduccion* ("reduction," or Spanish settlement) during the Colonial Era. However, in Cosma, the Indigenous community bore down hard against the Spanish, first against forced removal from their homelands and then against the exploitative hacienda system taking hold of the majority of Peru and the rest of the valley. The Cosmeños never gave up their community, reinforcing territorial, masculine attributes. This is something that can still be felt and read from the imbedded landscape, not just by myself and other anthropologists but by anyone willing to follow their story.

Kimberly Munro, PhD, Assistant Professor of Anthropology
New Mexico Highlands University, Las Vegas, New Mexico
2/26/2023

Reference Cited

Stone, R. (2017). "Dialogues in Thread: The Quechua Concepts of Ayni, Ukhu, Tinku, Q'iwa, and Ushay." In *Threads of Time: Tradition and Change in Indigenous American Textiles*, Michael C. Carlos Museum, Emory University, 2017. Digital catalogue online at http://threads-of-time.carlos.emory.edu/.

Introduction

RAPUNZEL

Once upon a time, there lived a woman and a man who longed to have a child but were unsuccessful. After many years of disappointment, the wife at last became pregnant, though the pregnancy proved difficult. Unwilling to eat, she became very weak. The one food she craved was the root of a plant called rampion, or rapuzel, which had a tiny purple flower and happened to grow only in the garden of a witch. The husband, more frightened he might lose his wife than of the witch, resolved to sneak into the garden and snatch a handful of the herb. He convinced himself that he'd be quick and quiet, and the witch would be none the wiser.

That evening, he set off just as a full moon rose. A high wall surrounded the garden, but trees grew on either side, so he climbed up one, scrambled over the wall, and climbed down another one into the garden. The world inside seemed darker, but the moon was bright, and he soon found his way to a patch of purple rampion flowers that shone black in the wan light. Reaching down, he grabbed three handfuls, stuffed them into a bag, and escaped undetected.

Once home, he prepared the greens for his wife, who had grown quite frail. With great effort, she ate, and in a short while the color returned to her face. The husband was overcome with relief, and so he returned to the garden that same night to retrieve more rampion. But this time, the witch awaited him. Threatening his entire family with a spell, she also offered a deal: She would let him go in peace and the couple could have all the rampion they wished—if they agreed to give her their firstborn child to raise as her own. With the lives of his family at stake, he reluctantly accepted her offer.

In due time, the wife gave birth to a girl and named her Rapunzel after the herb. But the couple had not forgotten the husband's promise. Tearfully, they presented their newborn to the witch, who took her back to her house in the garden.

As the child grew, the witch realized the girl might one day try to escape, so she took her to a tower deep in the forest. Situated at the very top of the tower was the only room, which had but a single window and no door. The witch, if she liked, could use her magic to come and go, but since Rapunzel's blonde hair was so long and robust, the witch instead decided to braid it and use it as a ladder. The witch brought food and supplies to Rapunzel each day by calling out to her in her gravelly voice, "Rapunzel, Rapunzel, let down your hair, that I might climb your golden stair!" Months became years, and Rapunzel grew into a beautiful young woman, though she was very sad and very lonely.

One day, a prince was riding through the forest when he heard Rapunzel's plaintive voice as she sang from her window. Through the foliage, he caught sight of her and immediately fell in love, but he was also wary of such a beautiful woman locked away in a mysterious tower so deep in the forest. For the rest of that day, he watched from a concealed location and noticed the witch who approached with food, and how she gained entrance. So, early the next morning, he sneaked up to the base of the tower and imitated the witch's gravelly voice, bidding Rapunzel to let down her braid. Ignoring a flash of uncertainty, Rapunzel obeyed the summons, and the prince climbed up. Upon seeing him in her room, she panicked and prepared to scream, though her fears vanished when he smiled. She was instantly smitten with the handsome young prince and fell in love.

In the following weeks, the prince continued to visit Rapunzel in secret, and as the two shared their love, they planned her escape. However, the witch noticed how Rapunzel's dress had become tight across her stomach—Rapunzel was pregnant! Furious at being deceived, the witch chopped off Rapunzel's braided hair and magically cast her out into the wilderness.

Later that day, the prince arrived with a rope to help Rapunzel escape, but the witch was waiting for him. She let down the severed braids, and the prince climbed up. Full of visions of his future with Rapunzel, the prince was shocked when he came face to face with a witch. Tumbling back from the window, he fell into a thorn bush below, which blinded him.

In this condition, he wandered the hills on horseback for years, each day searching for his love. Until one day, as the sun was setting and his horse had turned toward home, he called out to her one last time. Doubting her own ears, Rapunzel stood from the stream where she'd been collecting water and called back to him, and he, too, returned a frenzied reply. Overjoyed, she ran through the forest to meet him, and as they embraced, her tears of love restored his sight, and she told him her story: After she gave birth to their twins—a girl and a boy—the three of them lived in the forest, in a hut she had built. Now, at last reunited with his family, the prince led them back to his kingdom, where they all lived happily ever after.

* * *

It's no secret that sociopolitical institutions the world over operate in ways that are often unfair and occasionally barbaric. They hurt nearly everyone and everything at some point. But they're especially unjust toward women, people of color, the poor, animals (both livestock and wild animals), and the natural environment, which ultimately harms even those who control said institutions. So, it comes full circle.

What if I told you that it hasn't always been this way? And I'm not just talking about fairy tales like "Rapunzel" in which everyone lives happily ever after. Mind you, there has never been a utopia per se. When sixteenth-century philosopher Sir Thomas More coined the term for the title of his book *Utopia*, he gave a fictional account of a people who lived on an island in the Atlantic Ocean. He created the word from the Greek *ou* ("not") and *topos* ("place"), thus rendered as "nowhere." Utopia is a fiction.

However, barring any paradisiacal fantasies, there was indeed a place and a time in which human life was more equitable, and today we have the wherewithal to revive and modernize our most ancient predilections for peace—if we so choose. We'll return to this notion and the story of "Rapunzel" in a moment. But before we leave the station, let's look at the map and talk a little more about what you can expect to discover in the pages ahead.

First, this book's overarching goal is to shed light on the reasons why men—more precisely, certain types of masculinity—have dominated most of the world for the last six thousand years. We will also look at some of the effects of this domination and, as we have discovered more recently, its limits and what may be the beginning of its end.

Next, each section of this book begins with a story or a synopsis thereof to help lead you into the material that follows. As you'll see, we have evolved the tendency to learn best via stories, perfected thanks to the age-old craft of storytelling.[1] We read stories in books, newspapers, magazines; we watch them on television; and we pay ridiculous sums of money for a bag of popcorn and a ticket to see them played out on the silver screen. We absorb brief renditions of them in songs and TV commercials and longer versions in live theater performances. In a similar vein, the politician voted into office is often the one who can tell the best story, and the attorney with the finest elocution may be the deciding factor in a jury trial. Reflecting on your childhood, you may recall being hypnotized by a campfire and a titillating ghost story. This last instance may represent storytelling's most enduring venue and its oldest form.

This approach works well for our purposes here. But remember that although this book draws on arguments made by professional curators of fairy tales, it is not intended to provide professional analyses of fairy tales, legends, or myths. It makes use of only a few select examples for the purpose of illuminating social geographies of inequality—historical and modern.

Finally, while this book takes a historical approach to social geography, the dates and time periods used are approximate. This is intentional, for it is my hope that you will gain an appreciation of the broader patterns of social and environmental changes without getting "lost in the weeds." (For weedier material, please refer to the notes at the end of the book.)

We've started off with the fairy tale "Rapunzel" because its imagery is classic and gendered. The familiar Brothers Grimm version was published in 1857. But the plot summary above is of a slightly bawdier version published in 1812, complete with fornication and children born out of wedlock. Many people today might consider a story from the early nineteenth century to be ancient. However, the symbolism at the heart of "Rapunzel" is much older. In fact, certain thematic elements predate the emergence of the Indo-European languages, which include Latin, Hindi, and the Celtic language group. Scholars believe the core of this story reaches back to goddess-worshipping cultures that thrived more than six thousand years ago.[2]

"Rapunzel" is perhaps the most familiar example of the "maiden in the tower" archetype in Western fairy tales. This rendition has been compared to *hieros gamos* ("sacred marriage") between a goddess and a god, as well as said to allude to societies dominated by women in prehistoric Europe and western Asia.[3] However, these themes are shrouded beneath more recent social trends that value men and demonize women, especially independently minded women. Anthropologist Sherry Ortner has studied how women are depicted in many of the Grimm Brothers' fairy tales and concluded that female characters who have clear goals and take active roles are nearly always portrayed as villainous.[4] Wicked witches and evil stepmothers use poison and magic to achieve immoral, antisocial ends, while maidens, such as the protagonist in "Rapunzel," often play heroic roles, though on passive terms as victims. Their heroism is dependent on their passivity. Other scholars contend that the rivalry between the maiden and the witch represents the contrast between life/springtime and death/winter.[5] Yet others suggest that the wife/mother is the precursor to the biblical Eve, craving fruit from the garden. Following this theory, the witch is analogous to the serpent.[6]

This may be, but I would further suggest that the mother/wife character symbolizes an ancient divine feminine, which draws its power from green and living things, represented here by the rampion flower. The mother/wife can reproduce her magic only by consuming this organic proxy of Earth. In contrast, the witch's magic is intentional rather than natural and instinctive; it comes from cast spells rather than vegetation and childbirth. When the witch takes the child as her own, she demonstrates a masculine behavior—seizing the procreative impulse of the feminine. The tower itself is a phallic metaphor. It suggests a male-dominated ideology that subconsciously indicates the insecurity of the masculine world in which this version of the story is set.

Once cast out into the forest/wilderness, Rapunzel takes charge of her own life (masculine initiative), making her own decisions and raising her family. The last line of the story shows the prince "saving" Rapunzel and their children as he leads them back to his kingdom. This scene was added long after men began to dominate most societies. The morals of many similar stories, such as "Jack and the Beanstalk" and "Rumplestiltskin," were likewise revised in recent history.

So, the witch, the tower, and the father/husband are masculine, and the rampion/garden, forest/wilderness, mother/wife, and Rapunzel are, on balance, feminine. All represent common elements among stories that have filtered down through the ages, and we will discuss them further throughout this book. Forests, gardens, towers, walls, castles—these and many other features of the landscape are spatially gendered archetypes. They're important because archetypes carry powerful subconscious meaning for us today—meaning that comes to us honestly, that is, prehistorically.

Prior to 12,000 BP, no distinction existed between the natural environment and us. (BP years are years Before Present, as calibrated from 1950.) In the misty transition between that time and the advent of writing, about 6,000 BP, our entire worldview turned upside down. In those six millennia, we went from being communal, egalitarian, goddess-worshipping pacifists to xenophobic, hierarchical, god-worshipping warmongers. And under the direction of our ruthless gods of war, we (mostly men) proceeded to turn the planet red with violence.

But why, exactly? Why should men and masculinity have taken charge in the first place?

In his book *Sapiens: A Brief History of Humankind*, author and historian Yuval Harari puts it this way: "[T]here is some universal biological reason why almost all cultures valued manhood over womanhood. We do not know what this reason is."[7]

If you think you know the answer, think again. Explanations have fallen into three categories: brute force (men are stronger), violence (men are naturally more aggressive), and competition (men fight with other men to gain access to fertile women to impregnate). Some scholars have argued that all three tendencies may have coevolved and thus contributed to our ancestors' reproductive success—hence the natural selection of a "patriarchal gene."[8] For these scholars as well as popular culture in general, this is a classic example of confirmation bias, i.e., we see what we want to see (or what we've been conditioned to see). Different versions of this position have become so deeply embedded in everyday life that few of us think twice when we hear colloquialisms such as, "Boys will be boys," or, "Man up," or, "Grow a pair!" We unconsciously accept sayings like these and respond in customary ways because "it's in our DNA." Or so we believe.

The fact of the matter is that we have no good explanation for gender inequality and that all current hypotheses are easily debunked. Of course, we could reference queens, women presidents, and women CEOs here and there, but they are the exceptions that only serve to prove the rule: men have dominated nearly every aspect of social, economic, and political life in most cultures throughout recorded history. And in modern times, it's been mostly white men. So we are left scratching our heads, asking: How did it end up this way? What caused it? And will it go on like this forever?

This much is known: During the last Ice Age, worldwide environmental quality declined. (Biodiversity, climate, and water resources are measures of environmental quality.) This had two critical effects on humans. First, it created a selective pressure for genetic mutations in our thinking (i.e., our imagination and curiosity); and second, it inspired us to migrate in search of food.

Here's where this book comes in. As we go along, we'll investigate what I call the Gendered Landscapes Theory, or GLT, and to show how it works, I've assembled research from the social and natural sciences. In short, the GLT asserts that geography shaped our minds, which in turn shaped our cultures.* So let's break it down:

1. Human cerebral mutations that occurred during the last Ice Age greatly expanded the human ego.
2. The ego perceived our separateness from the natural world.
3. The ego interpreted landscapes as distinct, separate entities in terms of genders.
4. The masculine nature of harsh landscapes encouraged us to rely on corresponding masculine behaviors for survival.
5. *In certain critical instances*, an emphasis on masculine behaviors would culminate in punitive gods and religions, patriarchal socioeconomic structures, environmental devastation, and social inequalities.

A patriarchy is a society that is politically, economically, socially, and institutionally dominated by men and masculine values. Another useful term to bear in mind is *paradigm*. A paradigm is a mental framework of the world that's based on a central, unifying theme, such as the American Dream or the assumption that men are naturally better at math. It colors

---

* Gendered Landscapes Theory is related to, albeit distinct from, the concept of gendered spaces. Gendered spaces are areas where normative expressions of gender are organized, e.g., men's restrooms, women's locker rooms, or the separate prayer rooms for men and women at a mosque (when women are allowed to attend at all). In these and many other situations, biological sex divisions are merged with gendered categories.

one's perception of reality. One more term for now is *misogyny*—an animosity shown toward women that often results in sexual harassment, violence, and institutional oppression.

As you will see, misogyny provides something of a touchstone in our investigation of the Hyper-Masculine Paradigm, or HMP for short. But general violence, racism, gender disparities, environmental degradation, and animal exploitation also orbit our theme of inequality, and we'll investigate how each is a result of the HMP.

An obvious question you might be asking is: Did it have to be this way? Is human society as we know it simply a product of blind evolution, such that the "law of the jungle" was inevitable? In short, no. Archaeology reveals that early foragers and farmers in Europe and Central Asia worshipped goddesses, and there is little evidence of physical conflict among them even though they lived in unforgiving environments.[9] However, these peoples were ultimately overrun by cattle-herding tribes and hyper-masculine empires (a term that's probably redundant).

Even so, remnants of relatively peaceful alternatives remain today, exemplified by the Malwa of India and Nepal, the Minangkabau of Indonesia, the Aranda of Australia, the Khoisan of Namibia, the Arapesh of Papua New Guinea, the Bathonga of South Africa, the Hopi and Navajo of the American Southwest, and several others. Nearly all of these peoples live in the tropics or subtropics. But more significantly, all are matrilineal, meaning wealth and family name follow the mother's side of the family, and/or matrilocal, meaning newly wedded couples live with the wife's side of the family. Of course, even these cultures are affected by globalization, and their ways of life are endangered and changing.

Now you've gotten a preview of where we're headed. But before we go on, it's important to stop and remind ourselves of something that's easy to forget. Despite questionnaires and application forms that often confuse the matter, gender per se does *not* equal female or male, which are biological sex terms. Rather, gender, normally thought of as feminine or masculine, is socially constructed—that is, we learn and master its concepts, which are peculiar to the social milieu in which we grow up. And that's not all: gender is also fluid and recombinant and may change throughout our lives, which means it is ultimately non-binary, not merely one or the other. Finally, we use gendered traits not only to describe ourselves and other people but also to interpret and relate to certain architecture, clothing, furniture, colors, landscapes—basically everything around us.

So, when we talk about gendered landscapes, we'll be referring to features of the Earth's surface that we typically perceive as having some combination of masculine and feminine qualities. As ecopsychologist D. L. Merritt contends: "Every landscape has a soul, a particular character. What impression does one get of the total landscape? Does it feel dry and barren, rugged and challenging, or lush and nurturing?"[10] As we go along, we'll learn that lush natural environments with greater biodiversity contain more feminine qualities. They're what we tend to gravitate toward when we seek rest and relaxation. Harsh and rugged environments are masculine landscapes. We might deem them no man's land, although they may also function as portals into our most essential selves.

At this point, you may suspect me guilty of something called environmental determinism. This concept claims that cultures are mere products of their environments—no more, no less. In the nineteenth century, environmental determinism was the prevailing view on how cultures evolved, with geographer Ellen Churchill Semple, for instance, declaring that monotheisms (religions that espouse belief in one god) were a direct result of the monotonous landscapes of sand and sky in which the desert Arabs lived.[11] Peoples of the Middle East had no choice *but* to perceive and worship one god.*

---

* Environmental determinism of the nineteenth century grew out of a notion called social Darwinism. Both claimed that human cultures respond to the same forces as does biological evolution; therefore, a racial group that holds power is innately superior to one that does not. Environmental determinism, which wholly credited climates and landscapes for racial superiority and inferiority, implicitly supported imperialism, colonialism, and white supremacy. It was largely discredited after World War II due to its use in Nazi racial propaganda and eugenics.

By the mid-twentieth century, social scientists had found that environment has less to do with creating culture than does culture itself— that is, when people migrate to new places, they take their histories, preferences, and taboos along with them. Environmental determinism fell out of favor and was replaced with something called probabilism. The thinking here was that while environment certainly constrains human choices and makes some outcomes more probable than others, people still have freedom of choice. (Environmental determinism, however, has been revised and gained new traction in the twenty-first century.)

So, to answer the charge, yes, the statements I made about "Rapunzel" and those I'll make in the chapters ahead draw on environmental determinism. However, as I hope you'll see, when human technologies were simple and comprehension small, environment was indeed an all-powerful force that shaped not only our choices but also our cognition. As we and our technologies evolved, environment determined less and less of what we thought and how we lived. Even so, to this day, it still tugs at our primeval emotions, our sense of safety and danger, and it certainly casts a vote in many of the decisions we make.

Geography is a critical element in most stories. It informs characters' personas and may even function as a character itself. Rapunzel is a product of the forest and the tower: these are images that trigger emotions in our subconscious because their meanings are contained within us. These and other archetypes will be our guides as we explore how the human mind and geography reflect one another. This is the Gendered Landscapes Theory, and with the stage now set, our story begins.

PART ONE

FORESTS AND SAVANNAS: >60,000–12,000 BP

Big Picture: Modern humans evolve in areas of Africa with high environmental quality. Although they hunt, they obtain most of their calories from plants and live in small, egalitarian bands of hunter-gatherers, also called foragers. The landscapes they inhabit are comprised of tropical and subtropical forests, valleys, savannas, and caves. However, the Ice Age dries out equatorial Africa and pushes humans to the brink of extinction. A mutation in human cognition rescues the survivors by giving them the ability to imagine and invent. The descendants of some migrate to other continents.

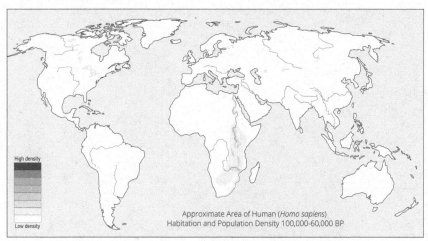

Approximate Area of Human (*Homo sapiens*)
Habitation and Population Density 100,000-60,000 BP

High density

Low density

Illus. 1: Approximate area of human (Homo sapiens) habitation and population density, 100,000–60,000 BP

CHAPTER 1

THE GENESIS TREE

Once upon a time, all the people and all the animals lived together beneath the surface of the Earth. The Great God Kaang had created everything, and even though the underworld had neither sun nor sky, Kaang's presence produced bountiful daylight that kept everyone warm. Food and water were plentiful, and no one wanted for anything. There was no sickness, no death, and all the animals and humans understood each other when they spoke. Everyone lived in harmony and was happy.

This age of bliss lasted for a very long time. But all the while, Kaang dreamed of creating even greater wonders on the surface of the Earth, which he hoped to share with the animals and the people. One day, he went to the surface and made an enormous tree whose branches stretched from one horizon to the next. He then made smaller trees that produced fruits and nuts, as well as grasses with seeds, streams with cool, clear water, and many other wonderful things. Finally, at the base of the enormous tree, he dug a hole so deep that it reached all the way down into the underworld where the people and animals lived. Climbing down into the underworld, Kaang took a man by the hand and led him up through the hole to the surface. As the two of them sat under the tree to rest, a woman found her way up through the hole. The man and the woman were excited to see the new world, and together they began to explore it.

After a while, they returned to the base of the great tree. They were so pleased with what they'd found that they called down through the hole to the others to come and join them. First, a curious giraffe climbed up. His long neck allowed him to see farther than anyone else, and so he looked around for some time. The giraffe enjoyed the view so much that he called back down for more to climb up. Soon, all the people and animals had climbed up through the hole onto the surface. Birds flew up into the branches of trees, lions leaped onto rocks and roared, and other animals jumped and scrambled up to see for themselves.

Illus. 2: Cave painting created by the San people, Cederberg Cave near Stadsaal, South Africa

Pleased with how they enjoyed his creation, the Great God Kaang called all the people and animals together under the great central tree to give a speech. "I will tell you the laws of this new world," he said. "As before, you are to live together in peace and harmony. You will talk together and listen to each other. But this is a new world, and it is very fragile."

Turning to the humans, he continued, "Under no circumstances may you make fire; to do such a thing would bring great evil into this beautiful world." In solemn agreement, the humans promised they would never make fire. Satisfied, Kaang left them to explore their new world, although he watched in secret from afar.

For a while, all went well, and as the sun began to set, everyone gathered to watch this strange new phenomenon. This, too, was beautiful and everyone smiled. But from the moment the sun disappeared, the world began to grow cold and dark. The humans could not see in the dark, so they could not find their way back to the safety of the hole under the great tree. Furthermore, they had no thick coat of hair or layer of feathers like the other creatures, so they huddled together to keep warm and share their fears with one another. "What is happening?" they asked. "Will the sun never return?" As it grew colder, their fears turned to panic. "We are going to freeze to death! How can we live if we cannot see?"

Finally, the man who had climbed out of the hole first shouted: "We must make a fire! Then we will have light and warmth, and we can survive."

"Yes," the people agreed, forgetting their promise to Kaang, "that's what we must do!" Soon, they had built a great fire and gathered round it. In its light, they could see each other, and they could feel the warmth of the flames on their chilled bodies. As they began to relax, they turned to their friends, the animals, only to find that they had run away, terrified of the fire.

"Come back!" shouted the people. "There is nothing to fear!" But the animals could no longer understand them and heard only howls and whoops that terrified them more. In no time at all, every creature had run away to hide.

Of course, Kaang had watched all of this transpire, and so with a great quaking of the ground, he sealed shut the hole under the tree. Only then did the people remember their promise to him. They realized that by disobeying him, they had broken their relationship with the Creator and with the animals forever.[1]

Illus. 3: Khoisan rock art of tree and humans, Lake Chivero, Zimbabwe

* * *

This creation story belongs to the Khoisan peoples—sometimes called Bushmen—of southwestern Africa. The Khoisan are foragers whose ancestors inhabited most of sub-Saharan Africa until only three thousand years ago, when Bantu agriculturalists from the north pushed them into drier areas in the south. Today, the few remaining groups of Khoisan live in the semi-arid Kalahari Desert. Each group speaks one of the so-called "click" languages, which contain far more phonemes (sounds) than does any other language, making them likely the oldest languages on Earth. Linguistic studies corroborate genetic testing that shows that the Khoisan's ancestors are ancestors to us all. The Khoisan are the original Indigenous peoples on Earth.

Officially, the story above has no title. I do not suggest that it should be named "The Genesis Tree" or that the Khoisan should give it this name.

Instead, I use it here simply as a thematically useful way to reference the story as we go forward in this book.

As you read this story, you may have picked up on some of its symbolic elements. The warm, wet underworld is analogous to the womb, and the progenitors of all humans and animals are "born" from it into the everyday world on the surface. Among Indigenous peoples, this motif is nearly universal, appearing as the underworld, a cave, a spring, or a hole in the ground. More familiar motifs include an all-powerful god, a utopian paradise, a central tree, a man and a woman, temptation, and the people's separation from that primeval paradise. When we put it all together like that, you probably see where I'm going.

I originally began this chapter with a retelling of the Genesis story of the Garden of Eden. But that story is so well known that I instead decided to relay something fresh—albeit ancient. That said, creation myths in many cultures revolve around motifs shared by these two stories, and so it's important we circle back and include the big-picture symbols contained in the story of the Garden of Eden too. Each story is relevant, and each is trying to tell us something that we think we already know. But do we?

"The Genesis Tree" begins after the supreme god Kaang had created the world, presumably from primordial nothingness or chaos. (The Khoisan pantheon contains many lesser spirits.) Like "The Garden of Eden," it portrays an original *paradise*, a word that comes from the ancient Persian *pairi-daêza*, meaning "enclosed garden." In fact, the word *Eden* comes from the Hebrew expression for "place of beauty" or "delightful place," and perhaps from an even older Sumerian word for "garden." This motif is not unique; it is nearly universal. More importantly, both myths explain how a fundamental shift occurred early on in humanity's understanding of itself and its relationship with nature: we fell from grace when we tried something new. The question is: Why are creation myths—and this garden theme in particular—so ubiquitous?

The mythological motif of order created from chaos likely originated from the Late Paleolithic (the Old Stone Age), around 60,000 BP, and continued well into the Bronze Age, which spanned from 3,000 to 1,200 BCE (Before Common Era, equivalent to BC). Evolutionary psychologist Marie-Louise von Franz explains how this was a natural result of the human psyche experiencing its own ego-consciousness coming into being as "world-becoming."[2] Psychoanalyst Carl Jung agrees, stating, "Cosmogonic [creation] myths are, at bottom, symbols for the coming of consciousness."[3] In other words, our emerging self-awareness first expressed itself in symbolic stories, songs, and art. Much later, people would recast this emergence in their creation myths as the point at which the world itself came into being.

The biblical version describes how the Great God Yahweh created the heavens and a chaotic, watery earth. Depending on the translation used, he then "hovered" or "brooded" over the formless deep. As we'll explore more fully in the next chapter, water, chaos, and darkness are all archetypal feminine symbols. Light, order, and dry land—especially desert—are masculine. Many of our oldest symbols involve features of the physical landscape.[4]

Yahweh went on to speak all things, including people, into being (Adam was first, Eve was second).* In Genesis 1:29, Yahweh gave humanity "every seed-bearing plant on the face of the earth and every tree that has fruit with seed in it . . . for food," so people could move about and go wherever they wished. However, the Garden was special. It contained streams, animals, and plants, not the least of which were two rather conspicuous fruit-bearing trees at its center.

---

* Lilith is the name of a woman who many myths contend was created before Eve. Lilith is mentioned in the Christian Bible, the Jewish Talmud, the *Epic of Gilgamesh*, and other Mesopotamian texts. How she is described in stories varies greatly, from being created at the same time and from the same clay as Adam to magically embodying the serpent who later tempted Eve. Most stories generally agree that Lilith chose to leave Eden after refusing to become subservient to Adam.

Tree symbols are another universal. Nearly all such symbols represent an *axis mundi*, or world axis. Mythologically, a world axis is an eternal still point around which the cosmos turns and where all dualities are resolved, including female/male, night/day, good/bad, right/wrong, cold/hot, and so on.* This idea is portrayed in "The Genesis Tree" when the Great God Kaang created a tree that spanned the sky. In Islam, the Qur'an describes a *shajarat al-khold*, or Tree of Immortality. In Hinduism, the Bhagavad Gita names an *Ashwatta*, or Tree of Life. Aztec, Olmec, Toltec, and Mayan cultures also hold central tree motifs. Tibetan Buddhism has its *Bodhi* Tree, or Tree of Enlightenment. Old Norse mythology tells of *Yggdrasil*, a tree that binds together the Nine Worlds. Yet the sacred trees portrayed in the Judeo-Christian tradition are an exception. The Tree of Life and the Tree of Knowledge in "The Garden of Eden" do not unify and harmonize. Rather, they contain latent chaos and disruption.

However, the Christian New Testament adds a twist. The Cross of Crucifixion connotes the reunification of Heaven and Earth. Its horizontal axis (beam) draws together the mundane dualities of quotidian life, while its vertical axis (post) draws together the spiritual above and the corporeal below. The fulcrum at its center represents a non-dual harmony. So, in Christianity, the cross symbolically heals the wound of division between God and humanity and the damage done by all those feminine archetypes in days of yore.

The serpent in the Garden represents intentional, active chaos. In particular, it personifies Leviathan (or the goddess Lawtan/Lotan of Canaanite mythology).[5] The Talmud in Judaism describes Leviathan as a watery female serpent, while the Christian New Testament equates it with Satan. (Behemoth, who is a dry-land monster, is its male counterpart.)[6] These Abrahamic faiths, as well as the religion called Zoroastrianism, foretell that Yahweh (masculine) will finally and utterly crush Leviathan (feminine) on an undisclosed future Day of Judgment. Ironically, the root

---

* Dualities are contrasted opposites, also called binary opposites. Binaries are asymmetrical, however, and often imply that one opposite has a greater value than does the other. More on this in Chapter 5.

of the word *Leviathan* is *Levi*, which also refers to the Levite priest-kings. The Book of Leviticus, too, derives its name from the same root and is one of the most misogynistic books in the Bible, yet the polytheistic history of the Levites is thought to have originated with serpent priests of the Great Mother and the World Dragon of the Goddess.[7]

Those who wrote and later edited the Bible intended to explain how, why, and through whom chaos was made manifest in the world. The notion of a primordial chaos suggests a deep fear and loathing of the unknown (feminine). Therefore, chaos, the serpent, Leviathan, Satan, the Tree of Life, and the Tree of the Knowledge are all feminine archetypes, and all are focused through Eve, the most overtly feminine symbol in Genesis. We see this theme expressed in many similar creation stories.[8]

In "The Genesis Tree," the central tree and the underworld are feminine gendered landscapes. The Great God Kaang used his masculine procreative powers to penetrate the earth under the tree and extract the life he had installed there. The Khoisan creation myth describes how the male god Kaang caused the first man to be "born again" when he took him by the hand and led him through the hole under the tree and out onto the surface. A woman next emerged of her own accord and without aid. The metaphor is clear: Girls are spontaneously reborn as women when they experience their first menstrual cycle. But the transformation of boys into men is less certain and requires cultural effort. Rites of passage for boys are often dramatic and bloody, as with puberty circumcision, whereby boys are reborn—that is, they are intentionally "birthed" into adulthood. This ceremony imitates women's menstrual cycle and ability to give birth.[9]

"The Genesis Tree" next diverges from the myth of the Garden of Eden in two important ways. First, instead of the first woman being duped into transgression, it is the first man who disobeys Kaang's proscription against making fire. And second, instead of defiling the original paradise/underworld/inner sanctum as Adam and Eve defiled Eden, humans pollute the new-and-improved upper/outer world and become stranded there.

In the biblical version, Eve eats the fruit, and because she is thoughtful and likes to share, she later offers it to Adam, who also eats some. All of this happens while they are still in the Garden. Of course, Yahweh discovers their infraction and expels them. This transgression comprises the original sin, offered as an explanation for all manner of evil in the world. For our purposes here, this myth shifts the blame (in an egoic tactic called projection) onto the archetypal feminine at every level, including unformed chaos, a garden of fruit-bearing trees, a serpent, and the first woman. We are led to believe that Adam would not have made the same error in judgment. As a result, in cultures modified by the Abrahamic faiths, women—and feminine traits more generally—have been demonized and treated with enmity ever since.

All cosmogonic myths harken back to a time of mystery, seeking to explain suffering in the world. It is impossible to say how old the Khoisan story is, but the biblical version was written down about 2,500 years ago. This was roughly 10,000 years after the Horticultural Revolution and 60,000 years after the Irrational Revolution, both of which we will explore next. Between these two turning points, humans perceived the world as supernatural and pangendered, and its spiritual agents were either zoomorphic (all animal) or therianthropic (half animal, half human). This vast stretch of time is salient to our story, for it was when we acquired all of our most essential human capacities, some of which might surprise you.

CHAPTER 2

PANGENDERED LANDSCAPES: THE DEEP BACKSTORY

If you're reading this in a chair or on a couch, or in some other spot that's snug and stationary, take a moment to shift around and make yourself as comfortable as possible. Next, take a long, slow breath . . . pause . . . and then exhale. As you exhale, picture a safe and restful place, perhaps one you're familiar with, one that quiets your mind and relaxes your muscles. Imagine that you are in that place, letting it soak into your skin, into your bones, until a deep sense of "ahh" comes over you. You are part of its rhythm.

At this point, you may feel like taking a nap.

In all likelihood, your imagination has taken you to a sunny town park or a picnic area in a meadow, maybe overlooking a lake or a forest, with mountains in the distance. If you were to describe the place in your mind using a single word, you might choose a word like "sublime," or "tranquil," or "heavenly."

Landscapes matter. It's no accident that urban planners design parks and greenways and even cemeteries to consist of open spaces punctuated with tall, green trees, a water feature or two, and places where you can sit in the shade and rest. Often, they're located on a hill or a gentle rise in the terrain that grants a pleasant view of the surrounding area. In congested urban areas, pocket parks help to satisfy this predilection while at the same time conserving space. Any fragment of "nature" will do. But when we get the chance, many of us prefer to leave the stress of the city behind to recreate—and re-create ourselves—in places enclosed in less intentional tracts of nature, such as national parks, national forests, and even wilderness areas.

The spatial qualities we seek in the natural world rest on a fundamental human instinct for contact with Mother Nature. It can be argued that any natural setting carries a certain aesthetic appeal, but those we are most fond of tend to consist of an open area (for a safe buffer from predators), yet with sufficiently tall trees (for shade but also escape routes), plus reliable water sources and food options. This preference evolved in forested environments where hominins (ending with an "n," this group being our direct ancestral line) lived 7 to 5 million BP. The fossil record indicates this was when we began spending more time on the ground than in the trees. It marked the beginning of our shift toward habitual bipedalism— that is, walking on two legs more than half the time yet not all the time (that would come later). Scientists refer to three of these ancestors by their Latin genus taxa as *Sahelanthropus*, *Orrorin*, and *Ardipithecus*, in chronological sequence. At that time, we had small brains—around 350 cc (cubic centimeters), or about the size of a softball—few or no tools, and we ate mostly fruits, leaves, berries, and nuts. However, we wouldn't have turned up our noses at a rotting zebra carcass, killed by a saber-toothed cat who had gotten her fill.

Between 4 and 2 million BP, we began spending nearly all our time on the ground, which translated to less time spent in the forests and more on the savannas. This group of hominins, the australopithecines, came in several different makes and models, each being finely tuned to their local environment. And toward the end of this epoch, just as we were evolving a slightly larger brain of around 450 cc, we began fashioning tools in abundance: simple stone tools at first, used to crack nuts and dig for roots.[1] We likely also made tools from wood, though scientists may never know for sure, since wood usually decays before it has a chance to fossilize.

As bipeds, we moved around a lot, and being so mobile made us hot. Individuals who happened to be endowed with less body hair and more prolific sweat glands stayed cooler. These folks could travel farther for food, which means they were healthier, lived longer, and passed their traits down more often than did others who lacked such traits. Just to be clear, we still have about the same number of basal hair cells today as do other primates in our wider hominid (ending with a "d") family, such as gorillas and chimpanzees, but most of our body hairs are tiny by comparison. In the meantime, our trajectory toward relative hairlessness was matched by the evolution of more melanocytes in our dermis, giving us darker skin to protect us from the equatorial sun.

By 1.8 million BP, we had become obligate bipeds—that is, we walked on two legs full-time. The *Homo erectus*, or "upright walking human," had a brain size in the neighborhood of 1000 cc. Although we were never very good at sprinting, we could walk or even trot all day long, outdistancing most other mammals. Some of us used our locomotive talent to leave Africa for the first time, migrating to northern Europe, eastern Asia, and even as far as today's Indonesia. At that time, the weather was nice and there was plenty to eat, so we may simply have been following the rains and the proliferation of plant and animal foods.

However, our main ancestral line evolved into anatomically modern *Homo sapiens* by about 200,000 BP. Our average brain size had grown to 1400 cc, our brow ridge and jaw had shrunk, we stood a bit taller, and we had acquired a handsomely chiseled chin. (One theory suggests the chin is a remnant of a larger jawbone, which shrank more in the area that held the teeth when we began to cook foods into softer mush, thus rendering a robust mandible unnecessary. Teeth, however, are under greater genetic control compared to jawbone size, which has resulted in many of modern humans' dental malocclusions.)[2]

Archaeologists and geneticists concur that around three million of us were alive on the planet in those days, and we all lived in Africa. (Earlier *H. erectus* populations that had migrated to Eurasia evolved into species and subspecies that would either interbreed with us later or go extinct.) Based on the average rate of mutation in our DNA, called the "molecular clock," geneticists have traced the ancestor of all living women to a "mitochondrial Eve," who lived in southeastern Africa around 148,000 BP. The ancestor of all men was a "Y-chromosome Adam," who lived in eastern Africa about 156,000 BP. (Studies continue to refine these calculations.)[3] These were the most recent common ancestors of everyone alive today, though technically, they were not individual people but related kin groups.

In those days, life was good. Global temperatures were warm, and there were rainforests teeming with life near ponds, lakes, and rivers across what are now the Sahara and Kalahari deserts. As always, we foraged for all our food. Our bodies had evolved to prefer these high-quality environments, and this time, on a verdant continent three and a half times larger than the United States, we saw no reason to go anywhere else in search of anything—not just yet anyway.

Fast forward to recent history. Anthropologists in the nineteenth and early twentieth centuries claimed that modern-day foragers perpetually teetered on the brink of starvation. However, in 1966, groundbreaking work by Marshal Sahlins showed how foragers spent only fifteen to twenty hours per week getting food—far less time compared to agriculturalists and pastoralists—because they always knew where to find it. This granted them more leisure time compared to people in any other socioeconomic system. Foragers constituted, in Sahlins's words, the "original affluent society," in which "all the people's wants [were] easily satisfied."[4]

Of course, Sahlins had his critics, who noted how the availability of food depends on the quality of one's environment. This in turn depends largely on one's distance from the equator: lower latitudes equal higher-quality (feminine) environments, and higher latitudes equal lower-quality (masculine) environments.[5] Nonetheless, as with people, few, if any, landscapes can be called purely masculine *or* feminine. In most cases, they are composites that may fluctuate—literally—depending on the weather. Therefore, every landscape is to some degree pangendered.*⁶ Picture a dense, wet forest, where streams trickle through the low spots but grassy meadows open across higher patches in between. These are safe, feminine spaces. If you were to follow those streams to their source, you'd find that they narrow and steepen as they climb into misty forests nestled in cool mountain valleys. Indeed, the tallest peaks may rise into the realm of tundra, rock, and ice. This example thus moves from feminine to pangendered to masculine landscapes.

Illus. 4: Blyde River Canyon, South Africa. Pangendered landscape of river valley in subtropical forest with mountains

Early *Homo sapiens* perceived the character of each landscape in their surroundings in ways that were based on their experience of themselves—physically, socially, and psychologically. The landscape in Illustration 4 balances various gendered traits and may represent an approximation of the environment in which modern humans evolved. In other places, savannas supported abundant populations of ungulates

---

* Even the concept of "landscape" is socially constructed, a fiction we continuously modify and attach to deeper symbols. "Landscape is a cultural term pertaining to the earth itself as it is perceived and conceptualized by a particular culture."—David S. Whitley (hooved mammals) as they congregated around water holes lined with acacia trees. But those grasslands were also punctuated with drier areas of rock outcrops, devoid of trees and water. These were pangendered landscapes that tilted toward the masculine.

You'll recall that the sacred trees we discussed in the last chapter emphasize feminine archetypes. However, large, conspicuous trees like the one portrayed in "The Genesis Tree" may be perceived to contain both feminine and masculine qualities, which makes them pangendered. For example, in pre-Christian Britain, Celtic druids associated oak trees with the myth of the Green Man, which emphasized (and praised) the masculine archetype. This woodland myth symbolized the masculine traits of strength and protection *while also* praising the feminine traits of reproduction and life.

Illus. 5: The Druid Grove, artist unknown. Sacred Celtic tree, possibly an oak tree, in Old England: A Pictorial Museum by Charles Knight, c.1845

Gendered symbols are often reinforced with more explicit sexual metaphors. Among the Buhaya horticulturalists of modern-day Tanzania, men perform the vertical, upright work of tending tree crops. The tool of choice, the *olhuabyo*, is more than two meters long, with a double-sided, sickle-shaped iron blade hafted at one end. This tool is used to harvest mature banana bunches—all phallic symbols. Meanwhile, women tend to annual crops, including beans and field peas, which grow close to the ground, as well as tubers (such as cassava, yams, and potatoes) and legumes (such as peanuts), which grow underground—feminine symbols of the womb and Mother Earth. These practices conform to the Haya adage, "Men work above, women work below."[7] Remnants of pangendered histories also persist in traditional Haya iron-smelting technologies, with phallic-shaped tuyères (tubes for air induction) stoking the feminine reproductive power of the kiln.[8]

Perhaps one of the most explicit examples of sexualized landscape motifs is from the Dogon people of West Africa. The Dogon construct their villages in the shape of a supine, hermaphroditic human. However, their wider agricultural lands, which include villages, are shaped like the mythical Dogon cosmic egg. Furthermore, fields that encircle the villages are cut into spirals, but on the southern end of the fields is a cone-shaped shrine representing a penis. A stone located next to it is used to press nuts and fruits for oil. This stone is the vulva/vagina. Menstrual huts (used to house menstruating women) on the east and west sides of the fields represent hands. And both men and women engage equally in agricultural work for the community.[9]

At this point, you might be thinking: Sacred trees, fruit trees, and root crops all sound well and good, but what about all the meat those prehistoric cavemen ate? Didn't they live in the kind of dog-eat-dog world that, as the old saying goes, made men men and women glad for it?

The familiar story goes something like this: Early humans and their cousins, such as Neandertals, were savage carnivores who fed themselves almost entirely by hunting. Men brought home the bacon, and women fried it up in a pan—or rather, roasted it over a fire—while their brood of little moppets grubbed about. Art and acumen were dull, disease rampant, and death close at hand and always violent.

These convictions have saturated popular culture and our psyches since at least the nineteenth century and are so well worn in the American vernacular that they epitomize cliché. So you could be forgiven for believing them, even when nearly every word is wrong.

To begin with, before we *Homo sapiens* began leaving Africa around 60,000 BP, most of our diet consisted of plant foods. (We'll get back to this in a moment.) And although some symbolic behaviors did exist before 200,000 BP, before the evolution of our modern physical bodies, none of these behaviors really caught on. But something strange happened after 60,000 BP. Almost overnight, artistic thinking exploded onto the scene in the form of beads, necklaces, carvings, figurines, and cave paintings.

Finally, death from violence or disease was rare among early humans, with the exception of the Neandertals, our closest hominin cousins. Nonetheless, while most Neandertals did indeed eke out a living by hunting those large, dangerous animals, some ate nothing but plants.[10,11]

By the way, if you're wondering if all those cave paintings of wooly rhinos and mammoths and cave bears represent animals hunted by early *Homo sapiens*, sorry, but no. In the early twentieth century, French archaeologist Abbé Breuil proposed his "hunting magic" hypothesis as an explanation for what inspired Paleolithic people to paint on cave walls, such as those in modern-day Lascaux, France. Breuil thought that if people imagined an animal and then "captured" him by drawing his likeness, then his fate was sealed as an item on the dinner menu—a little like ordering takeout.

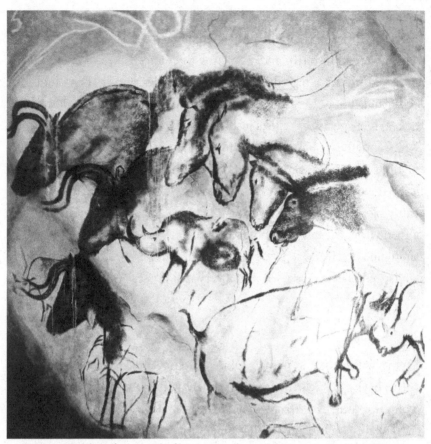

Illus. 6: Replica of pictograph of horses, aurochs, and rhinoceroses, Lascaux Cave, Chauvet-Pont-d'Arc, c.32,000 BP, in the Anthropos Museum, Brno, Czech Republic

The hunting magic hypothesis reflected the "Man the Hunter" or "conquest of nature" ethos of Breuil's day and, as such, received wide acceptance among academics and laypersons alike. However, recent studies in paleobiology and archaeology show that Paleolithic *Homo sapiens* killed and ate very few of the animals they painted on cave walls.[12] Instead, caves and cave art likely served religious functions or as part of fertility ceremonies. European cave art typically contains sexual symbolism, including animals in copulation: some are coated in red ocher (a paste of red soil mixed with a liquid), while others are anthropomorphic animals presenting genitalia. The art in these images concerns animals not as food, hunted by humans, but rather as gestures made to a life force responsible for reproduction. Other carvings and sculptures depict human male genitalia in tumescence, vulvas, women in birth, and women with enlarged breasts and hips. So, cave paintings were more likely a type of sacred scripture than prehistoric food menu. Today, Indigenous shamans consider these sites as portals into the realm of spirits that exists just beyond the rock wall veneer.[13]

Essentially, we have always eaten whatever food was available. Most of the time, this meant eating things that didn't bite back or run away from us. So the question becomes: How and why did we manage to distort the reality of prehistoric life so badly? This is a critical question in the story of inequality, because it exposes fictions on which the Hyper-Masculine Paradigm, or HMP, depends. Part of the answer lies in the Gendered Landscapes Theory, or GLT, and a very real process called socialization.

* * *

Playing with a beagle named Okie, watching my dad work with tools in the backyard, learning my ABCs from my mom, watching Walter Cronkite on the *CBS Evening News* present footage of soldiers in Vietnam. These were some of my earliest memories. I was no more than three years old when I experienced each, yet I still remember them because they were significant in the formation of my view of reality. I mention this because much of the foundation for how we as adults would see and understand the world is already in place by age three.

The people, things, and events we experience in our earliest childhood shape our character and our view of reality. They shape who we are. This phenomenon is called socialization: from the moment we are born (if not before), each of us is socialized to perceive and respond to the world around us.[14] One example in mainstream Western culture is reflected in the old nursery rhyme that reminds us how little boys are made of "snips and snails and puppy dogs' tails" and little girls of "sugar and spice and everything nice." One result of this mentifact (a shared idea of a culture) is that many people therefore assume baby girls smile more often than baby boys, a phenomenon supported by some research.[15] However, other studies show that those who interact with babies tend to smile more often at baby girls than at baby boys, because they expect girls to be sweeter-natured, being made of "everything nice."[16] These findings suggest that babies have a propensity to imitate whatever they see and hear, and so we learn to embody and perform scripted gender roles (feminine and masculine) from day one. This supports what we're discovering about ourselves as primarily cultural animals—that is, although we are products of a mixture of both environmental and genetic forces, it looks to be more nurture than nature.[17,18,19]

Illus. 7: "Happy 'Holladays,'" boys get guns at Holidays

Accordingly, research also reveals that children already show signs of racial bias by age three—again, learned from adults and others nearby.[20,21] Ego is well on its way to maturity by age three, and ninety percent of a child's worldview is in place by age five,[22] about the time parents reinforce their emphasis on popular gendered traits by, for example, purchasing toy guns for boys and Easy-Bake Ovens for girls. All of these are examples of socialization. It is strong, it is ubiquitous, and most of it happens subconsciously.*

* * *

Returning to our caveman fable, the popular notion of "Man the Hunter" is one of these deeply socialized mind patterns. Early-twentieth-century anatomist Raymond Dart inadvertently helped strengthen this belief while interpreting fossil tools. In 1924, Dart was teaching at the University of the Witwatersrand in Johannesburg, South Africa, when workers at a mine near the small South African town of Taung uncovered what they thought were the fossil remains of a baboon. Thinking the specimen might be of interest to the university, they mailed it to Dart. Upon investigation, Dart suggested the remains belonged to an infant member of a pre-human species he named *Australopithecus africanus*, Latin for "southern ape of Africa." At first discredited, his analysis of "The Taung Child" would eventually be vindicated.

Dart went on to interpret tools found with other australopithecine fossils. He concluded that early hominins had used these tools to kill for meat—both animals and other hominins. Dart's judgments, like Abbé Breuil's, supported the dominant worldview of his day, which portrayed prehistoric life as nasty, brutish, and short. However, Dart's conclusions would have greater consequences than did Breuil's.

---

* In the mid-twentieth century, French sociologist Pierre Bourdieu elaborated on an established concept called habitus. Bourdieu suggested that habitus is comprised of the sum of all our attitudes, habits, mannerisms, and intuitions, which are subconsciously shaped by our society. In this sense, habitus is created through socialization.

Dart had been a medic in World War I. He had witnessed firsthand the cruelty that humans are capable of inflicting on one another, and his interpretations of fossils may have sought a prehistoric motivation. In the late 1950s and early 1960s, science writer Robert Ardrey popularized Dart's theories in several publications, including *Playboy Magazine*. But perhaps most influential was Ardrey's book *African Genesis: A Personal Investigation into the Animal Origins and Nature of Man*, which begins, "Not in innocence, and not in Asia, was mankind born."[23]

Screenwriter and film director Stanley Kubric, a fan of Ardrey's work, famously drew on material from *African Genesis* when filming the opening scenes of *2001: A Space Odyssey*. In these scenes, two groups of hominins—possibly australopithecines—discover the use of tools as weapons, using them to kill animals and each other in competition for scarce resources. Kubric's film reinforced the popular notion of "Man the Hunter," confirming that humans are born predators and that violence is in our nature.

Again, none of this is true. In the decades since *2001*, analyses of the calculus (tartar) on fossilized teeth have shown that foods eaten by hominins consisted entirely of plant materials.[24] In fact, we were nearly always prey, seldom (if ever) predators.

To put this in perspective, consider that humans have always been social animals. We have no sharp claws or fangs, so living in groups and getting along with one another were critical to our survival. Charles Darwin, nineteenth-century naturalist and author of *On the Origin of Species*,[25] suggested that the best way for a species to survive and evolve is by being cooperative and friendly.[26] Aggression is costly, it can get you killed, and it is also stressful and weakens the immune system. Overall, aggression results in fewer offspring. So when Darwin wrote about "survival of the fittest," by "fittest" he actually meant "best suited" to any given environment and thus capable of producing the most viable offspring. Only rarely does it mean "biggest" or "strongest." This is why the most common strategy used for survival in nature is to be social.[27]

Thus, cooperation and friendliness are literally in our nature. Imagine what would happen if several unrelated tigers, hyenas, or polar bears—all obligate carnivores—were placed together in, say, your garage. The scene would explode in blind pandemonium. Yet we humans are able to move about with many other humans unrelated to us—for example, at a grocery store or on a bus—and for the most part, we remain civil, even pleasant. We do not tear each other apart. We could call this trait "human nature," because it is a direct result of our genetic makeup *and* our socially formative experiences as a species.*

* * *

You may now be wondering: If Paleolithic men were not killing dangerous animals like mammoths, and big, aggressive men weren't having the most babies, then why are men so much bigger and stronger and more aggressive than women?

Since the 1990s, paleoanthropologists have excavated numerous skeletal remains of anatomically modern humans (people who look like us). Fossils from these sites range in age, from 200,000 to 65,000 BP, and except for a single group found at Skhul Cave in Qafzeh, Israel (at 110,000 years old), all are in Africa, and all show very little sexual dimorphism (difference in size between males and females). Yes, a difference does exist, and it is statistically significant, but just barely. Fossils show that the average adult female weighed just sixteen percent less and stood just seven percent shorter than the average adult male—ratios that still hold true today. Of course, some females are taller and heavier than some males, and some males are much larger than some females, but we're talking averages.

This is important when we consider that the average adult male gorilla is approximately *twice as large* as the average adult female gorilla, and the

---

* Regrettably, as we will see in Chapters 8 and 9, when the HMP became dominant, we culturally overwrote this original programming. Since that time, we have descended into horrific bouts of warfare, terrorism, and barbarity. Our underlying predilection for peace endures, albeit subdued.

male orangutan is *ninety percent larger* than the female orangutan. Great differences like these remark on those species' residence patterns: In the case of gorillas, for example, a single male dominates several females, which is called a polygynous relationship. An alpha male must therefore be able to confront male aggressors who might wish to take his females, kill his young, and usurp his position. (The opposite residence pattern is called polyandrous.)*

But in species that adopt monogamous relationships, female and male body sizes average very close to parity. For example, male and female gibbons, who are monogamous throughout their lives, are essentially the same size. The male need not be bigger if the female pledges her heart to him and him alone. Humans' small degree of dimorphism likely indicates a long history of monogamy or something very close to it, or, as with bonobos, the complete opposite.

Once called pygmy chimpanzees, bonobos are one of our closest genetic relatives, with whom we share 98.6 percent of DNA. Females rule the roost and will gang up on a male if he steps out of line. But this rarely happens. Bonobos have little dimorphism and practice what might be called "free love" with either sex, often as a means of resolving an argument or sealing a friendship. In this way, it might not be entirely whimsical to appraise bonobo culture by the old hippie reference, "Peace, love, and which way to Woodstock." Bonobos are also renowned for their willingness to share food and tools with friends and strangers alike.[28] So, genetically and socially, humans and bonobos have a lot in common, and we might refer to both species collectively as "the sexy primates." (That is, for both species, sex fulfills psychosocial needs at least as often as it does biological needs.)

And that's all well and good, but we also share 98.6 percent of our DNA with common chimpanzees. Like bonobos, chimpanzees also mate promiscuously in what is called a multi-male, multi-female residence

---

* Polyandry refers to the residence pattern wherein one female cohabits with more than one male. This residence pattern is practiced by marmosets, tamarins, and some human groups, such as the Maasai of East Africa and the Malwa of South Asia.

pattern. However, chimpanzee society is decidedly male-dominated, and chimpanzees are much more aggressive than bonobos. Chimpanzees regularly fight, form alliances, wage war on other chimpanzee groups, and hunt for smaller primates to eat. And on that point, while both species eat very little meat, chimpanzees manage to kill and eat more than twice as many animals compared to bonobos; the average chimpanzee's diet is 5–8 percent meat, and a bonobo's is 2–3 percent meat.[*29]

So, chimpanzees are a male-dominated species and more prone to aggression and violence (although they do have a soft side too), while bonobos are a female-dominated species and more prone to friendliness and altruism. Though the two societies share similar elements, they produce very different outcomes. And one reason they may have evolved so differently is difference in environmental quality.

Bonobos and common chimpanzees are separated from one another by the Congo River; bonobos live on the south side, chimpanzees on the north side. Neither can swim. For this reason, they are never in direct competition. In addition, ecological studies show that fruits and herbs exist in greater abundance on the south side, where the bonobos live. This has led some primatologists to suggest that bonobo society evolved to be friendlier due to the higher quality of their local environment.[30,31]

As you read earlier, humans display a relatively small degree of sexual dimorphism. This suggests we evolved in ways that encouraged us to get along with one another. But there are other reasons why we are inherently a nonviolent species. Like most primates, we have long intestines. Adult humans' intestines are about twenty feet long, and our height- and weight-to-intestinal length ratio is the same as that of herbivores. This is because we evolved to digest mostly complex plant materials. Carnivores' intestines are much shorter, both because carnivores do not need a diverse range of foods to meet their nutritional needs and because meat digestion requires a quick transit time, so that harmful toxins do not accumulate in the gut.

---

* Gorillas, orangutans, gibbons, and most other primates are vegans—technically, folivores and frugivores—with the bulk of their diets coming from fruits, leaves, shoots, grasses, nuts, and other plant materials.

Also, our tooth structure is quite generalized—that is, our molars and premolars are best suited for crushing and pulping (with up-and-down *and* side-to-side motions, like in herbivores), not so much for tearing and ripping (with just an up-and-down motion, like in carnivores). So if you can move your jaw around in a circle, then you're essentially an herbivore. Anthropologist John Napier reminds us that human dentition "is poorly adapted for the flesh-eating habits of man, who still retains the tooth form of his fruit and vegetable-eating ancestors" and that "man's digestive system has all the physiological hallmarks of a vegetarian, not a carnivore."[32] That's right: we're not carnivores. In fact, the only true land carnivores are animals in the cat family, hyenas, polar bears, gray wolves, and mustelids such as ferrets and weasels.*[33] We are at the herbivorous end of the omnivore spectrum. Our bodies testify to it. Digestible carbohydrates from plants were even critical in increasing the size and complexity of the early hominin brain.[34,35]

This might be a good place to make a point about the usual modern diet. While our physiology performs best on a regimen of varied plant foods, we can—and many of us do—get away with eating an abundance of animal products and, nowadays, a plethora of manufactured "foods," neither of which are a healthy choice in the long run. (We'll return to this topic in greater depth in Chapters 8 and 11.)

You might object to all of this if you've ever read an article or seen a documentary film that showed how predators' eyes are situated on the front of their heads—just like in humans. This gives predators binocular stereoscopic vision, which is useful in judging distance when pouncing on or running down prey. However, we inherited our eye configuration by way of a very different route in evolution compared to carnivores.

---

* Even though dogs evolved from wolf-like ancestors, dogs have become omnivores, with physiologies that prefer foods made mostly of cereal grains and vegetables. Meat is not required. This is due to their association with omnivorous-herbivorous humans for at least the past 10,000 years, and perhaps much longer, eating what we eat. Dog food manufacturers, however, tend to promote meat-centric diets, presumably because they are marketing their products to humans who think that they, and their dog, should eat some imagined version of a "paleo" diet.

First, unlike carnivorous mammals, we and our primate ancestors were never terrestrial quadrupeds (four-legged, walking on the ground). Instead, fossil evidence shows that our ancient ancestors were first arboreal brachiators (arm over arm, swinging through the trees) and later arboreal quadrupeds (four-legged, walking on tree branches). Second, life in the trees required us to accurately judge the distance from one branch to the next, especially when our color vision identified ripe-looking fruits hanging in the next tree over. Misjudging aerial distances would have quickly eliminated someone from the gene pool. Thus, those with eyes nearer together passed down their genes.

So, our eyes, our gut, our teeth—in fact, our entire body plan—are formed around our physiology's predilection for plant foods. Today, the San, Hadza, and Ju/'hoansi foragers of Africa certainly hunt, several times each week, and they occasionally bring down a dik-dik, a baboon, or even a larger animal. Still, fully 75 percent of their diet is comprised of edible roots, fruits, nuts, seeds, berries, leaves, and honey.[36] The food they obtain is distributed among all members of a band, and malnutrition is virtually unknown.[37] And this on the more marginal (masculine) lands to which their recent ancestors were pushed.

Foragers like these, who live in the tropics, typically experience higher ambient air temperatures, have access to higher-quality environments, and therefore tend to gather more foods than they hunt. Women contribute more to such groups' diets and economies. Not surprisingly, foraging groups are also more egalitarian in their social structures, they tend to be matrilocal and matrilineal (husbands live with the wife's family, and wealth and name follow the female side of the family), and conflict is rare. As anthropologist Carol Ember points out, "It is widely agreed that, compared to [pastoralists and farmers], hunter-gatherers fight less."[38] When fighting does occur, it is almost always directed outside the group.[39] Other researchers, too, have found that matrilineal patterns are adaptive in higher-quality environments, where people are not threatened by conquest.[40]

Things change, however, as one moves from equatorial regions toward the poles. As environmental quality worsens and temperatures decrease, males contribute more to groups' diets (from hunting and fishing), and groups tend to be increasingly patrilocal and patrilineal, as with the Chukchi and Inuit. These social structures nearly always occur where resources are scarce, or where attacks from patriarchal invaders are common.[41] Warfare is not always greater in patrilocal communities, although it does tend to increase with wealth, status, and social hierarchies among less nomadic, more sedentary groups. And in addition to out-group conflict, more hostility is directed inward, toward neighbors and relatives.[42]

Data gathered since the nineteenth century has led notable scholars, such as J. J. Bachofen, Friedrich Engels, and Marija Gimbutas, to speculate on the existence of prehistoric matriarchies. A matriarchy is a socioeconomic structure in which women control all means of production, decision making, and power. No pure matriarchy exists today. But some research suggests that matriarchies were once ubiquitous and comprised the very earliest forms of true human culture.[43]

So, why all this talk about food, sex, and in-laws?

Generally speaking, cooler, drier climates with more barren landscapes (lower environmental quality) encouraged more hunting and, later, pastoralism for survival. (While this was true for early human groups with primitive technologies, it is less true today. Where such practice persists, it may be a mere historic relic.) In these landscapes, masculine traits of aggression and violence were fostered, even celebrated, while feminine traits of relationship and nonviolence were curbed and controlled. Think about it: a group of hunters certainly communicates, but in a completely different way compared to a group of people gathering fruits, digging for tubers, scaring animals away with their singing and laughing.

But as we say this, please remember: feminine does not necessarily equal female, and masculine does not necessarily equal male. Also, human decisions emerge from a combination of cultural and environmental ingredients. Nature cannot compel us to behave in any certain way; it can only offer options.

Of course, we must be careful when speculating about prehistoric peoples based on the habits of modern-day foragers. In a world of over 8 billion people, fewer than 250,000 foragers still exist, scattered around the globe on marginal "waste" lands. Arguably, all have been affected to some degree by globalizing popular cultures and socioeconomics. For example, it is no longer unusual to see San people camped near rural villages in the Kalahari during the dry season, finding employment with local kiosk owners and trading forest goods for kerosene, matches, candles, sugar, and bottles of warm Fanta Orange. The Mbuti of the Ituri Rainforest trade kola nuts and bushmeat with merchants along the Congo River for scrap metal that they then fashion into tools, trinkets, and weapons. Inupiat Natives in northern Alaska hunt caribou if the spring ice breakup is "late," conditions they once called normal (which allowed the caribou to migrate and Natives to hunt them). More and more, however, the Inupiat are taking up contract work in the oilfields with companies like ConocoPhillips and ExxonMobil, since the ice has been thawing a little earlier each year.

To sum up, when we combine data from across the sciences, we see that our species evolved in lush, garden-like landscapes, eating lots of fruits and veggies; but, if need be, we could get by on almost anything. Physical geography shaped our bodies as well as our mental perceptions of ourselves, each other, and the world. That is, our environment socialized us. It encouraged us to be monogamous and inherently friendly, to discern between places that were safe (feminine) and places that were not (masculine). This lies at the core of Gendered Landscapes Theory.

Yet, despite all our adaptations and clever tools, we were ill-equipped to cope with changes in global climate that began around 110,000 BP. So drastic were these changes that by 60,000 BP, our total population had dwindled to a mere few thousand souls scattered across southeastern Africa. We nearly became extinct. Luckily, we had an ace up our sleeve, or rather, a most peculiar mutation that occurred in our genes.

CHAPTER 3

THE IRRATIONAL REVOLUTION: SPIRITS, ART, AND LIFE

Once upon a time, people thought that they were fundamentally different from animals. This concept, known as human exceptionalism or speciesism, was accepted on faith because people believed not only that they possessed an immaterial quality called a soul, which animals did not, but also that they were shrewd and powerful and animals were not. You see, people were special because they could make stuff—lots of stuff—and to make all that stuff, they needed tools, which they also made. Animals lacked all these abilities.

The great majority of us continue to defend this human/nonhuman binary. One reason may be to justify the multitude of ways in which we ruthlessly exploit animals.[1] But the more we learn, the trickier it gets to defend our comfortable, self-appointed superiority, which is another symptom of the Hyper-Masculine Paradigm. In fact, by the late twentieth century, some writers had begun to question whether we had any solid claim for being different from animals at all.[2]

True, we humans certainly make lots of tools. We even use tools to make other tools, with which we make still more tools and an almost infinite constellation of materials and products. Despite this, researchers in the twentieth century began to notice something very peculiar: chimpanzees and other primates use stones as hammers and anvils to crack open nuts, and they fashion smooth sticks to "fish" for termites in termite mounds. Some even make simple spears with which to kill other primates. What's more, elephants use their feet and trunk to modify tree branches to use as flyswatters. Even finches use individual cactus quills to push insects through holes in tree bark, occasionally impaling them, in which case the quill becomes a fork. So yes, even though humans have fashioned a material culture several orders of magnitude more complex, many animals can and do make simple tools.

Fine. So, we took tools off the table, at least in the binary sense of "having tools equals human" or "not having tools equals nonhuman." But then what? What makes us so special, if indeed we are? Probing all known studies, artifacts, and data, social scientists at last hit the jackpot: humans have two extraordinary abilities—to imagine things not present and to perform complex symbolic behaviors. Together, these two criteria profoundly shape how we interact with each other and the world around us.

Perhaps the best example of these faculties is human language. Language involves richly symbolic forms of communication and may be our most purely human trait. It can be spoken, written, or expressed in how we dress and move our bodies, as well as in the many forms of art we create. We use it to remember the past, plan for the future, and imagine things not close at hand or even true; and most of the time, we do so automatically. Artifacts indicate we had begun to invent complex language by at least 60,000 BP, religious practices and art by 50,000 BP, and written language by 5,000 BP. And while few would suggest that any nonhuman animal exhibits truly religious behavior, Dr. Jane Goodall witnessed chimpanzees in their natural habitat shouting and shaking branches at the thunder of an approaching storm and the din of a great waterfall. She interpreted this as an indication that the "awe and wonder that underlie most religions may have originated in such primeval, uncomprehending surges of emotion."[3]

Imagination and complex symbolic behavior are our twin superpowers that make us human. Waterfalls and lightning may or may not have inspired them, but certain other elements of physical geography—and luck—clearly did.

* * *

One hundred and ten thousand years ago, average global temperatures began to fall—not by a lot, only 3 to 4°C (5.5 to 7.5°F) over the next few thousand years. But it was enough to allow snow and ice to accumulate near the poles and on high mountains. Slowly, glaciers grew to depths of nearly 3 kilometers (2 miles) and pushed outward from the North Pole to cover most of Canada and the US, as far south as present-day St. Louis and New York, as well as northern Europe and much of Siberia. As moisture became locked up in these vast sheets of ice, sea levels dropped by 120 meters (400 feet), the climate dried out, and tropical forests shrank. What had once been a veritable Garden of Eden in Africa grew thin and austere.

As if the Ice Age weren't enough, the surface of the Earth itself fractured, nearly resulting in humanity's *coup de grace*. Seventy-five thousand years ago, on the island of Sumatra in present-day Indonesia, Mount Toba erupted with a volcanic explosivity rating of eight—the highest rating of all eruptions known to have occurred on Earth—creating a caldera that measured 35x100 km (22x62 mi) in diameter and ejected some 2,800 km³ (672 mi³) of pyroclastic material and ash. That eruption is estimated to have been at least twelve times more powerful than any eruption in recent history, and it would have loaded the stratosphere with enough particulates to create a "volcanic winter." Global temperatures dropped an additional 3 to 5°C (5.5 to 9°F),[4] maybe more. The most severe effects lasted for 200 years, and a full recovery to pre-eruption Ice Age conditions may have taken 1,000 years.[5]

Due to a decline in available foods—both plant and animal—human populations followed suit, dropping from a pre-Ice Age global estimate of three million down to roughly 2,000 individuals by 60,000

BP. Our species teetered on the brink of extinction. Yet, over the next ten thousand years, fully modern *Homo sapiens* began to leave Africa in earnest. (Starting 110,000 years ago, fluctuations in climate spurred at least four waves of early humans migrating out of Africa. However, the only wave known to have succeeded in populating the rest of the world occurred between 50,000 and 60,000 BP.)[6]

The big question is why. What made us believe that unknown lands might have more to offer than those we left behind? After all, better the devil you know than the devil you don't.

Today, around 300 million people, or 3.6 percent of the world's total population, migrate *each year*.[7] So humans often give up the familiarity of the known for the dangers of the unknown. Social scientists call the motives that drive these moves "push-pull factors." Search for work is the leading cause of modern-day migration, followed by political persecution and natural disasters. If we can no longer make a living here, then we'll take our chances there, because we've heard stories or we can at least imagine better conditions that exist somewhere else. We might be wrong. It might be terrible. We might end up dead. But if we're certain that staying put will kill us, then we're willing to take that chance.

And here's why: around 60,000 BP, we began to get truly creative. Yes, we'd had the capacity to envision and craft stone tools from raw cores of rock for over three million years, making infinitesimal improvements along the way. By 100,000 BP, we'd begun to occasionally bury our dead, even paint them with red ocher. But none of these practices had really caught on. They had been merely one-off anomalies.

Only after 60,000 BP did truly symbolic art begin to flourish far and wide, and in a multitude of forms—first stones engraved with crosshatch patterns, as well as bone beads and necklaces, in Blombos Cave, South Africa, then the exquisite drawings and paintings applied to cave walls and rock overhangs in Africa, Europe, and Indonesia. Most rock art was drawn between 45,000 BP and 12,000 BP.[8] Therianthropic (part-human, part-animal) figurines were carved from ivory and bone and molded from clay between 35,000 BP and 6,000 BP.[9]

Illus. 8: The Löwenmensch, or Lion-man of the Hohlenstein-Stadel, an ivory figurine estimated to date between 35,000 and 40,000 BP

Scholars variously refer to this shift in human consciousness as the Cognitive Revolution or the Upper Paleolithic Revolution, among other names. Author Jared Diamond coined his own term, declaring it the Great Leap Forward.[10] I call it the Irrational Revolution, though not in a pejorative sense, for it was neither illogical nor a failure. Rather, we engaged our newfound magical thinking and imagined how it could work—which it did, insofar as it gave us comfort, confidence, and a more holistic conception of reality that helped us survive. Whatever name we use, this shift was truly revolutionary, as complex language and all manner of symbolic thought exploded into being. We had become fully human.

Yet we still haven't answered our earlier question: Exactly why did we gain the kind of imaginative consciousness and curiosity we take for granted today?

In his book *The Madness of Adam and Eve*, psychologist David Horrobin argues that certain "creativity genes" are responsible for both schizophrenia and creativity.[11] He suggests that clinical schizophrenia results from having too many copies of these genes. All humans have at least a basic capacity for creativity. However, those who express it more readily than do others often exhibit mood disorders, such as bipolar disorder, manic depression, unipolar depression, and schizoaffective disorder. All are characterized by delusions or hallucinations that indicate an alteration in one's apprehension of reality. It is well known how these maladies likely affected famous artists such as Vincent van Gogh, Jimi Hendrix, and Naomi Judd.

However, we must be careful not to declare an either/or infirmity. Many who are institutionalized for such disorders show no predilection for creativity, and not all virtuosos suffer from mental afflictions. Furthermore, there are artists who do harbor mild psychoses who manage to function well enough in society, often with professional help.

It wasn't long after psychologists proposed this theory that biologists found evidence to support it. In the early 2000s, a team working with geneticist Dean Hamer sought to identify genes associated with trance states and altered states of consciousness (ASC). Hamer's team correlated the personality scores of over one thousand people with their DNA, eventually parsing out a single gene that matched variables such as creativity, mood disorders, ASC, and religiosity. The gene is called vesicular monoamine transporter 2, or VMAT2, which Hamer euphemistically calls "The God Gene."[12] He claims that it's "a leading gene among many others written into our genetic code that predisposes people to religiosity."[13]

Hallucinogenic drugs can certainly help kickstart our God Gene, but ASC has also been induced by fasting, sleep deprivation, solitary confinement, sensory deprivation, dehydration, hyperventilation, marathon dance sessions around campfires, monotonous drumming, and temporal lobe (brain) seizures.[14] Mountaineers who climb into the "death zone" (typically over 8,000 m, or 26,000 ft) often experience hypoxia along with other physical infirmities. In such conditions, ASC may present as a "ghost" climber moving next to the climber, just beyond their peripheral vision.[15]

The VMAT2 gene mutation had entered the human genome by at least 60,000 BP, and at first, it was likely passed down to only a small number of people. However, it spread throughout our entire species, with a total population of only a few thousand individuals, in a mere five thousand to ten thousand years. This critical mutation affected at least three neurotransmitters that had long been part of our makeup and still are today: dopamine, serotonin, and norepinephrine. The new admixture of these hormones resulted in what anthropologist Stewart Guthrie calls our agency detection device,[16] heightening our awareness of external phenomena and augmenting our imagination. People endowed with it saw faces in the clouds, imagined creatures they could paint onto slabs of rock, and dreamed of places that might exist beyond a distant range of hills. Each one of us today is tacitly aware of how our gaze is often drawn toward the horizon, to the edge of what is known. Thus, our seemingly intrinsic curiosity to explore new places may very well be embedded in our genes. As *National Geographic* writer Eric Weiner puts it: "[H]ope lies in the very nature of travel. Travel entails wishful thinking. It demands a leap of faith, and of imagination . . ."*[17]

This evolutionary tweak in our neurotransmitter levels was a game changer. But a runner-up may have been the neurohormone oxytocin. Basically, when levels of our "happiness hormone" serotonin increase, oxytocin becomes more effective. This is important because oxytocin makes us, well, friendlier. Studies show that when human test subjects inhale oxytocin, they become more empathetic, altruistic, and trusting, and they can more accurately interpret other people's emotions.[18,19,20] Our ability to predict what others are thinking and our predilection to help strangers, which we share with bonobos, are called the Theory of Mind. This trait would have been critical to our species's survival when our numbers hovered near zero.

Evolutionary psychologist Justin Barrett and others have taken things a step further, calling this overwrought impulse of ours a hyperactive

---

* This mutation in our genome may not have been the first such occurrence to humans or other primates. In 2013, the discovery of Homo naledi, who lived in southern Africa approximately 250,000 BP, yielded evidence of symbolic behaviors, including a tool, cave art and, most significantly, the burial of their dead. However, it is not currently known if H. naledi was a direct ancestor of humans.

agency detection device, or HADD.[21] Inasmuch as this mutation may have also marked the flowering of the human ego—the conceptualizing of past and future, and distance—I suggest an alternate term: the hypersensitive egoic agency detection structure, or HEADS. This is how I will refer to it throughout the rest of this book.

In prehistoric times, people endowed with HEADS became our first dreamers, artists, and shamans, who may have been visited and instructed by "spirits."[22] According to evolutionary psychologist Scott Atran: "All supernatural agent concepts trigger our naturally selected agency detection system, which is trip-wired to respond to fragmentary information, inciting perception of figures lurking in the shadows and emotions of dread and awe. Mistaking a non-agent for an agent would do little harm, but failing to detect an agent, especially a human or animal predator, could prove fatal; it's better safe than sorry."[23] As it turns out, religion may have been an egoic byproduct that aided our adaptation and survival as well.[24,25]

Similar research by anthropologist Ernest Becker proposes what he calls the Terror Management Theory, or TMT.[26] Becker's main thesis holds that humans coevolved a psychological defense to buffer against the terror of their impending demise. That is, once our ego reaches maturity, around age seven or eight, we must sit with the realization that we will one day die. Most people manage this reality by imagining another, more pleasant scenario in an afterlife. If we can imagine an immaterial essence or soul that survives death to live forever with spirits or gods who possess and control everything, then the ego may be mollified. Thus, religion was born.[27]

Finally, this extraordinary mutation allowed us to radically expand our social construction of space. From this point on, there would never again be a *cognitively* "natural" or "wild" space, because the world was either controlled (home range) or uncontrolled.[28] And if it was uncontrolled—which meant nearly everywhere at that time—then it was populated by our imagination (HEADS), which in turn was socialized by the worldview we had learned from the day we were born. Spaces and places became gendered. Some landscapes were directly associated

with predominantly feminine or masculine gendered traits and female
or male sexual traits. From that moment on, every place, condition,
quality, and person became socially constructed. As geographer Howard
Stein puts it, "We project psychic contents outward onto the social and
physical world and act as though what is projected is in fact an attribute
of the other or outer."[29] (We will return to this concept in Chapters 11
and 12.)

Remember: this irrational yet favorable shift in cognition occurred
during one of the most brutal episodes of the last Ice Age, when plant,
animal, and human populations plummeted. At that moment, we
experienced a random mutation in our brain chemistry that just happened
to benefit our species in a novel way. It inspired us to imagine and
innovate—capacities we desperately needed to survive as we migrated
south to fish the shores off the Cape of Good Hope and north along the
Nile Corridor to the Mediterranean. It enabled those of us who moved
north to invent clothing and build the shelters we needed (in addition
to the evolution of lighter, more sun-absorbent skin tones to synthesize
vitamin D). Another group of us migrated along the coast of the Indian
Ocean. Ever curious to move on, this group invented boat technologies
that allowed us to paddle across 240 kilometers (150 miles) of open ocean
to arrive in Australia by 50,000 BP.

And what did we find? Where did all these new cerebral superpowers
lead us?

Well, not exactly to a Garden of Eden or into the shade of a Genesis
Tree. Yes, the rivers, lakes, and seashores teemed with life, but the
surrounding uplands were often drier and more desolate than the places
we had left behind. Of course, these migrations didn't happen over a long
weekend or even within a generation. We made these moves cautiously
and incrementally, doing what we knew and altering our behaviors as
little as necessary. The trip from sub-Saharan Africa to the Middle East
took five thousand years, and the journey to Australia took ten thousand
years. The peopling of the rest of Europe and Asia would require another
twenty thousand years. This latter migration was deterred by the presence

of a continent-wide ice sheet and perhaps the presence of certain locals—
that is, the Neandertals.

We encountered, along with strange climates, foods, and peoples,
profound changes in the landscapes as we left the narrow river corridors
and coastal plains of East Africa. Vast new terrains funneled our
migrations: the Sahara and Rub al-Khali Deserts; the Zagros, Caucasus,
and Himalaya Mountains; the Mediterranean and Black Seas; as well as
the great river systems of the Volga, Indus, and Ganges.

The gods had beckoned, and we climbed out of our birthplace to
confront new worlds. We quickly learned to cope with them, but
processing what they would mean to us and internalizing their realities
would come only slowly. The symbols contained in our art, religions,
stories, and cultures were in the process of evolving from a pangendered
matrix to a profusion of gendered binaries. Applying our enhanced
cerebral hardware, we worked to frame these new geographies in terms
of our new psychic content. And as we were about to discover, some
geographies would be friendly, while others would not.

PART TWO

RIVER VALLEYS AND COASTAL PLAINS: 12,000–6,000 BP

Big Picture: Small bands of humans grow into cohesive tribes and become dependent on agriculture. In turn, they migrate less, acquire more possessions, and divide labor among individuals with specializations, such as in farming, crafts, ceremonies, or leadership. Humans had long interpreted elements in their environment as parts of an integrated, pangendered whole. However, as this period progresses, they increasingly view all categories, including those of gender, as distinct, unequal, and hierarchical.

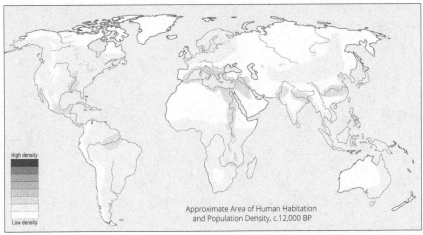

Illus. 9: Approximate area of human habitation and population density, c.12,000 BP

CHAPTER 4

PANDORA'S BOX

Once upon a time, there lived many goddesses and gods, the greatest of whom was Zeus. Together, these divine beings created a race of immortals called titans, but no mortal humans yet walked the Earth. As time went on, most titans proved to be an unruly breed and were always getting into trouble.

An especially precocious one named Prometheus had gone so far as to steal fire from the gods and give it to all titans. This angered Zeus greatly, who chained Prometheus to a rock, where an eagle fed on his liver each day. Still, the knowledge of fire could not be reclaimed. So, Zeus crafted a plan to punish the titans (and the humans to follow) for their unearned good fortune.

One day, Zeus instructed the god Hephaestus to create a daughter for him, but one who was unlike any other: this woman would be the first mortal. Obeying his command, Hephaestus took a lump of clay, fashioned it into a woman, and named her Pandora. But her body was still quite basic and lifeless, and so he asked the other deities for help. The goddess Aphrodite bestowed great beauty upon Pandora, Athena breathed life into her, and the god Hermes invested her with charm, deceit, and insatiable curiosity. Pleased with their work, Zeus sent Pandora to Earth to become the wife of a gentle and considerate titan named Epimetheus, who just happened to be the brother of Prometheus.

Epimetheus found Pandora positively charming and instantly fell in love with her. However, before Zeus released her, he entrusted her with a little box, and to Epimetheus he gave the key. Zeus instructed them to never open the box, but as for that he gave no explanation. After delivering his cryptic warning, Zeus left, certain that Pandora would soon open the box.

Epimetheus and Pandora dutifully put the box and the key on a high shelf for safekeeping. But true to her nature, Pandora yearned to know what was inside the mysterious little box. One morning, while her husband was away, she took the key down from its high shelf, fitted it into the box's lock, and turned it ever so carefully. However, imagining her husband's disappointment and Zeus's anger, she relocked the box without opening it and replaced the key on its shelf. It was only a few days later that she again took the key and fitted it into the keyhole, and once more, at the last moment, she relented and placed each item back in its proper place. She was happy she'd been able to resist the temptation, but each time it had gotten a little harder to stop herself from opening the box. The thought of it consumed her.

The very next day, she once more took the key, fitted it into the keyhole, and turned it ever so gently, but this time, she turned it until it clicked into place. And scarcely had she touched the lid that it burst open, releasing a tempest of specters—disease, inequality, poverty, hatred, jealousy, greed, death, and suffering without end.

Pandora screamed and slammed shut the lid, but all had escaped, save one. She sensed that the remaining entity within the box was somehow different from the rest. So she cracked open the lid and peered inside, and there, in the center, spun a tiny pearl of light, the only virtue the box had contained. Despite having released misery upon the world, she had at least preserved Hope so that she might instill belief, encouragement, and optimism in her children and in all children yet to come. For Pandora was destined to be the mother of all mortal humans.

* * *

Written by the Greek poet Hesiod around 700 BCE, "Pandora's Box" is a latecomer among the stories we've considered so far. Like the story of Eve in the Garden, this myth pins the ills of the world not only on women but, more deeply, on the feminine principle itself. The name Pandora may be translated to "all gifts," which sounds charitable and humanitarian but actually refers to the spate of misfortunes Pandora unwittingly releases upon the world. Hope is the only positive quality contained within the box, and the only one she preserves. Scholars interpret this to represent either humanity's redeeming qualities of aspiration and having the faith to carry on, or the bitter false hope of delusion, self-deception, and paradox. All these vices and virtues may be considered byproducts of HEADS.

The original Greek version of the story describes not a "box" but a "jar," referring to the large earthen vessels once used to store grain or olive oil. In the sixteenth century, the Dutch scholar Erasmus incorrectly translated the Greek word as "box," as in a casket or sepulcher. As such, the feminine was further made to imply sin and death with reference to Eve's original sin in the Garden: "For the wages of sin is death . . ." (Romans 6:23). Mythologists suggest that both metaphors may also refer to female sexual anatomy. In the same vein, notions of female inferiority are reflected in how the Greek word for "uterus," *hystera*, became *hysteria*, denoting irrationality (in the pejorative sense). Beginning in classical Greece, medical professionals throughout history have used *hysteria* as a clinical diagnosis for women's so-called uncontrollable bursts of emotion. The diagnostic term was dropped by the American Psychiatric Association only in 1952.

In the myth, Zeus is angry that Prometheus has taken fire from the gods without permission. You'll recall that a similar theme emerged quite independently in the San people's creation story, "The Genesis Tree." Worldwide, the "theft of fire" motif has commonly been used to explain the origins of civilization. Notably, the Jewish and Christian traditions tell of how "fallen angels" (later considered demons) taught humans to use fire in the Book of Enoch.[1] And as we've seen, fire is an archetypal masculine form of matter, and the light it emits is a masculine form of energy. Freud considered fire, as well as flame-shaped mountains such as Mount

Olympus, metaphorically phallic, because they tend to point skyward.[*2] In this way, Prometheus himself is a masculine symbol of conquest.

By contrast, the torch-body that supports the flame is analogous to the Great Tree in "The Genesis Tree" and the Tree of Life in "The Garden of Eden." It is used here as a feminine symbol, and Prometheus wields it to plunder the masculine symbol that is fire from the realm of the supernatural. The box, which is feminine, may also be viewed as a metaphor for the Great Tree as well as the Tree of Knowledge of Good and Evil—the source of both hope and suffering. All symbolize the forbidden fruit and that which comes with the awakening of ego consciousness.

Epimetheus plays a minor role in this tale. His career takes on greater significance in other myths, wherein he is tasked with creating all animals. Fathering some of the first humans is only his second-greatest project, courtesy of Pandora. I should, however, mention that when Epimetheus fulfilled his first job, he gave animals all the best traits and saved none for humans, an oversight he later denies. Hence, Epimetheus is also the god of excuses and negligence. This is an interesting example of the hyper-masculine propensity to deny culpability and responsibility for wrongdoing and to project blame onto others.

Our goal in this section of the book is to tighten our focus on the time when humans invented small-scale garden farming (horticulture) and the keeping of livestock (pastoralism). Together, these two systems of making a living are called agriculture, and so this period is often called the Agricultural Revolution.[†]

This was a critical turning point. Throughout this age, gender and other categories were reduced to egoic binaries, and while the sacred feminine continued to be venerated in most areas, the masculine gained traction. In a few places, myths like "Pandora" and "The Garden of Eden" scapegoated the feminine for all things evil in the world, and women were punished for it. Change, in the form of the Hyper-Masculine Paradigm, was in the air.

---

* This is especially true for actively volcanic mountains.

† Another term used is the Neolithic Revolution or the New Stone Age, because stone tool technologies were refined to a high degree during this time.

Chapter 5

FEMININE LANDSCAPES

Tales told round those prehistoric campfires likely involved suspense, humor, sorrow, and plenty of romance. But whatever its theme, every story was no doubt rich in allegory, with plots that contained symbols painted onto the world of the storytellers and their audiences. And every time, landscapes would have played a critical role.

As we saw in Chapter 1, the human mind is a master at parsing the world into discrete categories, the most obvious of which are binary opposites, or dualities.* This ability kept our ancient ancestors alive, allowing them to discern what was safe and what was dangerous, what was edible and what was poisonous, who was friend and who was foe; and it evolved to work automatically and instantaneously. In Chapter 3, we saw that HEADS is the cognitive structure that enables us to interpret symbolic meaning. Putting the two together, we get a world suffused with implicit value and bias. For example, most people would say that it is better to be alive rather than dead. This may be the most universal biocultural duality. But second place might go to the female/male divide, with likely agreement among people who live in patriarchal societies (which are most) that it is better—socioeconomically, at least—to be

---

* Twentieth-century French anthropologist Claude Lévi-Strauss developed the theory of structuralism to explain how the human mind organizes the world into binary opposites.

male rather than female. Other biocultural dualities include young/old, tall/short, thin/fat, able/disabled, light skin/dark skin, and animal/plant.

Below are a few more examples of dualities. As you read through each pair, pick one term you consider to be the better or more important of the two. Go quickly and try not to think about it too much.

> Compassion/indifference, caution/risk, strong/weak, soft/hard, assertive/passive, defiant/submissive, masculine/feminine; land/water, wet/dry, mountain/valley, forest/desert, cold/hot, north/south, east/west, center/periphery, high/low; up/down, light/dark, sacred/profane, eternal/temporal.[1]

Did you pause over some pairs longer than over others? Did the order in which they are written speed you up or slow you down? Most of your preferences likely required no thought at all and came to you automatically and instantaneously. This is because you internalized their symbolic value as a young child. They reflect a tiny part of your socialized mental content. However, some of your choices may have been trickier to make. They also symbolize part of your socialized mental content, but with added layers of social filters. Finally, you may have guessed that the pairs above are examples of social, geographical, and cosmological dualities, respectively. All are gendered, and by itself, neither term in any pair is inherently better or worse. Socially, however, the presence of one implies that there is indeed a better or worse opposite.

For example, the concept of *hard* is often seen as masculine, and the concept of *soft* as feminine. Among the Plains Indians, women worked with soft materials such as textiles and clay, while men worked with hard materials such as bone, stone, and metal.[2] However, these generalizations do not always hold true: among the Puebloan peoples of the American Southwest, men wove textiles on looms, and both women and men made stone tools. Since hard materials usually last longer, archaeologists who were socialized and educated in male-biased cultures traditionally assumed all such artifacts had been made by men.

In modern Euro-American cultures, the social sciences themselves were once called "soft" sciences, with implied feminine qualities. They often struggled to gain equal footing with the natural or "hard" sciences that based findings on quantifiable data and mathematics, which were interpreted as masculine.[3]

In reality, binaries do not exist in a vacuum; they are stacked and linked with other binaries in something akin to a web or a matrix. To take another example, the social construct of *feminine* may intersect with female-valley-water-east-earth-mundane. Its corollary is *masculine*, which may intersect with male-land-mountain-north-cold-center-spiritual. These illustrations are patently stereotypical. But in the broader matrix of apparent dualities, feminine-male-birth-periphery-forest is just as valid as masculine-female-death-east-mundane. In fact, any number of combinations is possible.*

There's more: each pair of binary opposites is mediated by a third term—or a spectrum of third terms—what Hindus call the *Ajna*, or the third-eye chakra. Third terms affiliate with neither of the opposites, yet they simultaneously join them and contain them. For example, yellow is intermediate on the visible spectrum between red and green. It is neither red nor green yet contains both. On a stoplight, it means neither "stop" nor "go" (unless you try to outrun it before it changes to red). In the same vein, pangender and transgender intercede between (and beyond) feminine and masculine, intersex between female and male, twilight between night and day, and Earth between Heaven and Hell. In terms of geography, coastlines are areas of transition between dry land and water, piedmont between mountains and plains, savanna between forests and deserts, and thresholds between inside and outside. In fact, all intermediate spaces are types of thresholds, being neither this nor that. In terms of social constructs, they comprise the greater part of the matrix, and we can refer to them as liminal spaces, conditions, and qualities.

---

* Today, *mundane* is commonly associated with *feminine*, while *spiritual* correlates with *masculine*. This has been the case only since the Hyper-Masculine Devolution, discussed in Chapter 9.

This concept reveals the special value assigned to the number three. Examples include the Christian Holy Trinity, the Hindu Trimurti, the three sons of Noah, and Neptune's trident. From its magico-religious origins, the number three has come to pervade popular culture: "three strikes and you're out," "third time's a charm," *The Three Musketeers*, "learn your ABCs," three-letter acronyms such as network television's CBS, NBC, PBS, and CNN, and now the GLT and HMP, and so on. Note also that some of the stories in this book revolve around the number three: Pandora opens the box on her third attempt, and as you'll see later, the Smith asks for three items from the Devil, and the boy in *The Lorax* chooses from three forms of payment to hear the Once-ler's tale. Examples are endless. Worldwide, only the number seven is more popular than the number three.*[4]

Many stories and myths attempt to mediate what might be called the ultimate duality—that of life and death.[5] However, in its grandest sense, life may be seen as the consciousness that contains both birth *and* death, which are opposites. As such, life is the ultimate liminal condition and has no opposite.[6]

The physical world itself was once thought to be comprised of elements found in opposition to one another. Water, fire, earth, and air (all of which are gendered) represented the four states of matter and may have been among the first symbols cognitively internalized by humans. These elements were derived from early beliefs in what were once called the "four humors" of the organic world: moist, dry, hot, and cold. As psychologist Carl Jung remarks, "Of the elements, two are active—fire and air, and two are passive—earth and water."[7] These pairs of opposites and their mediators are symbolized in Taoism's yin and yang. Water and earth represent the yin, which is the feminine archetype, of Chinese philosophy, while fire and air represent the yang, the masculine archetype.

---

* Regarding the number seven, think of the creation week in the Bible, "in seventh heaven," the lucky number seven, the seven dwarves, seven seas, etc. Its popularity extends back to antiquity, wherein it may have originally referenced the seven celestial objects visible to the naked eye that do not move in accordance with the stars, i.e., five of the planets plus the sun and the moon.

The earth element represents the everyday surface underfoot, as well as the fertile soil in which plants and food crops grow. Water is equated with streams, rivers, valleys, and bodies of water. The motion for each is downward and passive, and its disposition is cool, dark, and unconscious, i.e., associated with the inner Self. Darkness is further associated with the moon and its twenty-eight-day cycle of birth, death, and rebirth. This is allegorical of women's menstrual cycle, the reproduction of life, and therefore the generative cycles of nature.[*8] The downward-pointing triangle is a sexual symbol of the female, the feminine, and the goddess. (More on this in Chapter 6.)

Illus. 10: Feminine landscape: tropical rainforest with stream

Fire and air are associated with the sky and masculine, male sky-gods. Their motion is upward and active, their disposition hot, illuminated, and conscious—that is, they symbolize the ego-mind that operates in time and space. Daylight implies sunlight. This is allegorical of life in the

---

* Women's menstrual cycles average 28 to 29 days, with younger women and teens often experiencing longer cycles and women in their later reproductive years experiencing shorter cycles. As for moon cycles, the moon orbits the Earth approximately every 27.3 days but requires about 29.5 days to move through one complete cycle of its phases. Therefore, lunar calendars alternate between 29 and 30 days for each lunar month.

quotidian human world. The upward-pointing triangle is a sexual symbol of the male, the masculine, and gods. (More on this in Chapter 8.)

These basic gendered symbols correspond to a landscape's environmental quality—that is, its conduciveness to life. Some places are more conducive to life than are others. Landscapes may thus be classified based on how relatively wet or dry, low or high they are. Dryness and height are associated with the elements of air and fire, as flames and mountains point upward. Wetness and lowness are associated with water and earth, as valleys point downward. Well-watered tropical and temperate landscapes tend to be rounded by erosion, with gradual slopes and climates moderated by moisture. Dry tropical and temperate landscapes contain sharp angles, and their climates swing from frigid cold to searing heat, which implies fire. Air is ethereal and immaterial.

Illus. 11: Masculine landscape: Monument Valley, Arizona

Using these criteria, we can discern the natural world in terms of places that are predominantly feminine and those that are predominantly masculine. Feminine gendered landscapes of the world include oceans, lakes, and rivers, as well as forests and valleys (especially those containing streams or rivers). Masculine gendered landscapes are mountains (especially high mountains), circumpolar areas, deserts, steppes, and semi-arid plains. As stated above, although feminine–masculine liminal spaces occur at varying points between the opposites, the clearest junctures exist in canyons that contain perennial streams, in caves with subterranean streams and seeps, and in coastal areas. These transitional realms serve as liminal thresholds that both separate and join conditions tilting toward opposing gendered landscapes.

For example, among the modern-day Haya people of Tanzania, female spirits are usually propitiated at cave sites. One such cave, named *Kalyabagole*, or "The Cave That Ate the Bride," is steeped in myth involving a betrothed Haya woman. As the story goes, one day a woman went out into the tall *rweya* grasses to chase grasshoppers, a seasonal delicacy. Unawares, she tripped and fell to her death in the vertical entrance to this cave—a vast, multileveled cave complex now considered sacred by local villagers. The spirit of the woman, who is regarded as an ancestor, continues to be recognized in accordance with the seasonal emergence of grasshoppers, a prized source of protein.[9]

Another nearby cave is called *Lwemboijole*, or "The Cave of God." A story is recounted of a woman who went to draw water from the entrance of this water-filled cavern. While stooping at the water's edge to dip her pot into the water, she slipped, fell in, and was pulled into the subterranean current of the cave. Legend has it that her body reemerged on the opposite side of Rubafu Peninsula, some 12 kilometers (7.5 miles) west, in the Kaagya Bay of Lake Victoria-Nyanza. The horizontal entrance to this cave measures over 5 m (16.5 ft) and receives a perpetual "rain" of water that percolates down through the strata above. The spirit of the woman, who is now considered an ancestor, is propitiated for rainfall and agricultural success each month when the moon is new.[10]

In Chapter 2, we saw how our inclination toward inherent friendliness and imaginativeness forms the first layer of the Gendered Landscapes Theory, or GLT. These social traits grew from biological mutations. We built on these traits when we began to project everything in our unconscious ego-mind (HEADS) onto the world around us, whether it was other people, animals, or the surrounding landscape. As Carl Jung writes, "To the degree that the ego identifies with the persona, [our gendered subconscious] is projected into the real objects of our environment."[11] So, in the Late Neolithic, we projected our social subconscious onto, and experienced our world in terms of, the gendered binaries and liminal qualities outlined above. This forms the second layer of the GLT.

Before we go on, I must disclose an important exception to the neat and tidy associations already made, and so I approach this point with great care. People everywhere have long identified life with two primary sources: first, the heavens, that is, mostly the sun and rain, but also the moon and stars; and second, the earth, that is, rivers, streams, and fertile soil. After the Irrational Revolution, the sun and the sky were initially considered *not* masculine but rather feminine. Remnants of this original Hyper-Feminine Paradigm trickled down into the Bronze Age, with goddess myths from Sumer, Babylon, Egypt, Japan, China, and West Africa, and even to the modern day, with similar myths among the Indigenous peoples of Australia and Alaska.[12] Likewise, mountains may have long been the foreboding haunts of masculine spirits and gods, but they also generated the streams, rivers, and rain that people depended on, so they, too, were originally considered realms of the goddesses.[13] For instance, the Nepali name for Mount Everest is *Chomolungma*, which means "Goddess Mother of the World." In contrast, the *oldest* myths associate the moon and the Earth itself with male gods and masculine principles. For example, the Old Testament god Yahweh began his career as a lunar god and consort to a sun goddess.[14] One by one, these ancient precepts would be turned on their heads in the Iron Age. (More on this topic in Chapters 8 and 9.)

Illus. 12: Goddess on World Mountain, engraved gold, Minoan Crete, c.1,400 BCE

By 12,000 BP, global temperatures had finally begun to rise. This gave people the luxury of planting a little patch of ground with cereal grasses or root vegetables. We had likely known how to cultivate foods for a long time. We may even have experimented with it, planting edible greens such as *Oxalis pes-caprae* (wild sorrel) in a meadow one season before moving on. The next year, we would have returned to harvest enough of it to eat alongside some *Vigna frutescens* (ekwa root) we'd gathered.

If labor was divided according to sex, as it is among today's foragers, then women were almost certainly the first horticulturalists.[15] As a result, the female capacity, not only for human reproduction but also for food production, was amplified. Burying an edible plant, sacrificing it to the Great Mother instead of eating it, was a sort of women's magic. When a group returned to the same spot it had camped last season, and the women in the group discovered that food had grown where they had left its seeds, then the magic had worked. It reinforced the practice of sacrifice and provided a back-up source of food.

Most gathered foods had always come from forested, low-lying areas with good water sources. These feminine landscapes were most powerful—nutritionally, socially, and spiritually. Among modern-day horticulturalists and foragers—such as Polynesians and Australian Aborigines, respectively—supernatural power is concentrated in the landscape, and when plant foods are harvested, the spirits believed to reside in those places are praised.

In wet tropical and temperate regions, finding food was relatively easy. As rainfall and temperatures increased at the end of the Ice Age, experiments in farming added a nice bonus to our regular fare. We were most successful in low-lying river valleys, such as the Tigris-Euphrates, the Huang He, and the lower Nile. But no matter where we tried our hand at farming, it worked best in higher-quality, environmentally productive lands—that is, feminine landscapes.

Consequently, something curious began to happen around 12,000 BP. Eating plants that we had cultivated meant we could stay put longer before moving on to the next seasonal camp, and spending more time in one place meant we could afford to make things we would not otherwise carry around with us, such as ceramic pottery. This allowed us to cook our foods into a soft mush, not only for ourselves but also for our babies, and this resulted in earlier weaning and shorter birth intervals. In a few dozen generations, human populations soared to an estimated Paleolithic high of ten million worldwide.[16] Even so, we had lots of space to move around in, and shopping for groceries was a breeze, so there was more than enough food to go around. In fact, we'd never had it so good.

And then things got really interesting.

Chapter 6

THE HORTICULTURAL REVOLUTION: GODDESSES, MATRIARCHY, AND BIRTH

It was 11,000 BP, and just as the stories of an ancient Age of Ice were perhaps fading from our collective memory, the planet relapsed into the deep freeze. Paleoclimatologists call this thousand-year cold snap the Younger Dryas, so named after a tiny tundra flower, the *Dryas octopetala*—one of the few plants that flourished across northern Eurasia after temperatures dropped and glaciers once again advanced. The exact cause for the climate's cooling remains unclear, but it happened fast. One theory suggests the planet detoured back into the Ice Age because a large meteor crashed into the Greenland ice sheet, sending debris into the atmosphere that would have blocked the sun for years, thus cooling the climate.[1] Another theory cites evidence of an enormous lake in North America that had formed in the wake of retreating continental ice sheets. Due to higher temperatures, this lake breached its ice dam and flooded the Atlantic, disrupting warm-water ocean currents around the world.[2]

Whatever its cause, this sudden cold phase motivated people everywhere to scramble to make ends meet. Our populations had swelled during the good times, but suddenly, we were unable to feed everyone with only the foods we foraged. We were desperate, so we made a deal with the devil. Archaeological excavations around the world indicate that small clusters of us (mostly men) hunted more often, especially the larger animals. And where we could, in the protected river valleys, we (mostly women) also cultivated the ancestors of wheat, millet, barley, rice, and corn—not just experimentally, as we'd done before, but with intention and urgency.[3]

This period saw the swift extinction of many species of megafauna: mammoths, mastodons, camels, and horses in North America; giant ground sloths in South America; and species of rhinoceros, lions, and bison in Europe and Asia. Like us, they, too, were struggling to deal with the colder climate, although we humans are thought to have been a contributing factor in their demise.[4] Two smoking guns support this accusation. One is the great number of animal bones found in middens (trash piles) near Neolithic camps and homes. The other is the content of the bones of the actual inhabitants of those homes. Here's why: Strontium is a naturally occurring element that is found in groundwater and absorbed by plants. Herbivores absorb some of it into their cells when they eat plants, but omnivores and carnivores absorb very little of it when they eat the flesh of those herbivores. As Paleolithic foragers, we had high levels of strontium in our bones right up to the beginning of the Younger Dryas, indicating we ate loads of plants—some 150 varieties—which made up the bulk of our diet. But during the cold snap, strontium levels in our bones plummeted. We ate mostly animals. Later, after things warmed up again, we returned to eating plants for most of our calories, although this time those plants were cultivars (domesticated crops), which numbered only about eight varieties.[5,6]

By 10,000 BP, the Younger Dryas had passed, and we settled down into the first permanent villages—first in Southwest Asia and the Far East, a little later in West Africa, Central America, and Europe. These were horticultural communities, wherein all the farming was done by hand. Many of these small populations lived in the middle latitudes, which are semi-arid today but which experienced a warmer, wetter climate at that time. Consequently, the environmental quality of these places was moderate to high. Most of the larger animals were gone, so we hunted smaller ones and planted more crops. Soon, someone (perhaps a man, since men did most of the hunting) hit on the idea of domesticating certain animal species instead of hunting for them all the time. In temperate, semi-arid regions, this idea took off, and some of us became the first pastoralists.

Goats and sheep were first domesticated in the drier regions of Anatolia (Turkey), while chickens were popular in Southeast Asia. About the same time, we began living in more confined spaces, often together with our livestock to protect them from nighttime predators. This resulted in a host of communicable diseases that we acquired from those livestock, afflictions called zoonoses, from the Greek words *zoon* ("animals") and *nosos* ("disease"). Over the course of the past ten thousand years, human populations have contracted twenty-sex such diseases from chickens, forty-two from pigs, forty-six from sheep and goats, fifty from cows, and still more from wild animals.[7] Recent examples include tuberculosis, zika, Ebola, influenza, small pox, measles, mumps—a list that has grown to account for nearly 75 percent of all human diseases that exist today.[8] All this because a hunter (probably male) thought of domesticating the animals they hunted. Mythologically speaking, Epimetheus or Abel were far more likely to have ushered these contagions into the human world than Pandora or Eve.

Two primary worldviews emerged from this watershed moment. On the one hand, foraging peoples and horticultural peoples who lived in greener, more feminine environments tended to worship goddesses, continue to be egalitarian and matrilineal (possibly matriarchal), and esteem the social traits of relationship, community, and conciliation. On the other hand, pastoral peoples who lived in drier, more masculine environments tended to worship masculine gods, become hierarchical and patrilineal/patriarchal, and esteem exclusion, xenophobia, and aggression.

In the late twentieth century, anthropologist Peggy Sanday wrote ethnographies on over one hundred Indigenous societies still living much the way they always had. Her research found that women possess more economic, social, and creative power in cultures whose food is primarily plant-based, as compared with those whose food is animal-based. As Sanday states, "In societies dependent on animals, women are rarely depicted as the ultimate source of creative power."[9] Furthermore, in animal-based societies, wealth and name follow the male side of the family, male gods are worshipped, women are solely responsible for childcare, and women do more work than men, although their work is valued less.[10]

This crossroads in our evolution was perhaps our first large-scale encounter with social inequality. But wherever we lived and whomever we worshipped, our dependence on the new state-of-the-art crops and livestock-based foods carried unforeseen consequences: dental caries (tooth decay) from drinking goat's milk and eating corn; maloccluded (crowded) teeth from eating softer, cooked foods; and malnutrition from maintaining a less diverse diet. Together, our new habits negatively affected our height, bone density, and overall health. (Today, only about 25 percent of adults worldwide can digest milk products.[11] Contrary to Western popular attitudes and marketing campaigns, the greatest occurrence of osteoporosis and bone fractures is found in countries where milk products are most widely consumed. This is due to the body's extraction of calcium from its bones as a buffering agent against the increasingly acidic blood pH that occurs in response to dairy consumption.[12]) Origin myths that tell of the "fall of man," such as "Pandora's Box" and "The Garden of Eden," may be pointing back to this moment in time.

We had more food than ever before, and it did keep us alive long enough to have more babies, but we worked harder to get it and suffered after we ate it. The pendulum had swung, and things again looked grim. Contrary to most creation stories, two things appear to have saved us from oblivion: women and the moon.

* * *

As a field instructor for National Outdoor Leadership School, I once guided groups of novices—mostly college-aged—through wilderness areas in various corners of the world. Courses lasted anywhere from two weeks to three months, and most were comprised of both young women and young men. In my experience, on orientation day, a female co-instructor normally took the women aside to brief them on the finer points of maintaining good feminine hygiene in the wilds. And by the end of those longer expeditions, my co-instructors often confided in me that, yes, it had happened again—all the women's periods were in sync. (It gets easier to talk about bodily functions after having lived with someone for months in a tent, endured hundreds of miles of backpacking, and survived storms, illnesses, injuries, and emotional breakdowns—usually mine.)

But that's just an anecdote. Science has verified what all of us have known since the dawn of time: women who live in close proximity to one another experience closely aligned menstrual cycles.[13] What you may not have heard, however, is that women who live near the equator tend to ovulate around the time of the full moon.[14] It seems reasonable, then, to surmise that prehistoric women who lived in small bands of foragers in equatorial Africa ovulated during the full moon and menstruated during the new moon. Analogous myths that began in ancient Africa would have traveled with us as we migrated to temperate regions. This fits well with classical mythology that associates women with the moon.[15]

Since women and moon cycles were further identified with the creation of human life and most food production, it becomes clear why Neolithic peoples worshipped a pantheon of goddesses.[16] Meanwhile, men defaulted to the masculine gender role of hunting and killing, and with the advent of agriculture, these gendered divisions of labor became ever more pronounced. Nevertheless, most landscapes from which people wrested their livelihood continued to be verdant and riverine. These were feminine landscapes, so with horticulture and reproduction, the primary power of life continued to reside with women.

And yet, this portrayal misses the mark. People did not merely worship their imaginings of some distant, ethereal goddess, although this happened too. Rather, woman herself embodied the divine feminine. She magically created new life, and so she *was* the Mother Goddess, the Genesis Tree, and the Tree of Life. Woman and the feminine *were* the *axis mundi*, the center of the universe, and the universe *in toto*.[17] Human reality revolved around her.

Illus. 13: Venus of Laussel, Dordogn, France, c.23,000 BCE

Discovered in Dordogne, France, and estimated to be roughly 25,000 years old, the famous Venus of Laussel is a low-relief rock carving that shows a woman with pendulous breasts, a large stomach, and wide hips. In her right hand, she holds an upward-pointing crescent that has been inscribed with thirteen notches. Remnants of red ocher coat the carving. Prehistorian Andre Leroi-Gourhan interprets it as a representation of a goddess figure holding a bison horn, which is associated with the moon and hence with women, reproduction, and life. The notches represent the thirteen lunar months of the year, and the ocher represents menstrual blood. Many similar carvings have been found in places from Spain to Russia.[18]

Indeed, goddess figurines like this may serve as early examples of anthropomorphism—our propensity to view anything that is not essentially human as having human form or attributes. For example, when you were a child, you may have been sad when you saw a leaf fall from a tree, because you thought it must be afraid. In this instance, you would have interpreted the leaf's falling with your own human emotions, imagining what you might experience if you were to fall from a tree. You had anthropomorphized the leaf and, in so doing, also expressed your human capacity for empathy.

Likewise, we adults may name our car and feel sad when the day arrives when we no longer own it. Some of us may even wonder if the car is sad too. In this example, we have anthropomorphized—and probably gendered—our car. We do the same to pretty much everything else. If you discern the face of Jesus Christ in the crispy wrinkles of a tortilla flatbread, then you have anthropomorphized the tortilla. This is an especially apt example, since we humans have a talent for anthropomorphizing and gendering not only the things in our immediate experience but also the divine beings in our stories, songs, dances, and visual arts. Deities we pray to tend to look like us, behave like us, and unsurprisingly, display the same foibles to which we are prone. And not only gods, cars, and flatbread, but we also anthropomorphize and gender the landscapes around us—all compliments of HEADS.

Sigmund Freud suggested that overall, humans pattern their religions after the parent–child relationship. This is readily apparent in the nature of gods, who serve as larger-than-life parental figures and moral exemplars.[19] More recently, psychosocial anthropologists have expanded on Freud's theory to include landscapes. In anthropomorphizing nature, we humans have worshipped gods of thunder, of mountains, of the sea, and so on; it was but a short step for us to add human qualities—especially those of our parents—to gods and the geographic domains over which they preside.[20] If the environment is a certain way, and so are our parents, then so are the gods—whether that's harsh and punitive or mild and forgiving.

So, the sacred pervaded all of existence, including how we got our food. Sites in Asia Minor provide some of the earliest examples of this custom. In the 1950s, archaeologist James Mellaart began excavating a site in southern Turkey called Çatalhöyük, which is dated to 9,500 BP. Ancient pollen samples indicate the staple food was emmer wheat. At the height of its population, this town may have housed between 5,000 and 8,000 residents with a town plan that resembled a Southwest Native American pueblo. Homes were built very close to one another, with entrances on the roofs. No home was very much larger or smaller than any other, and artifacts show that each person carried about the same social status as everyone else. This was an egalitarian society.

Illus. 14: Artist's depiction of Çatalhöyük

Human skeletons buried in the floor of homes in Çatalhöyük are likely the remains of former occupants. Terracotta goddess figurines, also found throughout the town site, tend to accentuate breasts, hips, and vulvas—icons of physical birth. In addition, snake and frog figurines have often been recovered from inside the homes. These artifacts represent transformation or spiritual rebirth. Carvings of pigs and bulls are also ubiquitous. At that time, pigs had recently been domesticated and resembled wild boars with upward-pointing tusks. Aurochs, the progenitors of cattle, had also been recently domesticated and had horns that also pointed upwards. People considered these features analogous to the crescent moon, a metaphor for the waxing and waning of women's monthly cycle and reproductive life.[21] Sky-god cultures would later convert horns, tusks, and hooves from symbols of the goddess to that of the devil and evil itself. All misfortunes in the world would thus become further associated with women and the feminine.[22]

Archaeologists James Mellaart and Marija Gimbutas interpret artifacts from Çatalhöyük, Hacilar, Göbekli Tepe, and other Neolithic sites as representative of a matriarchal, Mother-Goddess culture. (Scholars fiercely debate this theory.[23]) Excavations reveal that these cultures installed no defensive outer walls around their towns; there are also no signs of warfare or weaponry, or of animal slaughter within the towns.[24] Small populations across Europe and Southwest Asia had survived the Younger Dryas by cooperatively adapting to local physical geographies, and everyone deified the feminine and focused heavily on horticultural and gathered food sources.[25,26]

However, other tribal peoples forged a different way. On the open plains of Central Asia, called the Pontic-Caspian Steppes, lived a people who survived by hunting. They obtained most of their food by killing migratory mammals, such as antelope, onagers, gazelles, foxes, gray wolves, Bactrian camels, and brown bears. They also hunted the great herds of horses that roamed the steppes.[27]

Illus. 15: Mother Goddess, Çatalhöyük, seated on lioness/leopard throne while giving birth, c.6,000 BCE

And here's where our story takes a turn. Around 6,000 BP, these tribes of Scythian and Turkic peoples—called the Yamnaya by anthropologist David Anthony,[28] or more broadly, the Kurgans by Gimbutas—first domesticated the horse.* Kurgan culture was highly patriarchal, with

---

* The word *kurgan* comes from an old Turkic word that means "fortress," "embankment," or "mound-grave." It was later adopted into East Slavic-Russian. Eighty percent of kurgan mound-graves were built for men.

men holding all the power.[29] Kurgans were also bronze smiths, and they equipped their horses with panoplies of bronze armor and their warriors with bronze weaponry.*[30] Accordingly, some authors refer to them as "battle-axe cultures."[31]

Over the next 3,000 years, wave after wave of Kurgan peoples would roll down from the steppes, obliterating everything and killing or assimilating everyone in their path. They spoke early forms of Proto-Indo-European—or PIE—languages, which were ancestral to all Germanic, Romance, Slavic, and Indo-Iranian languages spoken today. In time, their territory would range from the British Isles in the west to the Gangetic Plains of northern India in the east.† And as we might predict, they worshipped masculine sky-gods. Indigenous peoples of South Asia absorbed the Kurgans' hierarchical caste system and pantheon of gods into their pre-Vedic Hinduism, including a new deity named Vishnu, the God of Destruction. In 1945, Robert Oppenheimer, "father of the atomic bomb," said he reflected on the words of Vishnu when the first nuclear weapon was tested at the Trinity Site in New Mexico: "Now I am become Death, the destroyer of worlds."

We will revisit the Kurgans throughout Part Three of this book. But before we go on, I should point out that at about the same time, a second patriarchal tribe was gathering strength on the deserts of the Sinai-Arabian Peninsula. Between the Red Sea in the south and the Dead Sea in the north lived several Semitic tribes that also worshipped male deities, herded goats and sheep, and waged wars over scarce resources. One of these cultures would crush the feminine principle like no other, not even acknowledging a female consort for its supreme patriarchal sky-god.[32] We had entered a new socioeconomic landscape, where the hyper-masculine would expand to the near exclusion of the feminine, destroying all in its path. The Hyper-Masculine Paradigm had been born.

---

* A 2015 genetic study of the remains of horses and humans of Central Asia supports Gimbutas's Kurgan theory.

† The Indo-European language family is now the largest on Earth, comprising approximately 46 percent of all spoken languages.

PART THREE

DESERTS, PLAINS, AND MOUNTAINS: 6,000 BP–PRESENT

Big Picture: The Hyper-Masculine Paradigm, or HMP, expands from small source areas in western and southwestern Asia to become globally dominant, culminating in the Euro-American Imperial Era.* Near the end of this age, the human population soars to unsustainable levels due to exploitative capitalism and cheap fossil fuels. Today, the HMP shapes social values and economic principles in such a way as to produce inequality based on gender and sex, racial bigotry, environmental destruction, animal cruelty, and unprecedented human savagery.

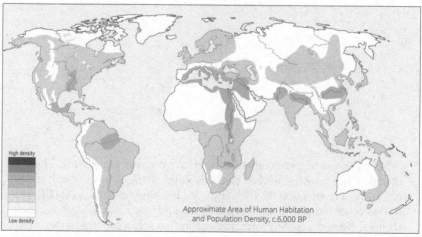

Illus. 16: Approximate area of human habitation and population density, c.6,000 BP

* Other cultures independently became effective agents of the HMP. These included, but were not limited to, the Xia and Shang dynastic civilizations of East Asia from 4,000 BP, the Olmec of Mesoamerica from 3,000 BP, as well as other Indigenous cultures of North and South America. Still, many retained elements of their formative egalitarian socioeconomic structures until they were overwhelmed by Euro-American colonialism.

Chapter 7

THE SMITH AND THE DEVIL

Once upon a time, there lived a man named Smith, who was a good and honest farmer. In those days, no one had yet learned how to fashion metal tools, so people like Smith farmed the land using sticks, sharpened stones, and their bare hands. It was miserable, backbreaking work that made everyone bitter—everyone, that is, except Smith.

Now, the Devil was pleased by the way in which hard labor made people grumpy, because it encouraged envy and hatred, which greatly increased the number of souls bound for Hell. But the Devil had also taken notice of Smith, whose equanimity troubled him. So, he made a plan.

One day, the Devil walked out into the barley fields where farmer Smith worked and said to him: "Why do you work so hard, sowing and reaping from the land with your bare hands, when I could give you secret knowledge that would make life so much easier for you and your family? All I ask for in return is your soul."

Smith rubbed his chin and thought for a moment. His young family was not unhappy, although it was true, they did work very hard. He would like nothing more than to ensure that their lives were easier and more fulfilling. For that reason, he agreed and pledged his soul to the Devil in return for his help.

Soon after, the Devil sneaked into God's workshop in Heaven and stole a kiln that would help Smith get started in his new career as a blacksmith. Now, the Devil had been vague in his initial offer, so with this, he met his obligation to Smith. But by itself, the kiln was useless, so in exchange for more tools, Smith also pledged the souls of his three older children. Satisfied, the Devil next delivered a bellows, a hammer, and an anvil. But even with these new tools, Smith found himself unable to work the metal with any skill. Furthermore, working in the shop exhausted him, and he still had to help his family farm the fields so they would have enough food to eat. He thought, *If only I had a tool that allowed me to grasp the metal as I worked it, things would be much easier.*

He talked this over with the Devil, who immediately saw the problem. After another covert trip to God's workshop, the Devil brought Smith a pair of metal tongs and explained how they would help him safely and efficiently work the red-hot metal. In return, Smith pledged the soul of his last and youngest child. With this, the Devil was content. "But," he warned Smith, "these tongs are very special, as they have the power to hold anything fast for all eternity, even a raging boar if you choose. So be very careful how you use them."

Years passed, and Smith became a prosperous metalworker. He taught his children the art of metalworking and sold his wares to farmers, soldiers, and kings—for his clients requested not only farm implements but also wheeled chariots, armor for men and their horses, and deadly weapons with which armies could conquer peoples in distant lands. Smith's reputation for making tools of war spread far and wide, and soon everyone was greedy, cruel, fearful, and suspicious of one another, all of which greatly pleased the Devil.

At last, the day arrived for Smith to give up his soul, so the Devil returned to the workshop. There, he found Smith laboring over the embers, using the same hammer over the same anvil and the same divine tongs the Devil had given him so many years before. But now Smith had grown old, and the Devil told him it was time.

Smith had long prepared for this moment. Nodding in resignation, he gently laid down his hammer, then quenched the hot metal he'd been working in a bucket of water at the Devil's feet. And through the great billows of steam that erupted from the bucket, Smith thrust the tongs into the Devil's face and latched them onto his nose. The Devil screeched and writhed in pain as the power of good in the tongs clashed with the evil in his bones. Knowing he could never escape, he begged Smith to release him.

"Devil, old friend," said Smith, "you have helped me and my family live such happy lives, of course I will release you—*if you release me from my debt to you of my soul and the souls of my family!*"

The Devil knew he'd been beaten at his own game, so he relented. Never again would the Devil bother Smith or his children.

But Smith's association with the Devil had tarnished his soul, so when he died, he was forbidden entry into Heaven, no matter how honest his life may have been. Neither would the Devil allow him to enter Hell. Thus, to this day, Smith's soul wanders the Earth as the Spirit of Blacksmithing, an art that will forever bear the black mark of the Devil.

* * *

From Germany to Greece, and from India to the British Isles, the story of "The Smith and the Devil" has appeared in many iterations. Phylogenetic linguistic studies indicate that this story is at least 6,000 years old and originated from somewhere between today's western Russia and Turkey.[1] This makes it contemporary with the source area of the PIE languages. You'll recall that this region was also the homeland of the Kurgan horse-warriors.

Here we have a story that arose before the advent of writing and that describes how humans learned to fashion metal tools for both good and evil. The plot tells how the Devil tempts humanity with this knowledge— knowledge possessed only by a sky-god, who has withheld it from humans. Nonetheless, it comes into their possession by way of a trickster deity. (Notice similarities with "The Genesis Tree," "The Garden of Eden," and "Pandora's Box.") However, it is curious that with the exception of the barley fields, no mention is made of a wider landscape—no trees or vegetation, hills or streams, only a wild boar. Neither are any women present or ever mentioned but merely implied as part of Smith's family. (This element was altered in the 2017 motion picture *Errementari: The Blacksmith and the Devil*. All dialog in the film is in Basque, an ancient pre-Indo-European language still spoken in the western Pyrenees.)

In a Scottish version, the story takes place during a winter storm, with Smith bringing beef broth to a saint disguised as a bedraggled old man who has stumbled in from the snow. The soup strengthens the old man, who then departs into the snowstorm. Moments later, the Devil appears. In still other versions, Smith is vile, is an alcoholic, or loses his wager with the Devil. And in the oldest versions, an evil spirit, a genie, or Death plays the villain. The Devil character in the account given above was likely a later adaptation following the introduction of monotheism, possibly Christianity.

Smith works in the fields, as does his family, but the story suggests that men are the primary breadwinners. It also suggests that when men first learned the metallurgical arts, they fashioned metal plows and hoes that were more durable than those made from wood and stone. Indeed, by 6,000 BP in western Asia, men had begun to switch from being full-time pastoralists to being livestock-agriculturalists (using animals to pull plows) and smithies. Sexual dominance is also implied: men plowed the tender soil with their pointed instruments and planted their seed. Thus, men began to take control of their societies—sexually, socially, economically, and politically.

It's worth noting that at the end of the story, Smith's spirit is condemned to forever wander the Earth—a liminal plane of existence—since neither Heaven nor Hell would grant him permission to enter. The essence of his spirit would continue to appear on the skin of smithies everywhere as the black mark of the Devil. Thus, in this telling, the color black—that is, darker skin—is already associated with evil. Curiously, blacksmithing has a long history of being equated with the "dark arts" of witchcraft, and the tools it produces are associated with masculinity and manipulation of livestock: the tongs had "the power to hold . . . even a raging boar."

(Recall that boars were a symbol of the sacred feminine in the Neolithic.) Therefore, we may think of blacksmithing as an occupation imbued with liminal qualities that symbolize thresholds and transformation.

Yet it wasn't only plowshares. In the Late Neolithic, many cultures around the world had already begun to smelt copper to make trinkets and ceremonial artifacts. This transitional period, sometimes called the Copper Age or Chalcolithic, began around 6,500 BP or 4,500 BCE, the chronometric we'll start to use as we shift to more recent times. By the time we reach the Bronze Age, around 3,000 BCE, we start to see swords, spearheads, armor, and chariots. (More on metals in Chapter 9.) According to forensic investigations of human skeletons and depictions preserved in rock art, instances of murder or group conflict were exceedingly rare prior to the Horticultural Revolution. The arc of violence rose only slowly after that time, involving mostly pastoralists who lived in drier lands.[2] However, by 4,000 BCE, as livestock-agriculture became primary and more power was transferred to men, rates of violence exploded.

One of the first known incidents of mass murder occurred in Kilianstädten, Germany, around 4,700 BCE, in which twenty-six adults and children died from arrow wounds or blunt trauma to the head. Such savage acts of violence were unprecedented. But over the next thousand years, they became commonplace, and by the Bronze Age, terrorism, warfare, and standing armies were facts of life. Walls were built around towns and resources directed to defense. Graveyards dominated the landscape, and the graves of men were far richer than those of women. After excavating Neolithic sites in Hungary, archaeologist Ian Hodder concluded, "The emphasis is on burial, men, cattle, and individual display."[3] By this time, throughout most of Eurasia, men—that is, the hyper-masculine ego—had usurped the feminine power of the previous age, inaugurating the HMP.

Many authors suggest the increase in violence at this time was a result of more complex forms of government being used to control larger populations competing for finite resources.[4] As the story goes, if men were better suited for controlling more territory to gain more resources—being bigger, stronger, and as some still say, smarter too—then they could feed more people and control more territory. Perhaps violence, they say, is in our genes after all. Violence is natural and inevitable.

As we've seen, this argument is patently false. At most, it may be interpreted as an attempt to perpetuate biases against not only the feminine in general but also women, people of color, animals, and the Earth itself in particular. It is an argument given in the interest of keeping those in charge comfortable and in charge.

On the contrary, the biological and social sciences show that we humans are predisposed to working together for peaceful solutions that require teamwork, relationship, and community. Only with Herculean effort have we managed to train ourselves to favor and enact a suite of hyper-masculine social traits without question, each generation unwittingly passing them down to the next. It is not natural; it is cultural. Or as anthropologists like to say, "We do what comes culturally."

So, what changed? What turned us from communal, goddess-worshipping egalitarians into xenophobic, god-worshipping warmongers? What deal did we make with the Devil that sent us down the road to perdition—one we are still on today?

Chapter 8

MASCULINE LANDSCAPES

"We don't see things as they are; we see things as we are." The gist of this familiar saying, usually attributed to early-twentieth-century writer Anaïs Nin, is that we each build our own one-of-a-kind view of reality based on the social conditioning we receive throughout our lives. An objective world might exist out there, but we will never know it. We can only ever see the world subjectively, through each of our unique—and uniquely socialized—lenses. The experiences we internalize through those lenses—experiences that in turn comprise the same lenses—are what psychologists call our mental content.[1]

That's one way to interpret the above quote. But its deeper truth, which may be less apparent, is that the off-the-rack cognitive architecture each of us comes equipped with is identical across our species. This means that regardless of our individual circumstances (i.e., our "lenses"), we tend to make sense of the world in certain predictable ways. If you recall from Chapter 2, we saw how our ancient ancestors learned to identify some landscapes with food, shelter, and safety, while others spelled disaster. The qualities inherent in those distinctive landscapes galvanized the human mental framework as it evolved. Psychologists refer to this framework as our cognitive structure.[2] So, to put it all together, each of us possesses a unique mental *content* that fills our universal human mind *structure*.

This sounds straightforward enough, although it's not always easy to know where one ends and the other begins. For example, when you read the word "cowboy," the image that springs to life in your mind's eye is formed by a suite of impressions you've collected over the course of your life that are associated with that term. They are part of your mental *content* and may include romantic ideals of the sexy "manly man," the salt-of-the-earth pioneer, the macho "tough guy," the rugged American individualist, or some combination of these stereotypes. They are stereotypes because they're ordinary, and they're ordinary because marketing ventures have capitalized on them by portraying the cowboy on a horse, riding out across the plains or through the desert or into the mountains. In this popular image, he (and it's traditionally been a "he") wears a pistol on his hip, and he might smoke a cigarette as he squints into the sun with determined grit. He could be the Marlboro Man, or the hero from a John Ford film.

Similar impressions are conjured by the word "hunter." Again, it's usually a "he," although sometimes it's a "she," especially in more recent ads. In that case, she might wear camouflaged clothing as she focuses her binoculars over a ridgeline, a rifle slung across her back. Or maybe she rides a horse through the wilderness with three mules in tow. Successful in the hunt, she has field-dressed a bull elk and strapped portions onto the packsaddle of each mule. The last mule carries the elk's severed head and his impressive rack of antlers.

It's worth pausing here to point out that men still appear in hunting ads and sports ads 50 percent more often than do women. In advertising generally, women are 48 percent more likely than men to be shown in a kitchen and six times more likely to wear revealing clothing, and are usually in their twenties. In contrast, male actors represent a broad age range in commercial ads, are 62 percent more likely than female actors to be portrayed as smart, and receive twice as many acting roles.[3]

Cowboy and hunter scenes typically depict masculine landscapes. When this happens, the lead character is perceived as absorbing that landscape's masculinity into their own nature as they become hardened by the elements. When cowboy and hunter scenes are set in feminine landscapes, with forests or rivers, the landscape is juxtaposed with the protagonist, who is taming the place and its inhabitants, and by proxy, the protagonist's own inner feminine, to conform to her or his (and the audience's) masculine ideal.

Illus. 17: "Men Are Better Than Women!"

Marketing agents know well how icons like these sell certain products: rifles and knives, as well as sweaters, wristwatches, cologne, charcoal briquettes, whiskey, and trucks. But let's not forget that the landscapes in these images first meant something to us biologically, and our biology produced our social traits of cooperation and imagination. This is the first layer of the Gendered Landscapes Theory, or GLT, and it forms part of our cognitive framework or *structure*. We then filled this structure with subconscious *content* (e.g., the above imagery of cowboys, hunters, and mountaineers, as well as anthropomorphic gods) by projecting it onto everything and everyone around us. This is the second layer of the GLT. And when we shared these ideas and behaviors with others and taught them to our children, they became part of human culture, the third layer of the GLT. In this chapter, we look at how the landscapes we had wandered into during the Late Paleolithic began to change the ways in which we thought about ourselves and others.

* * *

Bounded by some of the harshest deserts and highest mountains on Earth, a great swath of grassland once stretched 11,000 kilometers (7,000 miles) from eastern Europe, across Central Asia, nearly to the Pacific Ocean. Recall from Chapter 5 that dryness and height are associated with the elements air and fire. In various ancient philosophies, including those of Ancient India, China, Greece, and Egypt, these two elements or "humors" are metaphorically masculine. They are also associated with masculine gendered landscapes, such as mountains, deserts, plains, steppes (high, semi-arid grasslands), and circumpolar regions of tundra, snow, and ice. As for those last three, it may be helpful to remember how very cold temperatures or ice applied to bare skin can impart the sensation of burning. Alternatively, controlling fire is necessary for survival in any wilderness situation, but most critically in cold climates.

Professor of theology Belden Lane calls masculine landscapes like these "places on the edge . . . more given to being emptied than to being filled," which are "harsh, lean in imagery, beggarly in [their] love." Lane goes on to describe them as paradoxical, saying they "remind us that what we long for and what we fear most are both already within us."[4]

Plains, steppes, and deserts overpower the senses on the horizontal plane; mountains and canyons threaten to swallow us whole on the vertical plane. All tame the ego, which makes them well suited for vision quests and other rites of passage. Central Asia abounds in all these landscapes.

Geographers often categorize world climate regions based on a system pioneered by Russian-born climatologist Wladimir Köppen (1846–1940) called the Köppen Climate Classification System. This system (now modified) is based on mean values of annual and monthly temperature and precipitation data gathered from around the world. In brief, it first divides world climates into six general types—wet, dry, mild, continental, polar, and highland/mountain—and assigns a letter value to each. It further adds a second or third letter that denotes a refined range of precipitation and temperature.

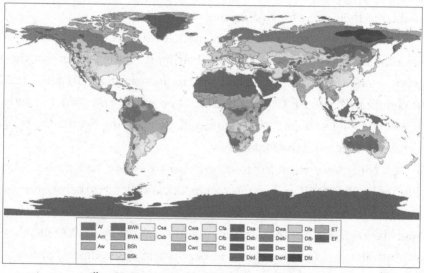

Illus. 18: Köppen World Climate Classification System*

---

* Generally speaking, the A-climates (blue) represent tropical rainy regions; the B-climates (red to tan) represent arid to semi-arid regions; the C-climates (green) are mild mid-latitude regions with seasonal variations; the D-climates (pink, lavender, indigo, teal, and turquoise) are continental regions with severe winters; and the E-climates (gray) are tundra, polar, and highland regions.

According to Köppen, Central Asia is dominated by climates that are dry mid-latitude, severe continental, and severe subarctic. In other words, it has hot summers, brutally cold winters, high icy mountains, and windy plateaus that are dry as a bone. Consequently, it's a kind of no man's land unless, of course, you're willing to kill for it.

Anatomically modern humans had been living in Central Asia for a long time—since 45,000 BP—long before the Kurgans fell into hyper-masculinism. In Chapter 6, we saw how the Kurgans were a collection of PIE-speaking peoples, who depended on hunting before they invented pastoralism. During this time, their populations increased, resulting in a decrease in the populations of the animals they hunted. This inspired the Kurgans to focus on livestock, especially cattle and horses. But great herds of livestock need lots of space to roam, especially when it's dry. Thus, by 6,000 BP, the Kurgans had begun to wage wars on peoples near and far in their quest for grazing lands.

Since the 1950s, archaeologists have excavated artifacts that tell us a lot about the Kurgans. Perhaps their most telling trait is that they were among the first to organize their cultures around patriarchy. This is significant, because Central Asia was one of the first predominantly masculine environments we encountered after leaving behind the river valleys of Africa and the Middle East.

Of course, we migrated to other places too. We had pushed into Europe by 35,000 BP, and yet our sociopolitical structures there remained egalitarian, perhaps even matriarchal, until the Kurgans arrived.[5] We had also traversed South Asia, arriving in Australia by 50,000 BP. Most of Australia was (and continues to be) an arid environment, although edible plants and animals were sufficient to support foraging populations of Indigenous Australians well into the modern era. People there also practiced unique and blended forms of matriarchy-patriarchy. But these Indigenous systems would devolve into the dominant patriarchal order soon after European colonialism arrived in the eighteenth century.[6,7]

Farther afield, biodiversity had always been scant and resources few in the Arctic and Subarctic. Consequently, our populations there were relatively small. With so few people spread across such vast, empty spaces, you might expect we would have gotten along better with one another. Yet in-group warfare (within and between clans) was often higher among circumpolar Indigenous peoples than among larger foraging groups living at lower latitudes.[8] Conflict was most prevalent among cultures dependent on hunting and fishing, wherein men made greater contributions to the food economy than did women.[9,10,11]

Human physiology typically prefers a diet comprised of 60–80 percent carbohydrates, 10–20 percent fats, and 10–20 percent proteins.[*†12] A diet containing more than 35 percent protein results in protein toxicity, and modern-day foragers intuitively avoid exceeding this threshold. Arctic Indigenous hunters historically obtained carbohydrates from the glycogen present in muscle tissue and the stomach contents of caribou and other terrestrial mammals, and also from tundra plants and kelp.[13,14] Additionally, Arctic peoples have evolved larger livers that convert larger amounts of fats and proteins into carbohydrates, and they excrete the resulting surplus of ammonia in their urine.[15] Still, their upper limit for protein intake is close to 40 percent, and for fat, it's about 50 percent.[16]

Among cultures of the far north, myth and ritual help to ameliorate the act of killing animals for food. For example, Inuit hunting rituals are much more elaborate than the rituals of plant-foraging peoples and are conducted by religious specialists, generically known as shamans. The Inuit believe that animals have souls, and before a hunt, shamans contact the spirits of a specific prey species to make deals with them. The transaction runs something like this: Animals will supply humans with food if, in return, humans eventually give their own flesh and blood to the spirits of those animals by way of sickness and death. After killing a

---

* Examples of healthy carbohydrates are found in whole vegetables, fruits, grains, and beans; healthy fats come from foods such as nuts, seeds, and olives (i.e., containing monounsaturated and polyunsaturated fats, and high-density lipoproteins); high-quality proteins are, for example, found in lentils, beans, quinoa, and many other cereal grains and vegetables.

† Under a medical doctor's supervision, certain physical conditions may warrant a departure from these dietary benchmarks.

seal, a hunter will pour a little fresh water into the seal's mouth to atone for the act, thanking the seal and thereby appeasing the animal's spirit so that future seals will allow themselves to be killed.[17] Subconsciously, the Inuit may recognize that killing animals is tragic and regrettable, though, in their landscape, unavoidable. This ritual act of atonement lets Inuit hunters assuage their own conscience as much as it satisfies a rite of religious intensification in the Inuit quest for food. (This tradition is decreasing in frequency as more Inuit find work in towns.)

Cultures and cultural traits, like those above, do change, albeit slowly. Goddess cultures and matrilines that had originated in Africa held out longest in West Africa, the Mediterranean, and the Indian sub-continent. Still, most would eventually be displaced or absorbed by patriarchies that had originated from either Central Asia or the Arabian Peninsula.[18]

Scholars argue that worldwide, most cultures had become patriarchal by around 6,000 years ago.[19,20,21,22] By that time, most people understood that a woman could become pregnant *because* she'd had sexual intercourse with a man—in other words, they understood paternity. The notion here is that before this time, people assumed that women alone embodied the mystical powers of human reproduction. Men had nothing to do with it. Yes, males had sex with females, males with males, females with females, and intersex people with everybody. (Results from studies of babies born with ambiguous genitalia vary widely. Most show that 0.1 percent, or 1 in 1000 babies, are born intersex, that is, with genitalia that do not conform to the male/female binary.[23] Differences in sex hormones and chromosomal complexity show similar percentages.[24]) Remember: we humans are the "sexy primates." However, a female did not become pregnant every time she had sex, and besides, people saw animals having sex all the time too. So what?

It may sound hard to believe, but until quite recently, some of the more isolated foraging groups in the world remained unaware of paternity, at least as most of us understand it. For example, well into the twentieth century, some Australian Aborigines considered pregnancy to be the result of actions taken by a totemic animal spirit. Conception was thought to take place at watering holes and wells (feminine landscapes), where a spirit entered a woman's womb. Elders later questioned the woman to discover which spirit might have impregnated her, thereby indicating the child's totemic-clan affiliation.*[25] Other examples include the Trobriand Islanders, first described by anthropologist Bronislaw Malinowski in the early twentieth century,[26] and the ancient Lycians of southeastern Europe, whose portrayal by Herodotus was later investigated by J. J. Bachofen in the late nineteenth century.[27] All were matrilineal cultures.

It may be reasonable, then, to speculate that after we began to feed, water, tend, and protect goats and cows on a regular basis, keeping them inside the home at night (as some pastoralists still do today), we would have taken note of their habits. We would have observed, among other things, their estrous, sexual, and reproductive cycles.

Research suggests that men were likely the first domesticators of animals.[28] If men oversaw livestock, they likely put two and two together, and in what may have been one of the most profound revelatory moments of all time, it dawned on men that they, too, contained procreative power. To put it mildly, this would have been a game changer. Things might have gone differently. But as it happened, after women had invented horticulture and men had lost their economic cachet with the demise of "big game" hunting, the male version of the masculine ego may have considered itself, well, emasculated. Now armed with this new paternal awareness, men who practiced pastoralism demanded their place in the sun, as it were. And apparently, they did not want just their fair share; they wanted all of it.[29] These earliest forms of pastoralism and patriarchy, which are socially biased toward men, only became feasible after we had migrated into lands that were hotter, colder, higher, and drier. This fits well with the Gendered Landscapes Theory.

But how does it fit with our story of Smith? After he sold his soul (essential self, good will, humanity) to gain transformative, magical

---

* I must qualify this by stating that Aboriginal peoples did not think that men were not involved whatsoever in pregnancy. A spirit could only impregnate a woman after she had "opened" herself to a man.

knowledge (metallurgy, pastoralism, paternity), he used it to subdue the Devil (animals, farming, the feminine). Now we can see that this is more than a mere story about the invention of blacksmithing and warfare; it is a story of how the masculine subdued the feminine when men usurped and controlled the power of women. It heralds the rise of the Hyper-Masculine Paradigm, and with this rise we see something new appear on the landscape: trilithons (such as Stonehenge) in Britain, megaliths in Brittany, pyramids in the Nile Valley and Mesoamerica, and a bit later, temples, pillars, ziggurats, towers, and steeples around the world. The vertical becomes egoically superior to the horizontal, masculine to feminine, male to female, fire and air to earth and water.[30] Vertical structures of the built environment are metaphorically phallic and epitomize wealth and power; they are for men, not women or children, and symbolically demonstrate men's masculinity. They are intended to distill and amplify the power of masculine archetypes of the natural environment in the human/built environment.

I want to be careful here, however, and point out that masculinity per se and masculine behavioral traits are not *inherently* unjust, destructive, or evil. Rather, the human masculine ego that exists in every one of us had, by that time, expanded onto landscapes where it could *potentially* prosper to the near exclusion of the feminine. Deserts, plains, and mountains substantiated in our physical reality what those archetypes symbolized in our subconscious minds. As it turned out, the collective human ego began to tilt toward extreme forms of masculinity. The resulting gendered imbalance yielded a feedback loop that devolved into the stark inequities of hyper-masculinity that would include sky-god religions, misogyny, racism, chauvinism, animal cruelty, and all manner of human violence. And even though none of these traits was in our biological nature (our cognitive structure), we imagined they were noble and honorable, even spiritual (our cognitive content), because an alpha god and the alpha men he put in charge told us so.[31]

Chapter 9

THE HYPER-MASCULINE DEVOLUTION: GODS, PATRIARCHY, AND DEATH

The bronze star. The bronze bull. The brass ring. As bold as brass. Brass balls. The Iron Curtain. The Iron Cross. Ruling with an iron fist. Iron Man. The Man of Steel. True as steel. Nerves of steel. A mind like a steel trap.

These and similar idioms demonstrate the masculinized valuation of certain metals. They imply strength, virility, intellect, and, oftentimes, violence; during the Bronze Age and the Iron Age that followed, the worldview from which these sayings sprang was considered the law of the land throughout much of the Old World. To be clear, bronze is an alloy of copper and tin, and brass is an alloy of copper and zinc. By itself, elemental iron is just iron, but steel is an alloy made from iron and one of several other elements. Ingredients may include copper, manganese, molybdenum, or carbon, depending on what qualities the metallurgist has in mind.

Due to its ductility, low melting temperature, and relative ubiquity, copper was the first metal known to have been smelted. Sites dated to 4,500 BCE in Anatolia and the Balkans have yielded copper hammers, axes, needles, hooks, and bangles. People in those regions began to smelt gold, silver, tin, and lead over the next thousand years, with all these metals having been hammered and worked in their raw, elemental forms without smelting for at least a thousand years prior.

Copper is one thing. Bronze is quite another. It is harder and more durable and can be used for much more aggressive purposes. The earliest bronze artifacts come from Mesopotamia, an area situated between the Tigris and Euphrates, its Classical Latin toponym (place name) meaning "Land Between the Rivers." As in Çatalhöyük, early peoples in Mesopotamia fed themselves by foraging and farming, and their towns needed no exterior fortifications against attack. Both women and men comprised ruling councils of elders, and there is little evidence of warfare.[1]

But in 3,200 BCE, the climate started to dry out. The marshlands of Mesopotamia became hemmed about by deserts and semi-deserts, much as the region is today. It is a marginal landscape, and here's the critical point: human populations there increased just as its environmental quality began to decrease. During this time, Mesopotamians developed bronze weaponry and started to fortify their towns with towers, walls, and moats.[2] Bronze relics from this region date to 3,000 BCE. In Sumer, the preeminent civilization that emerged, Sumerians crafted bronze swords, axes, spears, knives, helmets, scale mail, and armor, which they used to wage a long series of military campaigns against neighboring tribes, chiefdoms, and city-states.[3] They legitimized it all by envisioning punitive, hyper-masculine gods who were ruthless and demanded no less from their loyal subjects.[4] After all, the physical landscapes that surrounded the Sumerians were punitive, ruthless, and masculine.

Curiously, at about the same time and in the same place, the first form of writing, called cuneiform, was impressed into soft clay tablets. Sumerians first used cuneiform to catalog legal codes and tabulate payments and debts. Today, no one would dispute that written symbols and systems of writing are invaluable in condensing information (and disinformation) and facilitating its diffusion, and they are imperative for encoding meaningful dialog. However, as the Greek dramatist Sophocles cautioned, "Nothing vast enters the life of mortals without a curse."[5] And as anthropologist Claude Levi-Strauss added, "The only phenomenon which seems to be linked with the appearance of writing . . . is the establishment of hierarchical societies."[6] In his book *The Alphabet Versus the Goddess*, author Leonard Shlain took these conclusions to the level of controversy when he argued, "But one pernicious effect of literacy has gone largely unnoticed: writing subliminally fosters a patriarchal outlook." In Shlain's view, "*holistic, simultaneous,* and *concrete*" are "essential characteristics of a feminine outlook" while "*linear, sequential, reductionist,* and *abstract* thinking defines the masculine" (emphasis is Shlain's).[7]

Illus. 19: Sumerian cuneiform tablet: A Private Letter

Living around 2,300 BCE, Sargon the Great (or Sargon of Akkad, a Semite) was the first true Akkadian monarch of Sumer, although his roots were humble. As the story goes, Sargon's mother was a simple woman who lived along the Euphrates. Soon after her son was born, unable to keep the

child, she wove a little basket of rushes, sealed it with bitumen, and placed
him inside. She then set him adrift on that great river, where he floated
into the gardens of the King of Kish. (Kish was a Sumerian city-state.) A
gardener pulled the basket from the river and presented the child to the
king, who loved him and raised him to become Sargon the Great. If you've
ever been to Sunday school, this little story should sound familiar, as it's a
prototype—one of many—for the story of Moses on the Nile.

From Sargon to King Hammurabi a few centuries later, the Akkadians
were a ferocious fighting people. Clay tablets document their allegiance
to a pantheon of hyper-masculine sky-gods, among whom was Marduk,
their supreme male deity, who went to battle with Tiamat, their supreme
female deity, and killed her.[8] But to become king of the gods, Marduk had
to pass one final test:

Then they placed a garment in their midst;
To Marduk, their first-born, they said:
"Verily, O lord, thy destiny is supreme among the gods,
Command 'to destroy and to create,' and it shall be! . . .
By the word of thy mouth let the garment be destroyed;
Command again, and let the garment be whole!"
He commanded with his mouth,
And the garment was destroyed.
Again he commanded, and the garment was restored.
When the gods, his fathers, beheld the efficiency of his word,
They rejoiced and did homage, saying
"Marduk is king!"[9]

—*Enuma Elish*, Fourth Tablet, pp. 60–61:17–28

To our ears, this story may sound a trifle banal. Marduk destroys a shirt or
something and then reassembles it. Big deal. But to see the vital element,
we must read between the lines. The myth symbolizes how the male sex
and the masculine gender overcame their inability to create, a power
that only the female and the feminine had previously commanded. And
they did so by engaging the power of the word—that is, of the abstract,

symbolic mind. By simply uttering a word, Marduk is able to both erase something from existence and remake it—that is, create it *ex nihilo* (out of nothing). This crystalizes the moment in which the male and the masculine assumed superiority over the female and the feminine. The biblical story of the Garden begins where this one ends, when Yahweh creates the world by speaking it into existence.[10]

The Anatolian Hittites, who succeeded the Akkadian Empire, had a revised brand of cuneiform that would use the same glyph to represent "man," "iron," and their name for one of the more famous gods of war, "Mars."[11]

From Akkad to Egypt, and from Greece to India, hierarchical creation myths would seek to explain how and why a supreme male deity usurped the power of a supreme female deity. The upshot was that women and slaves became commoditized: they were considered *things*, to be bought, sold, or destroyed. And one of the foundational principles of patriarchal societies rests on their intrinsic control of *things* as resources.[12]

Literate Sumerians, Akkadians, and Hittites may have been the first to smelt bronze, but the impact of this innovation remained local. The Kurgan horse-warriors carried bronze technology over a far greater territory. Their weapons and panoplies of armor allowed them to swiftly overpower farming communities throughout Anatolia and Mesopotamia, along the Indus and Ganges Rivers, and across Europe into Scandinavia. Episodic waves of Kurgan onslaught continued well into the second millennium BCE, when hordes of the horse-warriors finally crushed the island goddess civilizations of the Mediterranean.[13,14]

Before going on, we should remind ourselves that the term *Kurgan*, coined by archaeologists only in the twentieth century, refers to the mound-grave builders of western and Central Asia and thus covers a number of pastoralist tribes. It overlaps with another generic term you may be more familiar with, that is, Aryan. The word *aryan* derives from many archaic Indo-European lexicons and translates as "noble."[15] You may also be familiar with one of these groups' primary symbols. It consists of four equidistant arms, or rays, that issue from a central point. The arms each turn clockwise at the end, giving the impression of a spinning wheel or whorl. Scholars interpret this symbol to represent the sun, for the solar deity Surya was the supreme god of the Aryan pantheon. Once called the gammadion, this symbol is now more commonly known as the swastika.[16]

Wherever the Aryan Kurgans roamed, they took with them their PIE languages, metallurgical technologies, patriarchal social orders, and sky-god polytheisms. Persia sat near the epicenter of the Aryan Kurgans' sphere of influence. By the time state-level polities developed in Persia, around 2,000 BCE, the concept of a *single* all-powerful god had emerged in the writings of the prophet Zoroaster, also called Zarathustra. The religion known as Zoroastrianism, or Parsee (Parsi), was likely the world's first monotheism. It continues today as a minority religion in isolated pockets of southern and southwestern Asia.

Other Bronze Age peoples on the Arabian Peninsula and along the southern Mediterranean coast likewise gained strength and envisioned an imperial worldview. These tribes spoke Semitic languages and represented related ethnic groups of Bedouins, Assyrians, Arabs, Hyksos, and Akkadians (to which Sargon the Great belonged). All were nomadic, and all practiced pastoralism. They lived in arid and semi-arid environments, migrating seasonally to cooler places with adequate water and pasturage for their livestock. Much as the Kurgans, they were also polytheistic, worshipping a pantheon of sky-gods and their subservient goddess consorts.

The Hebrews were one of these small, dispersed tribes of polytheistic desert nomads, who kept sheep and goats and migrated with the seasons. They authored various sacred writings, including the Torah and the Old Testament. Much later, an Arab who would become known as the Prophet Muhammed referenced both texts, plus the Christian New Testament, when teaching Islam's Qur'an. (Tradition holds that Mohammed was illiterate and received the Qur'an verbally from the Angel Gabriel. Muhammed later dictated the Qur'an to his literate disciple-companions, who wrote it down.) All of these holy books tell how the patriarch Abram (later called Abraham) adopted monotheism and spent the remainder of his life struggling to quash the older polytheisms throughout the region. Judaism, Christianity, Islam, and Baha'i are all monotheistic world religions that trace their shared heritage back to the story of Abraham. Thus, all are classed as Abrahamic faiths.

By 1,500 BCE, the Israelite branch of the Hebrews had begun to annihilate other desert peoples in what is now the Southern Levant. As recorded in the biblical Book of Joshua and Book of Judges, the Israelites conducted a particularly gruesome series of campaigns in which their god Yahweh instructed his chosen people to "kill everything in the city." This mandate advanced their cause of establishing the Promised Land.

According to legend, the biblical warrior Goliath wielded a spear tipped with an iron point. This was unusual, as most weapons of the day continued to be made of bronze. Many scholars point to the Hittites as the first to routinely smelt iron, since at least 1,000 BCE. Recently, however, archaeologists found that people in West and Central Africa invented iron-smelting technologies earlier than did Europeans.[17] The conventional use of iron technology—and therefore the Iron Age itself—reached Europe and China approximately 500 years after it emerged in sub-Saharan Africa.

What is perhaps most peculiar about the Hebraic traditions is how they so completely erased the sacred feminine from their worldview. For instance, Yahweh—whom Muslims would later call Allah—is the only supreme deity on record who was never identified with any sort of female counterpart.[*]

As for mortals, the Hebraic creation story tells of how woman came from man (Adam's rib), instead of the other way around. Here, the

---

[*] Recall from Chapter 5 that Yahweh was once a minor lunar consort to a female sun goddess. At that time, he was called El, before his meteoric rise to supreme godhead as El Shaddai-Elohim-Yahweh.

hyper-masculine ego finally reduced gender to an absolute binary. (See Chapter 1 for commentary on Lilith, the first woman.) Wholly divorced from its opposite, the Hyper-Masculine Paradigm, or HMP, rendered the feminine not only inferior but contemptible by further associating it with compassion, relationship, nature, life, and the Earth itself—all anathema to the HMP. For example, Ezekiel 28:17 quotes Yahweh, speaking to Satan: "So I drove you in disgrace from the mountain of God . . . I threw you to earth." The "mountain" referred to is a masculine landscape archetype, symbolic of Yahweh and the seat of his power. Earth was corrupted as the Devil's tomb (womb); thus, the feminine was merged with ultimate evil. Legitimated in sacred mythology, the hyper-masculine determined that the feminine must be controlled in all its forms at all costs.

Most of the New Testament was written late in the first century CE (Common Era, equivalent to AD). It is arguably less misogynistic than the Old Testament, and certain scenes from it describe Jesus defending a prostitute and befriending Mary Magdalene, who some believe may have been his wife.[18,19] As for Jesus, many of his behaviors are feminine, reflecting relationship, community, altruism, compassion, and so on. Still, the New Testament is clearly gender-biased, as these examples attest:

Wives, submit yourselves to your own husbands, as is fitting in the Lord.
—Colossians 3:18

A woman should learn in quietness and full submission. I do not permit a woman to teach or have authority over a man; she must be silent.
—1 Timothy 2:11–12

Women should remain silent in the churches. They are not allowed to speak, but must be in submission, as the Law says.
—1 Corinthians 14:34

Now I want you to realize that the head of every man is Christ and the head of every woman is man . . .
—1 Corinthians 11:3a[20]

The apostle Paul wrote 1 Corinthians. As a Jew who persecuted and condemned Christians to death, his given name was Saul. However, after he experienced a vision of Christ on the road to Damascus, he converted to the new Christian cult. Other than from this report, we do not know if he ever met the person called Jesus, and yet he is credited with writing at least half the books of the New Testament.

As a citizen of the Roman Empire, Paul was no doubt influenced by Greco-Roman gender roles as well as Jewish customs, both of which were deeply misogynistic. Paul's writings, fraught with this gender imbalance, would go on to shape Christendom and its colonial footprint down to the present day.[21] Legends abound of Christian religious committees that later debated whether women should be recognized as being fully human. The Ecumenical Council at Mâcon finally laid this contentious issue to rest in 906 CE when it concluded, by a one-vote margin, that women did indeed have souls.[22]

For its part, Islam is credited with granting widows property rights and affording women certain social protections they did not previously enjoy under hyper-masculine desert polytheisms. Still, the Qur'an relegates women to a subservient position and states that husbands may have up to four wives, that they should feel free to beat their wives, and that one man equals two women in terms of social value.

> Men stand superior to women in that Allah hath preferred some of them over others, and in that they expend of their wealth; and the virtuous women, devoted, careful [in their husbands'] absence, as Allah has cared for them. But those whose perverseness ye fear, admonish them and remove them into bedchambers and beat them; but if they submit to you, then do not seek a way against them; verily, Allah is high and great.
>
> —Qur'an 4:34[23]

Sharia Law (Islamic religious law) was a later addition to Qur'anic teachings. Although many specifics of the Law are not found in the Qur'an, Sharia and other Muslim texts, such as the Hadith, are used to justify restrictions on women's access to education, employment, mobility, and the democratic process.

> Allah's Apostle said, ". . . a man is the guardian of his family and is responsible for his subjects; a woman is the guardian of her husband's home and of his children and is responsible for them; and the slave of a man is a guardian of his master's property and is responsible for it . . ."
> —Hadith Sahih Bukhari 9:89:252[24]

These male-authored holy books are clearly hierarchical and hyper-masculine. They deny women any self-determination, instead ensuring that women remain reliant on men for their fundamental human rights and that misogyny would accompany warfare and other forms of violence. This was apparent in the genocidal wars waged in Ancient Persia, Egypt, Assyria, and Israel, as well as their modern-day counterparts.[25]

As we've seen from some of the stories recounted in this book, the HMP was mythologized and made instructional by monotheisms in the medieval age and early modern age. A quick peek at other stories reveals the same pattern: Scandinavian folktales explain that Lucifer and his entourage were expelled from Heaven into earthly forests (feminine landscapes) to then haunt them as wood sprites and trolls.[26] Russian, Czech, and Slovak stories tell of how the forests were inhabited by monsters with the face of a woman, the body of a pig, and the legs of a horse.[27] In yet another myth, a wild woman was said to plague the forests of the Bavarian Alps and Austrian Tyrol; locals described her as a giant with bristly hair that resembled wire, enormous, pendulous breasts, and a ghoulish smile that stretched from ear to ear. Her favorite habit was stealing babies.[28]

* * *

From this point on, we know the story all too well. Or do we? A selective list of major social upheavals over the past one thousand years might include the Christian Crusades, the Spanish Inquisition, Euro-American colonialism, witch trials, the triangular slave trade, two world wars, radical Islamic jihads, and the global merchandising of war. Each of these low points has provoked a multitude of collateral atrocities, including ethnic, racial, and gender discrimination, animal exploitation, pernicious capitalism, climate change, the sixth mass extinction, and nuclear proliferation. Spiritual teacher Eckhart Tolle calls our ability to achieve these ends "intelligence in the service of madness."[29] What few people may realize is that all these plagues of humanity stem from the very same source. To make it clearer, let's use the events just listed to connect some dots.

Starting in the eleventh century, Pope Urban II instigated the Christian Crusades, a long series of military campaigns that would continue into the fifteenth century. The pope initially rallied Europe's monarchs by contriving an urgent need to establish safe passage to Jerusalem for Christian pilgrims. Yet Christians and Jews already lived in the holy city, as Muslims considered both groups "People of the Book." Most scholars now believe the pope's ulterior motive was to unite the Eastern and Western branches of Christianity—Catholicism and Orthodoxy—and appoint himself supreme head of the Church. In this way, the Crusades may be counted as another power-grabbing scheme authored by the ego—specifically, the "immature warrior" archetype of the insecure hyper-masculine ego.[30]

As it turns out, the Crusades were costly—in terms of both finances and lives—and most campaigns failed. The pope and the rulers of Europe were therefore eager to replenish their coffers and regain their prestige. So, with backing from the Church and the legitimization of a patriarchal godhead, the stage was set for the European Colonial Era. Economic slavery had long been practiced in many regions, and ethnic rivalries had long fueled ethnocentric supremacist ideologies. But the concept of "race" as defining immutable *categories* of human beings got off the ground only in the fifteenth century.

The Catholic Church greased the wheels of racism by authoring a series of papal bulls (decrees) that supported territorial claims made by European rulers. Important in this discussion is the Doctrine of Discovery of 1452 and the Romanus Pontifex of 1455, both granted by Pope Nicholas V. The Doctrine included the papal bull Dum Diversas, which gave colonizers the right to "capture, vanquish, and subdue the enemies of Christ, to put them into perpetual slavery and to take all their possessions and property." The word "race" (*race* in French, *razza* in Italian, *raza* in Spanish, and *raça* in Portuguese, meaning "breed" or "lineage") was thereafter used to commoditize and render inferior the peoples who inhabited foreign lands. Then, in 1493, Pope Alexander VI issued the papal bull Inter Caetera to further justify Christian European explorers' claims of "discovery" in promoting Christian domination and supremacy. Colonial governments and settlers would successfully apply these policies in Africa, Asia, Oceania, and the Americas.

In the case of the Americas, disease would prove a powerful, if unintended, aid to colonialism. Diseases that were often not fatal to Europeans proved exceptionally contagious and deadly to Indigenous peoples. Within a single generation of contact, beginning with Columbus's expedition in 1492, diseases such as smallpox, measles, and typhoid killed an estimated 44 million, 90 percent of the Indigenous population, in North and South America. Europeans were immune because many of these (zoonotic) diseases had been transmitted to their ancestors from livestock during the Neolithic—animals who hadn't existed in the Americas at that time.

However, people of European ancestry were not immune to every such pathogen, and the fallout from keeping livestock is still with us today. The Centers for Disease Control and Prevention now estimates that historically, over 60 percent of human infectious diseases originally came from our contact with animals, and today, nearly 75 percent of newly emerging infectious diseases come from animals.[31] This includes, most recently, the COVID-19 global pandemic.[32,33]

The long arc of these histories shows how the state of the modern world is the result of a severely imbalanced valuation of gender. Researcher Bryan Husted investigated how masculine/feminine attitudes affect environmental policies by differentiating between feminine values that emphasize relationship, community, and quality of life and the masculine values of competitiveness, ambition, power, and materialism. His research found that governments that institutionalize masculine values have fewer policies that advocate environmental sustainability.[34] A body of similar research shows that when countries espouse predominantly masculine values, educational standards and environmental protections fall.[35] As yet another study concludes, "since people in feminine cultures emphasize values, as typical female members do, such as caring for others, interdependence and quality of life, as compared to goal achievement, they tend to care about public goods, including the environment, which is so vital to the well-being of other members in the society."[36]

Feminine landscape archetypes, which embrace symbols of and metaphors for the Earth itself, continue to inform the collective unconscious, which we all share.[37] As feminist philosopher Eva Kittay puts it: "In these metaphors, man mediates his engagement with the world through a representation of it as Woman and metaphorically transposes his relation to Woman to his relation to the world. Many of the metaphors are transcultural and transhistorical. Man speaks of conquering the mountains as he would a woman, or raping the land, of his plough penetrating a female earth so that he can sow his seed therein."[38]

This burden of proof might lead us to blame men—at least white men, or certain corporations, industries, nations, and religious institutions controlled by white men. But such an exercise would devolve into yet another opportunity for the ego to identify opponents and assert superiority. The real culprit is the hyper-masculine that each of us contains to some degree. It is comprised of learned (socialized) egoic perceptions that retaliate in the form of not only armed conflicts, terrorist attacks, and mass shootings, but also increased violence against transgendered people, women, the billions of animals penned, raped, and slaughtered each year, and a planet pushed to the edge of endurance.[39]

Illus. 20: "It's Nice to Have a Girl around the House"

In this section of the book, we saw how the HMP was born in rugged, arid landscapes where plant foods were meager and the climate harsh— masculine landscapes. Women and the feminine, once considered divine and synonymous with life itself, were denigrated, maligned, and scapegoated for the suffering that the HMP manufactured. This ruse comprised an epic projection of the insecure hyper-masculine ego.

Today, we live with the consequences of our Bronze Age sins. Einstein recognized our propensity for madness when he commented thus on the development of the first atomic bomb: "We shall require a substantially new manner of thinking if mankind is to survive." That "new manner of thinking" has always lived inside us. It is small, yet tenacious, and it is inspired by Eve's free will, Rapunzel's grit, and Pandora's hope. This is the focus of our final chapters.

PART FOUR

PANGAEA: IT TAKES A PLANET

Big Picture: The Hyper-Masculine Paradigm succeeds in damaging or destroying much of the planet's life-support system, expanding the geographic extent of low-quality, masculine environments. Nevertheless, feminine environments and qualities endure. This is not, however, the feminine of the Paleolithic; the landscape has changed. Six thousand years of social heat and pressure have metamorphosed the feminine into a "wise warrior" archetype, the only paradigm with sufficient courage to lead humanity to a more humane future.

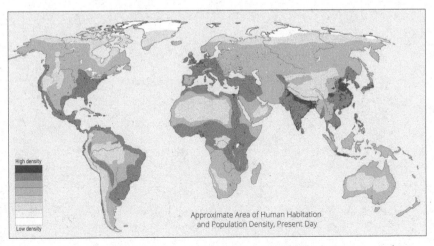

Illus. 21: Approximate area of human habitation and population density, present day

Chapter 10

THE LORAX

"At the far end of town
where the Grickle-grass grows
and the wind smells slow-and-sour when it blows
and no birds ever sing excepting old crows . . .
is the Street of the Lifted Lorax."[1]

So begins Dr. Seuss's children's classic *The Lorax*. Since most readers are familiar with this story, I will dispense with retelling it here. After all, it is by far the most junior member in our lineup of fairy tales, and because its content is copyrighted, I am precluded from printing the story in its entirety.

But in case you're fuzzy on the plot, here's a recap: A young boy visits a mysterious, hermit-like creature called the Once-ler, who lives at the top of a dilapidated tower on the outskirts of town. After the boy pays "fifteen cents, and a nail, and the shell of a great-great-great grandfather snail," the Once-ler proceeds to tell his story. He says that upon his arrival, the landscape was idyllic and unspoiled, filled with all sorts of animals and a forest of bushy-crowned Truffula trees. Immediately, he realized the trees possessed great commercial value and could be resourced to manufacture a type of clothing he dubbed "Thneeds." So, after hastily building a factory, he set about cutting down Truffula trees. The Once-ler then explains to the boy it was at this point that the Lorax appeared and implored him to stop: "'Mister!' he said, with a sawdusty sneeze. 'I am the Lorax. I speak for the trees.'" But the Once-ler ignored him and proceeded to cut down every last Truffula tree. Environmentally, this resulted in erosion, pollution, and the extinction of species. Overcome with despair, the Lorax flew away, never to return. At the conclusion of the story, the Once-ler hands the boy the last Truffula seed, urging him to plant it and protect the tree that grows from it. "Unless someone like you cares a whole awful lot, nothing is going to get better. It's not."

Illus. 22: The Lorax

As with any other Dr. Seuss story, the artwork is playful and imaginative and imbues the tale with a sense of fantasy. Seuss, whose real name was Theodor Seuss Geisel, claimed that his stories arose organically as he sketched his observations of the world in cartoon fashion. He remarked that he never intended to moralize to children when writing a book, because "kids can see a moral coming a mile off."[2] Be that as it may, he was not against telling stories that contain lessons and even insisted, "there's an inherent moral in any story."[3]

Published in 1971, at the height of the Vietnam War protests, various social justice movements—including the Black Power and Red Power movements, movements for women's rights, disability rights, and what would become LGBTQIA+ rights—and the demand for environmental protection legislation, *The Lorax* calls attention to the consequences of capitalism run amok. (Socially progressive on most accounts, some of Seuss's books have recently been called into question for containing racist undertones, however.[4]) Nevertheless, *The Lorax* has since been adapted into a television special, a feature film, various audiobooks, and a Broadway musical.

Seuss likely never intended for this little story to intersect with so many social variables. Yet it manages to accomplish this feat, becoming an apt illustration for the consequences of the Hyper-Masculine Paradigm, or HMP, in the modern age. Seuss describes the story's titular character as ". . . shortish, and oldish, and brownish, and mossy," who "[speaks] with a voice that [is] sharpish and bossy." This characterization fits the archetype of the wise old man and intersects with conventional stereotypes of Indigenous persons, shamans, and pagan "green man" deities. He is also portrayed as being "sort of a man," but not exactly one. This associates him with ancient depictions of therianthropic deities or, we could also say, with anthropomorphized animal deities and the natural world in general. Indeed, Seuss is rumored to have received inspiration for the character of the Lorax from the patas monkeys and De Brazza's monkeys he observed while traveling in Kenya.[5] As such, the Lorax embodies a liminal quality based on the dualities of human and animal, civilized and wild, and most poignantly, self-imposed psychological captivity and freedom. The Lorax's exit from the story represents humankind's loss of its liminal touchstone for both nature and its most essential self, that is, its humanity. Only the stark opposites of egoic binaries remain. (Notice the parallels with Adam and Eve in "The Garden of Eden" and the first humans in "The Genesis Tree": all are separated from an original feminine gendered paradise.)

As we've seen, trees can represent a liminal composite of gendered qualities. But Truffula trees are described as having flowing crowns of leaves that are "softer than silk" and "[smell] like butterfly milk." Butterflies, milk, and softness are stereotypically feminine and/or female, and here they suggest stereotypical qualities of women's hair, implicitly white women's hair. The fruits produced by the trees are a staple in the diet of the brown barbaloots (bears). Therefore, Truffula trees take on a nurturing feminine and female quality in the story.

It is worth mentioning that after the trees are gone, the barbaloots get hungry and leave. The Once-ler admits he was sad to see them go, but not too sad, because "business is business." He goes on to explain: "I meant no harm. But I had to grow bigger," with a larger factory, more trucks, more roads, more shipping, and more profits. The effect is analogous to that of factory sweatshops or industrial park expansion into rural areas, including the subsequent decay of those areas' ecological health.

Truffula trees are also mechanically consumed by the Once-ler's "Super-Axe-Hacker," a poignant symbol of blind industrialism, another mainstay of the HMP. Additional consequences of the Once-ler's business include smog and "gluppity-glop" and "schluppety-schlop"—these invented, figurative words refer to liquid pollutants that are dumped into a pond and kill the fish. On a psychosocial level, the full impact of ravaged forests, polluted waters, and starved wildlife is also analogous to that of men's social consumption of women, which we'll discuss more in the next chapter.

During the factory's production surge, the Once-ler's motives are singularly profit-driven and unsustainable. After all, he is so named because he commoditizes an element of the natural landscape that is extracted until it is utterly depleted. His business model rests on the ability to manufacture an item that consumers are convinced they need, and in order to meet production demand, he rapes a feminine landscape, achieving a short-term gain for himself. If he considers the future at all, he imagines a cycle of more and plenty that will continue unabated. This is a classic egoic delusion, for the outcome is quite the opposite. Punished by his own avarice, he ultimately discovers he is unable to heal the devastation he has created, and so he bequeaths a seed of hope (recall "Pandora's Box") to a child. And although the child is a boy, we may regard him by his feminine qualities of curiosity, sincerity, and gentleness. (The

2012 motion picture *Dr. Seuss' The Lorax* features the boy's mother and his girlfriend, perhaps to help balance some of the gender asymmetry present in the original story. However, both the book and the film fail to redeem the lack of racial diversity.)

Shortly before his death in 1997, explorer-scientist Jacques Cousteau cautioned that humanity might have no more than a single human lifespan in which to either repair its relations with the planet or suffer dire consequences. "If we go on the way we have, the fault is our greed, and if we are not willing to change, we will disappear from the face of the globe, to be replaced by the insect."

Cousteau's warning sounds more like a prediction, as the overall tenor is conclusive. Even so, in the decades since *The Lorax* was written, we have witnessed an explosion in optimism, innovation, and altruism on an unprecedented scale. Disparate groups of people are coming together from across the globe to invent and invest in solutions to the crimes committed against the natural environment, animals, women, people of color, and the poor. Though the great majority of this work remains to be done, the voices of the oppressed are gaining strength. This is our Truffula seed of hope, and this is where we commence our final appraisal of the Gendered Landscapes Theory and the beginning of the end of the HMP.

"So . . .
Catch!" calls the Once-ler.
He lets something fall.
"It's a Trufulla Seed.
It's the last one of all!
You're in charge of the last of the Trufulla Seeds.
And Trufulla Trees are what everyone needs.
Plant a new Trufulla. Treat it with care.
Give it clean water. And feed it fresh air.
Grow a forest. Protect it from axes that hack.
Then the Lorax
and all of his friends
may come back."[6]

Chapter 11

TRANSFORMED LANDSCAPES

My wife and I love our home. Simple and cozy, it is nestled into the mountains of southern Colorado. Our nearest full-time neighbor lives a mile away down a dirt road, our post office is ten miles away, and the nearest grocery store is about thirty miles from our back door. During COVID, social distancing was not a problem.

In the winter, we like to cross-country ski, and in the warmer months, we enjoy bicycling and backpacking. We once backpacked into the Weminuche Wilderness of southwestern Colorado for five days. In the Weminuche, snowy peaks crest above forests of spruce and aspen, and it's not uncommon to see moose and mountain goats or to hear elk bugle on a crisp fall evening. The Weminuche is the largest Wilderness area in Colorado and boasts the state's most remote spot. How remote? To use the most common criterion indicating "civilization," that spot is 16 kilometers (10 miles) from the nearest public road. In this sense, we might conclude that the state of Colorado is rather civilized, as it contains over 135,000 kilometers (84,000 miles) of roads, enough to encircle the globe three and a half times at the equator.

Sixteen kilometers may sound like a lot, especially if you live in an urban area, but my wife and I drive twice that distance just to get our mail. Once, when I camped near treeline (a.k.a. timberline) in

Colorado's Mount Massive Wilderness, I could easily see the city lights of Leadville far below and the headlights of the cars and trucks on State Highway 24 over 11 kilometers (7 miles) away. Keep in mind that we're talking about Wilderness, spelled with a capital "W," which indicates a federally designated "roadless" area. It is not necessarily the same thing as wilderness, spelled with a small "w," as in places untrammeled by humans.

The most remote spot in the forty-eight states of the contiguous United States is found in Yellowstone National Park, at 34.9 kilometers (21.7 miles) from the nearest road. If we add Alaska, the most remote place in the *mainland* US is in the Arctic National Wildlife Refuge near the Canadian border, 136.8 kilometers (85 miles) from a road.[1] But beyond the confines of the US and even continental landmasses, the prize for the most remote piece of land on Earth goes to the island of Tristan de Cunha. Located in the Atlantic Ocean, halfway between South Africa and Brazil, Tristan de Cunha is a British territory whose nearest neighbor is the island of St. Helena, 2,414 kilometers (1,500 miles) distant. Even so, approximately two hundred seventy people are permanent residents of Tristan de Cunha.[2] (In comparison, Antarctica has no full-time residents, though many scientific bases are sprinkled across that vast landmass.)

The point I'm making is that in the twenty-first century, it is difficult to find truly remote places, and those that remain entirely untouched by humans do not exist. Whether it's the Great Garbage Patch of the North Pacific Ocean (twice the size of Texas),[3] hydrocarbon particulates from fossil fuel combustion in the snow on Mount Everest,[4] or the 130 million pieces of space junk in orbit,[5] every spot on and near our planet has in some way been affected by our presence.[6] Earth today is an anthropogenic (human-influenced) planet.

This chapter considers how the world's natural environment and its nonhuman citizenry have borne the brunt of our greed and violence, and how our crimes against them intersect with sexual, gendered, and racial inequalities. Some of these crimes have resulted, in part, from our sheer numbers. Recall that we were down to about 2,000 individuals at the height of the last Ice Age, but that we rebounded to an estimated 20 million just before the Horticultural Revolution. This may be the maximum number of traditional-styled foragers the planet can sustain. But thanks to a random confluence of climatic fluctuations and human biocultural evolution, we surpassed the landscape's old carrying capacity for our kind by inventing horticulture and pastoralism. By the time our worldviews and social structures tilted toward the hyper-masculine 6,000 years ago, our numbers had topped 100 million, before hitting 300 million by the year 1 CE. We reached our first billion by 1804, just as the Industrial Revolution really got cranking. And by 1965, the year I was born, we had zoomed to 3.5 billion, increasing at a rate of 2.1 percent per year, the highest rate on record. Over the next 41 years, we doubled that number, hitting 7 billion by 2011. Barring unforeseen catastrophes, our current rate of increase puts us on track to reach 10 billion by the mid–twenty-first century.[7]

The spectacular increase in our population over the past two centuries has been possible only thanks to a reliance on cheap and, initially, bountiful fossil fuels, such as coal, oil, and natural gas. Some argue that the growth of the middle class and the social evolution of ethics were likewise results of the exploitation of these nonrenewable fuels.[*] The energy from all these sources allowed industrialism, consumerism, and capitalism to prosper on a staggering scale, though with capitalism also came outrageous discrepancies in wealth. For example, 1 percent of the US population holds almost 40 percent of its total wealth,[8] and the world's eight richest people (all men, six of whom are white) control as much wealth as do half the world's poorest.[9]

---

[*] We must never forget that the birth of modern capitalism and the Industrial Revolution of the late 18th and early 19th centuries were also a result of the barbaric enslavement of Africans in chattel slavery.

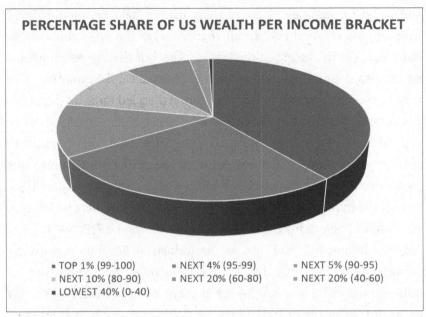

PERCENTAGE SHARE OF US WEALTH PER INCOME BRACKET

- TOP 1% (99-100)   ▪ NEXT 4% (95-99)   ▪ NEXT 5% (90-95)
- NEXT 10% (80-90)   ▪ NEXT 20% (60-80)   ▪ NEXT 20% (40-60)
- LOWEST 40% (0-40)

Illus. 23: Percentage share of US wealth per income bracket (after Wolff, 2017)

Capitalism ensures that most of the planet's human population languishes in poverty. Its lifeblood depends on the notions of hierarchy and class struggle, and on a few people controlling all the means of production. The only solution it can conceive is to double down on its own tack by investing in things like "trickle-down economics," an ever-ballooning military budget, and limits on social spending that encourage people to "pull themselves up by their bootstraps," which works only if you happen to inherit a good pair of boots. (One is reminded of a proverb attributed to Confucius: "To be wealthy and honored in an unjust society is a disgrace.") All are instruments of the Hyper-Masculine Paradigm, or HMP, reminding us that inequity and violence are okay and even necessary because our propensity for them is genetic: we came by our unjust nature honestly, and so we really can't help it. (As this book has made abundantly clear, hyper-masculinity is *not* genetic; it is a social construct.)

We are also an increasingly urban species. The year 2007 was the first time in history that more than half the world's population lived in urban areas, and by 2050, 68 percent of us will live in cities and towns.[10]

This is despite the fact that we were roaming the landscape in groups of twenty to fifty individuals until a mere five hundred generations ago. Very often, our cities are stratified by race, class, and gender, reflecting how we have egoically socialized ourselves since the Hyper-Masculine Devolution. For example, American towns and neighborhoods remain racially segregated, with marginalized communities often relegated to areas with the most polluted land, water, and air, usually downwind and downstream from factories and powerplants (to the east side or to the south side of US cities). Hence, these people, the majority of whom are poor, suffer more chronic illnesses due to social-environmental injustice. On a global scale, the United Nations estimates that one in three people on Earth will live in a slum by 2030.[11]

A 2011 report in the journal *Global Environmental Change* states that "perhaps white males see less risk in the world because they create, manage, control, and benefit from so much of it," and "perhaps women and nonwhite men see the world as more dangerous because in many ways they are more vulnerable, because they benefit less from many of its technologies and institutions, and because they have less power and control."[12] In 2018, Virginia Tech political scientist Cara Daggett identified the connection between the HMP and nonrenewable energy industries when she argued that "the concept of petro-masculinity suggests that fossil fuels mean more than profit."[13] According to Daggett and others, petro-masculinity and capitalism, which have resulted in egregious inequities between nations, socioeconomic classes, genders, and racial groups, are forms of hyper-masculinity.[14, 15]

Petro-masculinity also affects the production, distribution, and consumption of foods, especially highly processed foods. According to one estimate, if every human being on the planet consumed food and non-food products like your typical American does, we would require 4.1 additional Earths to fulfill our "needs."[16] As shocking as that figure may sound, several countries now rank even higher than the US on this ignominious index.[17]

Humans now make up 36 percent of all mammals on the planet, and livestock make up 60 percent. (Mammalian wildlife now comprise a mere 4 percent.)[18] To feed all of us, the UN Food and Agricultural Organization recommends that the *average* individual consume a minimum of 1,844 calories per day, with some variation based on age, sex, and activity level. Most people in developing nations average 2,800 calories per day, more than the required average, though a significant portion of that population still falls chronically short of this number. By and large, protein deficiency is not a problem in developing nations, as people there acquire most of their protein from plant sources, such as rice, corn, wheat, oats, peas, chickpeas, lentils, beans, nuts, seeds, quinoa, potatoes, sweet potatoes, yams, broccoli, spinach, asparagus, and Brussels sprouts. The real problem is total calories: on average, 20 percent of people in developing nations are unable to meet their daily minimum caloric needs.[19]

Meanwhile, the average American consumes 3,800 calories per day, the highest in the world. Still, between 1 and 3 percent of people in the US are undernourished.[20] This statistic is tragic, but paltry when compared with the 10 percent of Americans who are malnourished, i.e., who receive more than enough total calories, but whose nutrition is imbalanced and insufficient.[21] Other Western nations likewise consume large amounts of total calories.

These rates of consumption negatively affect not only individual health but also environmental health. In the United States, meat accounts for over 60 percent of protein consumption (not counting protein from dairy), meaning that the average American eats 222 pounds of meat each year.[22] This is twice the average of other developed nations and six times that of developing nations.[23]

Nevertheless, developing nations' food preferences are changing. As an article in the September 2014 issue of *National Geographic* states: "Simply put, a diet that revolves around meat and dairy, a way of eating that's on the rise throughout the developing world, will take a greater toll on the world's resources than one that revolves around unrefined grains, nuts, fruits, and vegetables."[24] Indeed, savannas and grasslands are being denuded by massive cattle feedlots, compounding the effects of desertification and groundwater depletion across the Sahel of North Africa, the Great Plains of North America, and the Loess Plateau of China.

By themselves, these data are sobering enough. However, they often fail to mention the sheer amount of water used in animal food production. For instance, one quarter-pound beef patty requires 660 gallons of water to produce,[25] and one gallon of 2% milk requires an input of approximately 1,000 gallons of water.[26] Whether raised for milk or meat, the average cow drinks 30 to 50 gallons of water each day. Multiplying this by 1.4 billion cows alive on Earth at any given moment yields 34 trillion gallons of water used each year in cattle production.[27] (The total world livestock population—cows plus all others—is estimated at approximately 80 billion.)[28]

But wait, isn't this supposed to be the blue planet? Isn't there plenty of water to go around? While it's true that over 70 percent of Earth's surface is covered with water, only 3 percent of that water is fresh, and only 1 percent is readily available. The rest is locked up in continental ice sheets, too deep underground to be accessible, or too dispersed (i.e., trapped in pockets of moisture scattered in rock strata).

According to David Robinson Simon, author of *Meatonomics*: "It takes dozens of times more water and five times more land to produce animal protein than equal amounts of plant protein. Unfortunately, even 'green' alternatives . . . can't overcome the basic math: the resources just don't exist to keep feeding the world animal foods at the level it wants."[29] Tropical rainforests absorb greenhouse gases, but two acres of the Amazon are cut down *each minute*. Ninety-one percent of that deforestation is done in the name of cattle ranches or crops used to feed cattle.[30] In addition, fully one-third of all land surfaces are devoted to either livestock or food crops grown for livestock, and another third of land is desert or semi-desert,[31] so the area we have to support our expanding population is, at best, modest. Finally, the methane from animal husbandry makes up 36 percent of all anthropogenic greenhouse gases.[32] (Methane is roughly 30 times more destructive than carbon dioxide as a greenhouse gas.)[33] As for fish, data show that the world's commercial fish species may experience a 90 percent collapse in populations by 2050.[34] Other aquatic species are not safe either: accidental "bycatch" or "bykill" from commercial fishing includes 300,000 whales, dolphins, and porpoises each year.[35]

According to data gathered by Will Tuttle in *The World Peace Diet*, 10 billion land animals are slaughtered each year in the world—300 every second in the US alone. This number includes both domesticated and wild animals.[36] In addition, approximately 15,690,000 people in the US—21 percent of the nation's total—hunted birds and land animals in 2018.[37] Nearly all did so with guns, as opposed to traps or bows.[38]

The learned behaviors of hunting and eating meat often rely on the belief that humans are intrinsically different from and superior to other animals—a belief that is foundational to speciesism. (See Chapter 3 for more on similarities and differences between humans and other animals.) Indeed, studies show that people who think they're superior to animals are more likely to rank human groups racially and hierarchically.[39] Children who are cruel toward animals are likely to be abusive and violent toward other people as adults—a well-known psychopathy.[40] In Ancient Greece, the mathematician Pythagoras already recognized this troubling association when he observed: "For as long as men massacre animals, they will kill each other." In the modern age, the same notion is apparent from this saying, attributed to Gandhi: "The greatness of a nation and its moral progress can be judged by the way its animals are treated."

Scholars who study cultures that primarily hunt to acquire food interpret their hunting and meat eating as subconscious patricide: a hunter metaphorically kills and eats his father.[41] (Among hunting cultures, hunters are nearly always men.) The greatest tension in patriarchal hunting societies exists in the father–son relationship. Killing animals assuages a hunter's hostility toward his father, and he usurps his father's social and spiritual power via the proxy of an animal. However, this interpretation overlooks the deeper symbolic connection of meat to mother, the one who mediates between father and son. In this sense, eating meat that is identified with the feminine reinforces male power and male dominance.[42]

This research refers almost entirely to foragers who live in cold, dry environments. As for hunters who live in modern developed nations, hunting often serves two psychological functions. First, hunters subconsciously believe they will appropriate an animal's power when they kill and perhaps consume that animal, thus assuaging their own masculine insecurity. The duration of this power is extended when hunters display parts of animals as trophies in their home. In so doing, hunters assert egoic control over themselves by ritually "killing" feminine aspects of their psyche (empathy, altruism, nonviolence, etc.). Today, in the US, 85 percent of hunters are still men, although the number of women increased during the first two decades of the twenty-first century.*[43] Second, the hunt is replete with sexual symbolism, not least because a predatory sexual act is reified when a hunter draws "first blood," using a phallic-shaped weapon to "penetrate" his prey.[44,45]

Women's minds are likewise controlled, dominated, and socially consumed, sometimes violently. In 2020, the gender pay gap in America stood at 81 percent; that is, women earned only 81 cents for every dollar earned by men. And as of 2021, women made up only 28 percent of members of Congress (increased from 20 percent in 2017). Based on economic participation, political empowerment, health, and education, the US ranked 46th in the world in terms of gender inequality in 2020, taking the spot between Slovakia and Moldova.[46,47]

---

* Recall that the terms "women" and "men" are not necessarily equivalent to the gendered terms "feminine" and "masculine" or to the biological terms "female" and "male," respectively. Therefore, the above statistics may indicate an increasingly internalized hyper-masculine socialization—and a perceived threat to that identity—among American women.

Illus. 24: "Do You Still Beat Your Wife?"

To be fair, the rights of women and minorities have advanced further in the US and other Western nations than in Southwest Asia and North Africa, where women hold only 7 percent of seats in governing bodies. According to the World Economic Forum, nine out of the ten worst nations in terms of gender parity are Muslim-majority nations.[48] Proscriptions on women in those countries range from bans on voting, driving, and holding public office to exclusion from school (Afghanistan, for example, has an 85 percent illiteracy rate for women), forced marriages, child marriages, female genital mutilation (FGM), floggings, canings, the cutting off of ears and noses, scarring by acid, and death by "honor killings." (At least 5,000 women are executed each year for, say, having premarital sex or looking at another man.)[49]

Each day, some 6,000 girls worldwide suffer FGM, a barbaric means of controlling women and female sexuality. And in the United States and other "developed" countries, brochures that advertise women and girls as young as four or five years old—or even younger—are available to the discriminating tourist. Such businesses are part of a global sex-trafficking industry.[50]

In her book *The Sexual Politics of Meat: A Feminist-Vegetarian Critical Theory*, Carol J. Adams investigates the psychosocial connection between our treatment of women and our treatment of animals. In this now-classic text, Adams demonstrates how meat and women's bodies are cognate symbols of male power and domination. Animals are consumed literally, and women are consumed visually and sexually: a manly man eats meat and controls women.[51] Advertisements that substitute cuts of meat for parts of a woman's body seem playful and innocuous—to the conditioned mind. Adams suggests that eating meat (and eggs and milk, which she calls "feminized protein") substantiates the fragmentation and consumption of women themselves. This worldview is nearly universal and nearly invisible.[52] Just consider this often-praised quote from actor Paul Newman, when asked if he ever considered cheating on his wife Joanne Woodward: "Why go out for burgers when you have steak at home?"

The step from having this impression of women to taking violent actions against them is a short one. When a rape victim (male or female, though the gendered feminine is always the intended victim) says, "I felt like a piece of meat," the metaphor is taken to a deeper level. Obviously, no one can "feel" like meat since meat is dead and therefore cannot feel. Rather, the socialized impression of what meat represents is used to describe the victim's sense of violation in abstract metaphoric language. (Adams calls meat the "absent referent.")[53] Consider how an implement such as a knife is used to fragment an animal into more desirable and less desirable cuts of meat, while a rapist's erect penis similarly fragments a human body into more desirable and less desirable "cuts of meat," thus acting as a metaphorical knife.[54] Commercial slaughterhouses use over thirty-five varieties of knives, blades, and other implements to render animals into commodities, and meat-industry workers colloquially call the machine in which animals are inseminated a "rape rack."[55]

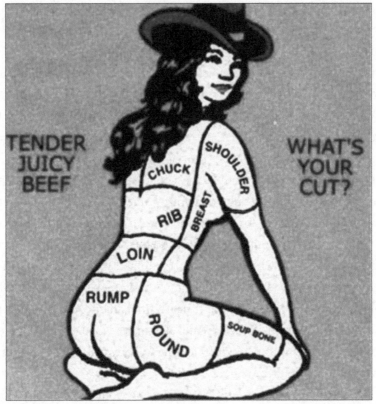

Illus. 25: "Tender, Juicy Beef. What's Your Cut?"

Marketing forces have learned to exploit women and the feminine to an appalling degree. The best-selling video game in America in 2013, *Grand Theft Auto: Vice City*, allowed players to have virtual sex with a prostitute and then beat her to death. *Call of Duty: Advanced Warfare*, another video game franchise that heavily featured male violence with guns, was the most popular in 2003 and remained in the top ten in sales through 2015, racking up over $11 billion in profit for its developer Sledgehammer Games, its publisher Activision, and other affiliates. Bearing this in mind, we can see it is no accident that the military uses violent video games to train soldiers. In addition, studies show that children who play violent video games become less sensitive to pain and suffering, more fearful of the world, and more likely to behave aggressively toward others.[56]

Even so, our culture and media continue to target boys with games that simulate womanizing, hunting, killing, shooting guns, joining the military, and pursuing wealth and power.

As of 2020, the total number of legally owned guns in the US was over 400 million, i.e., 1.2 guns for every individual.[57] This means that while comprising only 4 percent of the world's population, Americans owned 40 percent of all civilian firearms. Most gun owners cited personal protection as their reason for having guns, as only 38 percent of US gun owners used guns for hunting.[58] Consequently, gun sales spiked in early 2020 with the rise of the COVID pandemic, and again during the insurrection associated with President Trump's attempts to seize power from President-elect Joe Biden.[59] Many studies have begun to examine how the election and presidency of Donald Trump were predicted by the prevalence of the HMP in US culture. A 2021 research article by the National Academy of Sciences concludes: "The findings highlight the importance of psychological examinations of *masculinity as a cultural ideology* to understand how men's and women's endorsement of [hegemonic masculinity] legitimizes patriarchal dominance and reinforces gender-, race-, and class-based hierarchies via candidate support" (italics are mine).[60]

In the meantime, our lust for state-level violence continues unabated. In 2001, President George W. Bush initiated the Global War on Terror. Over two decades and $2 trillion later, US-led efforts have motivated that war to spread into eighty nations; US troops saw brief combat in fourteen countries in 2019; and prolonged active military engagement continues in Yemen, Syria, and Somalia.[61]

In 2015, total US military spending topped $736 billion, comprising nearly half the world's total military budget; by 2020, that figure had ballooned to nearly $936 billion.[62] As a side note, in 2019, the United States Space Force became fully operational as the sixth and newest branch of the armed services,[63] and to meet its fiscal requirements, $18.1 billion was added to the US defense budget in 2022.[64] These are enormous monetary figures that defy imagination. To put them in perspective, "ending [world] hunger by 2030 would come with a price tag of [US $330 billion]," according to a German study referenced in a 2020 article in *The Guardian*.[65] But warfare is an expensive business, and as of January 2024, the US had been engaged in military action somewhere in the world in all but 17 years of its existence since independence.[66,67,68]

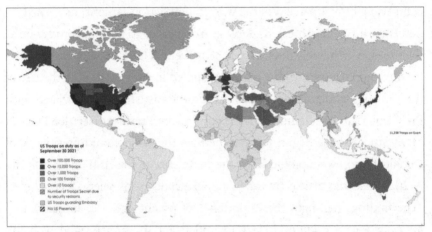

Illus. 26: Map of US military presence in US and abroad as of 30 September 2021

Considering America's near-constant state of warfare, which ensures the production of more warfare, such funds might more accurately be earmarked for an "offense budget." Indeed, in terms of peacefulness, *The Global Peace Index 2022* rated the U.S. at number 129 out of 163 countries assessed.[69] Thus, we are prompted to reexamine which nations are truly First World, developed, and civilized, and which are primitive and barbaric. In an apocryphal account, when asked by a CBS news reporter what he thought of Western Civilization, Mahatma Gandhi famously replied, "I think it would be a good idea."

Mountains of supporting data exist, but you already know, or at least have a sense of, these disturbing trends. We have spent the last 6,000

---

* This map may not include additional countries in which the US supports military operations with information, capital, or hardware, including military drones. As of March 2023, the US military was actively involved in Afghanistan, Egypt, Iraq, Kenya, Lebanon, Libya, Mali, Mauritania, Niger, Nigeria, Syria, Tunisia, and Yemen.

years killing each other and the environment, and we now stand at a crossroads. Our only sane recourse may be to remind ourselves who we truly are at our core—bioculturally—and resuscitate our better angels. Nearly everyone hopes for a better future. But what exactly does that mean? What does it look like, and how do we get there?

Chapter 12

THE CONSCIOUSNESS REVOLUTION: REBIRTH

In the introduction, I quoted historian and author Yuval Harari from his book *Sapiens: A Brief History of Humankind*: "[T]here is some universal biological reason why almost all cultures valued manhood over womanhood. We do not know what this reason is."[1] Although Harari's conundrum is compelling, and we used it to help build our investigation, we can now see a flaw in the way in which it's framed.

In the first section of this book, we reviewed evidence that shows early humans were *not* biologically disposed to violence, nor were men culturally valued more than women due to biological evolution. If anything, it was the other way around. We also saw how environmental quality declined worldwide during the last Ice Age, resulting in two critical effects on humans. First, genetic research indicates the human genome underwent a quantum leap in fundamental cognitive power during the Irrational Revolution between 60,000 and 70,000 years ago. Although this is fiercely debated, many scholars contend that the mutation caused a shift in our perceptual awareness that heralded the maturation of the human ego and HEADS (hypersensitive egoic agency detection structure). Second, while sparse and still in Africa, our ancestors survived because they socially enacted the effects of this biological mutation as it left an indelible imprint of archetypal landscapes on the human psyche. In other words, it manifested as art, religion, and impressions of gendered landscapes. In this watershed moment, the human psyche balanced the feminine/masculine binary with a constellation of liminal pangendered qualities.

In the second section of this book, we saw how our ancestors encountered strikingly different environments as some of them emigrated from Africa. Now "hard-wired" to interpret landscapes archetypally, they began to categorize places as more or less feminine and more or less masculine, accommodating their lifestyles to match. In Eurasia, lower-quality environments and the physical *structure* of landscapes encouraged them to invest in more masculine behavioral traits to survive. This process accelerated 12,000 years ago during the *Younger Dryas*, which resulted in the Horticultural Revolution, a surge in hunting, pastoralism, and the discovery of paternity. Taken together, the effects summarized in the first two sections of the book constitute the Gendered Landscapes Theory, or GLT.

Finally, in the third and fourth sections of the book, we saw how some cultures did indeed begin to value manhood over womanhood, *although this was a social decision, not a biological adaptation.* In a few critical instances, it would result in patriarchal socioeconomic structures that strengthened themselves by oppressing feminine "otherness" in terms of gender, ethnicity, race, and class, as well as by subduing the natural environment and life itself to the point of imminent ecological collapse. In allowing all of this to happen, we turned the planet red. We called this the Hyper-Masculine Paradigm, or HMP.

So, that's the recap. Taken all at once like that, our death spiral into the HMP certainly looks depressing. But here's the good news: The GLT suggests we evolved the capacity to imagine, remember, and project our minds into the future, and as a species, we originally engaged these superpowers for good. True, we later *chose* to abuse the same powers for evil. But our descent into violence and inequities was *not* imperative. Bioculturally, we have everything we need to consciously choose a more compassionate and equitable path "out of the desert." In fact, we've already started.

Even though the twentieth century may win the prize for most destructive and unjust on record, powerful pro-social forces sprang from it that continue to gain momentum. Every day, thousands of scientists and millions of concerned global citizens give their time, energy, and resources to solving profound social dilemmas—dilemmas that are intrinsically bound up in our relationship with planet Earth.

While the Amazonian rainforest continues to be logged at an alarming rate (2 acres every minute, as mentioned earlier), the Brazilian government has designated national parks and Indigenous territories, and the Brazilian Institute of Environment and Renewable Natural Resources (IBAMA) works around the clock monitoring and protecting those lands. And although humans have directly or indirectly affected every inch of the planet's surface, relatively pure, wild patches of Earth do still exist. Such gems are not mere playgrounds for ecotourists or even repositories of ecological health. More than anything else, these gardens of Eden are the very foundation of our humanity. Naturalist and author Terry Tempest Williams crystalizes this most human of sentiments when she writes, "Wilderness is the source of what we can imagine and what we cannot—the taproot of consciousness."[2]

Our consciousness was refocused in 2018 when Swedish environmental activist Greta Thunberg initiated climate strikes in schools around the world and challenged world leaders to stop using fossil fuels. (Burning hydrocarbons, such as natural gas, petroleum, and coal, releases carbon dioxide, one of the primary greenhouse gases responsible for anthropogenic climate change.) The UN Intergovernmental Panel on Climate Change (IPCC), the UN Environmental Programme (UNEP), and the World Meteorological Organization (WMO) are at the forefront of the fifteen international organizations, along with hundreds of national and local groups, committed to avoiding the worst effects of climate change.[3] And contrary to what skeptics might conclude, these groups are not always led by white, Eurocentric ideals and people. Among recent champions of this cause is Wanjiku "Wawa" Gatheru, a Kenyan-American woman who, in January 2021, founded Black Girl Environmentalist, an online community of Black women, girls, and non-binary people of all ages who are passionate about the intersection of climate justice, racial justice, and gender equality. Gatheru is the first Black person to be awarded the Rhodes, Truman, and Udall scholarships; she graduated from the University of Connecticut in environmental studies (with minors in global studies and urban and community studies) and from the University of Oxford in environmental governance.

Aside from carbon dioxide, two other primary greenhouse gases are methane and nitrous oxide, most of which are produced by the livestock industry. According to the Vegan Society, "If the world went vegan, it could save 8 million human lives by 2050, reduce greenhouse gas emissions by two-thirds and lead to healthcare-related savings and avoid climate damages of $1.5 trillion."[4] The same source cites Google trends that show how veganism increased seven times worldwide between 2014 and 2019. However, by eating vegetarian foods (which include eggs and dairy), one can already make a significant positive impact on the climate, human health, and animal welfare. Such impact toward intersectional equality is also the aim of La Via Campesina (LVC), an international social movement that defends "small-scale sustainable agriculture as a way to promote social justice and dignity" and that "strongly opposes corporate-driven agriculture and transnational companies that are destroying people and nature." Led by farmers and laborers from over eighty countries, LVC promotes equality through food sovereignty, environmental justice, international solidarity, agroecology, agrarian reform of land and water rights, and dignity for migrants and waged workers.[5]

As predicted by environmental philosopher Roderick Nash, the rights afforded oppressed genders (in particular women), races, ethnicities, and social classes, as well as animals and the environment have been increasing in scope, if haltingly, over the past few hundred years.[6,7] The Human Rights Campaign (HRC) has worked to alleviate the discrimination, fear, and violence suffered by marginalized people since its founding in 1980. (Originally the Human Rights Campaign Fund, it was rebranded in 1995.) The HRC now seeks "to ensure that all LGBTQ+ people, and particularly those who are trans, people of color, and HIV+, are treated as full and equal citizens." With equity as its goal, the organization's logo is the familiar equal sign in yellow, embedded in a blue square. In addition, as we became more conscious of our treatment of other animals, groups such as People for the Ethical Treatment of Animals (PETA) and the Humane Society of the United States (HSUS) were created to advocate for animals and oppose cruelty toward them.

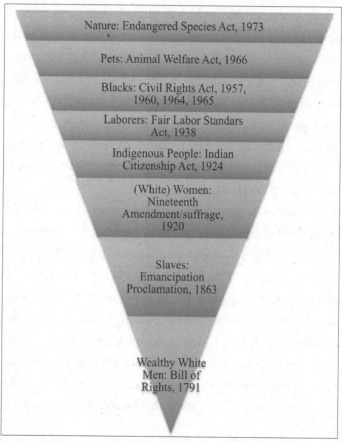

Illus. 27: The expanding concept of rights (after Nash, 1989)

While women have faced bigotry since the Hyper-Masculine Devolution, only since the nineteenth century have (white) women had sufficient leverage and influence over enough (white) male allies to successfully dispute gender discrimination (against white women). Movements for women's rights began with suffrage, grew to confront workplace discrimination, and continue today in the form of the struggle against income disparity and sexual abuse. Recent campaigns for gender equality include The Everyday Sexism Project (http://everydaysexism.com) and MeToo (#MeToo). "Me Too" was first suggested by Tarana Burke in 2006 as a phrase of solidarity for survivors of sexual abuse, but it only became the slogan of a national and global movement with the scandal surrounding American film producer Harvey Weinstein in 2017.* Since then, scores of high-profile personalities have joined the ranks of the MeToo movement, including Gwyneth Paltrow, Uma Thurman, Alyssa Milano, and many others. MeToo has grown to become the viral social media campaign #MeToo, as well as a society for women who have been sexually harassed or abused, giving them the courage to speak out. In 2022, MeToo celebrated its five years of success in discussing sexual violence and disrupting the HMP by expanding its mission with the campaign #BeyondTheHashtag.

Racial inequalities comprise yet another legacy of the HMP. Following the 2012 shooting death of unarmed Black teenager Trayvon Martin and the subsequent acquittal of his assailant George Zimmerman, social media platforms began using the hashtag #BlackLivesMatter in protest and solidarity. The movement gained further intensity after Minneapolis police officer Derek Chauvin killed George Floyd, an unarmed Black man, in 2020.† Black Lives Matter declares itself a nonviolent global organization "whose mission is to eradicate white supremacy and build local power to intervene in violence inflicted on Black communities by the state and vigilantes."[8] Since then, discussions about race and Critical

---

* New York Times journalists Jodi Kantor and Megan Twohey broke the story of the Harvey Weinstein sexual misconduct allegations in 2017, for which they won a Pulitzer Prize in Public Service. Their tireless work helped ignite Tarana Burke's MeToo movement.

† We mustn't forget that in the eight years between these two events, dozens of other Black people, including Sandra Bland, Tamir Rice, and Michael Brown, needlessly lost their lives at the hands of police.

Race Theory (CRT) have increased. Indeed, whether we realize it or not, white people, especially white men, benefit from an ingrained social hierarchy that puts them at the top and discriminates against everyone else to varying degrees. As summarized by author Dr. Paula M. Lantz, CRT affirms that the concept of race is a social construction and that racism is institutional, structural, and prevalent and creates numerous inequities in measures of health, education, and quality of life.[9] As such, CRT has certainly given the white patriarchy and its allies an easy target against which to push. At the same time, CRT has inspired grassroots organizations to raise awareness of systemic racism, as well as to launch programs and advocate policies to mitigate its effects. Through all this, African Americans still show a sobering amount of generosity, as they donate more money to charities than any other subset of Americans, including wealthy white Americans, who receive tax offsets on capital gains if they make large donations to charities.[10]

Racially and ethnically motivated wars cause the greatest harm to the poor and underprivileged, although international aid agencies alleviate some of the effects by feeding and housing refugees and internally displaced persons. Examples include the International Rescue Committee (IRC), Amnesty International, the United Nations Children's Fund (UNICEF), and *Médecins Sans Frontières* (Doctors Without Borders). Nonetheless, some agencies commercialize gendered and racialized images of women and children of color, while depicting white women as caregivers and white men as saviors. Oxfam International, Save the Children, CARE International, and Heifer International are among those that use online shopping platforms that perpetuate—and capitalize on—these stereotypical socioeconomic inequalities.[11]

However, grassroots programs driven and supported by individuals without a white savior complex do exist. A rising star in this arena is the Partners in Health program, founded by Ophelia Dahl, Todd McCormack, Tom White, and doctors Paul Farmer and Jim Yong Kim. Operating under the mission that everyone should have access to quality healthcare, these heroes partner with local community organizers to bring free or affordable healthcare and pharmaceuticals to impoverished people of color who suffer from diseases that have long been able to be cured or palliated in wealthy nations.

As for religion, its long-term effects are mixed. On the one hand, religious aid organizations and missionary programs have built schools, orphanages, and clinics for the world's poorest. On the other hand, the same efforts have privileged imperialist worldviews of exclusion, misogyny, xenophobia, and supremacy by demonizing Indigenous customs and ensuring that colonized peoples remain dependent on colonizers. Bearing this in mind, we can make the argument that humanity has outgrown any Paleolithic benefits of its religious conversion.

Yet this claim is simplistic. Our sense of spirit, art, beauty, and all things creative—that is, our humanity—first appeared as a genetic mutation that, though irrational, helped our species survive. So at least *our capacity* for religion is literally in our genes.

Estimates of the population of atheists and agnostics worldwide range from 7 to 13 percent; this means that the vast majority of us continue to pattern our lives around a belief in the supernatural.[12] According to a 2015 Pew Research Center study, 83 percent of Americans were "absolutely sure" or "fairly certain" there is a god,[13] 72 percent of Americans believed there is a heaven,[14] and roughly 71 percent were Christian.[15] And in a comprehensive demographic study of more than 230 countries and territories around the world, Pew found that 86 percent of humanity declared faith in one religion or another.[16]

So, in all likelihood, we will continue to be a religious species, although the timbre of our faith traditions will no doubt evolve. As it does, it's imperative that we reinterpret ancient scriptures with a more inclusive and compassionate global ethos in mind, for as in all things, the only humane way forward will be to foster diversity and acceptance.

* * *

The final section of this book is titled "Pangaea: It Takes a Planet." The word *Pangaea* comes from the Greek word *pan*, meaning "all" or "entire," and *Gaia*, meaning "Earth." In 1912, the German meteorologist Alfred Wegener attempted to prove that the world's major landmasses resemble pieces of a puzzle. Wegener coined the term *Pangaea* to suggest that all landmasses today might have once been joined together in a single supercontinent. This idea formed part of his theory of continental drift, which the scientific community of his day roundly dismissed. It is now known that the Earth is indeed fractured into seven large tectonic plates and dozens of medium-sized and smaller plates, all of which were joined together from roughly 350 to 200 million years ago, before they began to drift apart at the rate of 2.5 to 15 centimeters (1 to 6 inches) per year. Hats off to Mr. Wegener.*

I use the term here as a metaphor to show how our more recent technologies have allowed us to compress time, space, and social milieus into an integrated whole (and as a not-so-subtle allusion to the pangendered landscapes discussed earlier). A journey that once required months or years can now be accomplished in a matter of hours. More than a mere tool to improve our physical speed, technology also allows us to shop online, video-call with friends and family half a world away, and marvel at the surface of the red planet—Mars—through the "eyes" of NASA's rover Perseverance and the drone helicopter Ingenuity. In little more than a generation, our species has come together faster and shared more of our information, lifestyles, and economies than we had in all the rest of our evolutionary history. We have globalized, and we might even call some of this globalization—including our movements toward a global ethos of environmental justice, animal rights, human rights, anti-racism, anti-sexism, anti-capitalism, and decolonization—good. Some go so far as to suggest that national borders are all but meaningless in our postmodern world of multinational corporations, global trade, and omnipresent social media, and that the formal removal of those boundaries is inevitable if we are to create a more harmonious world.[17]

---

* Climatoligist Wladimir Köppen was Wegener's father-in-law and aided him in developing his hypothesis of continental drift.

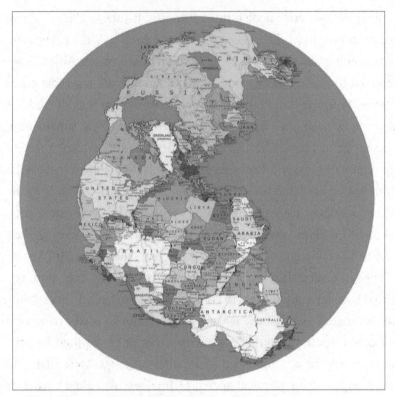

Illus. 28: Pangaea: Modern political map

So where do we go from here? We could learn from the bonobos and
thrive, or we could continue along like the chimpanzees and fight
our way back to the Stone Age (or more accurately, the Bronze Age).
New research suggests that when we intentionally change our stories,
we change our lives. At Duke University, Student Services found that
students who struggled with classes often did so because they thought
they were simply not cut out for university. This was the story they'd been
told, which they had repeated to themselves and believed. However, after
receiving intervention, these students understood that they just needed
more time to adjust. They were then more likely to raise their grade point
averages and less likely to drop out. This became their new story because
they believed in it.[18]

We have begun to write a new story for ourselves. As remarked by American politician and author Stacey Abrams: "We can't escape where we come from, but it's our responsibility to reshape what that story looks like." In a similar spirit, Dr. Wangari Maathai, who was a Kenyan environmentalist and women's rights activist, and the winner of the Nobel Peace Prize in 2004, said: "In the course of history, there comes a time when humanity is called to shift to a new level of consciousness to reach a higher moral ground. A time when we have to shed our fear and give hope to each other. That time is now." Dr. Maathai carried on her work in the face of constant and oftentimes dangerous opposition because she believed in a different story, a better story for us all.

Our tendency toward conflict and disagreement will always be part of the human condition. It comes with the package. But a desire for peace and harmony is also an elemental part of who we are—one of our most essential qualities, our better angels. To continue the work of reengaging these qualities will require tremendous imagination, belief, and faith in ourselves and each other. It will take a planet. Luckily, these are our superpowers. Tales of the Genesis Tree, the Garden of Eden, the Smith and the Devil, and the Lorax explain the world in terms of the HMP, but in the end, they're only stories. And stories can be rewritten. We have within us the characters and landscapes of an exhilarating, healing story. May we redraft ours in the image of a healthier, more pangendered, multicolored, and equitable planet—a new Pangaea.

RESOURCES

Introduction

Questions for Discussion

1. Which fairy tales had the most impact on you as a child, and what lessons do you remember learning from them? In retrospect, can you discern a bigger picture in which those stories were set or a deeper social reality that they conveyed, even if unintentionally?

2. Have you traditionally thought that humans are intrinsically good, bad, or somewhere in between? How do you think you arrived at that notion about humanity?

3. This book is predicated on the notion that hyper-masculine men have dominated most societies throughout recorded history. Do you agree or disagree with this statement? Why?

4. The Gendered Landscapes Theory suggests that humans' perception of themselves as complex gendered beings transferred to the natural landscape. Do you think this theory is supported by the evidence shown? Why or why not?

Recommended Viewing

- *Re-Enchantment: The Hidden Meaning of Fairy Tales*
- *Mustang*

Chapter 1—The Genesis Tree

Questions for Discussion

1. Can you identify other similarities or differences between "The Genesis Tree" and "The Garden of Eden"?

2. Chapter 1 states: "The mythological motif of creating order from chaos likely began in the Late Paleolithic. . . . Evolutionary psychologist Marie-Louise von Franz explains this was a natural result of the human psyche experiencing its own ego-consciousness coming into being as 'world-becoming.'" How does this statement make you feel about your own humanity and your understanding of reality? How might this fit into interpretations of "The Genesis Tree" and "The Garden of Eden"?

3. If/when you think of the Christian cross, what does it mean to you personally? Have you ever thought of it in terms of the symbols described in Chapter 1?

4. Name some things or concepts (e.g., places, landscapes, architecture, celebrity personalities) in your experience that contain gendered symbolism. How are those symbols used? Why might those symbols contain those gendered qualities?

Recommended Viewing
- *Dawn of Humanity*
- *Joseph Campbell and the Power of Myth*: Episode 1: "The Hero's Adventure" (first broadcast June 21, 1988 on PBS)

Chapter 2—Pangendered Landscapes: The Deep Backstory

Questions for Discussion

1. How is gender socially constructed?

2. What are your earliest memories of differences between the sexes? This could include anatomical differences, as well as different jobs, roles, and levels of relative importance assigned to different sexes. Additionally, would you say those roles are determined by sex or by gender? Why?

3. What are your favorite landscapes, and how do you feel when you visit them? According to the descriptions of landscapes given in the book, what gendered traits do the places you just named express?

4. Do your experiences of "human nature" fit the popular image of "Man the Hunter"? Think of an example of a human trait that does fit this archetype, and then try to explain why it exists.

Recommended Viewing
- *Miss Representation*
- *The Mask You Live In*
- *Raised without Gender*
- *Whale Rider*

Chapter 3—The Irrational Revolution: Spirits, Art, and Life
Questions for Discussion

1. Have you ever considered how humans and other animals are similar and how we are different? How do you feel knowing that according to science, humans are animals? Does this change how you view the traditional hierarchy of species? Finally, how might this be related to other hierarchies, such as those of gender and race?

2. Geographer Howard Stein is quoted as saying, "We project psychic contents outward onto the social and physical world and act as though what is projected is in fact an attribute of the other or outer." What psychic contents is Stein talking about, and how do they apply to the social and physical features of our world?

3. The end of this chapter states that the symbols contained in our earliest art, religions, stories, and cultures were in the process of evolving from a pangendered matrix to a profusion of gendered binaries. What is meant by "pangendered matrix" and "gendered binaries"?

Recommended Viewing

- *Journey of Man*
- *Two Spirits*
- *Joseph Campbell and the Power of Myth*: Episode 2: "The Message of the Myth"
- "How Mental Illness Changed Humanity—For the Better" (TEDx Talk by David Whitley)

Chapter 4—Pandora's Box

Questions for Discussion

1. What similarities do you notice between Pandora and Eve in the Garden?

2. As mentioned in the text: "Hope is the only virtue contained within the box, and the only one [Pandora] preserves. Scholars interpret this to represent either humanity's redeeming qualities of optimism, ambition, and having the faith to carry on, or the bitter false hope of delusion, self-deception, and paradox. All these virtues and vices may be considered byproducts of HEADS." How might these "virtues and vices" be results or side effects of HEADS?

3. Why is the "theft of fire" motif used so often in myths to explain the origins of civilization?

Recommended Viewing

- *Gender Revolution: A Journey with Katie Couric*

Chapter 5—Feminine Landscapes

Questions for Discussion

1. Most people tend to think in terms of either/or binaries. To your knowledge, which cultures have made binaries a cornerstone of their worldview, and which have not? Why might this be the case?

2. Think of some famous personalities, e.g., celebrities, musicians, politicians, or artists. Then try to construct a gendered matrix that would describe each one's public persona.

3. What would your gendered matrix look like? Do you think this is how someone else might describe your matrix? Why or why not?

4. What's your favorite number? Why? Also, now that you have read this chapter, what deeper reasons might exist for it being your favorite number?

Recommended Viewing
*   *City of Joy*
*   *Feminists: What Were They Thinking?*

Chapter 6—The Horticultural Revolution:
Goddesses, Matriarchy, and Birth

Questions for Discussion

1. Odds are you've been vaccinated against several zoonotic diseases. Were you aware that most diseases are the result of humans' contact with nonhuman animals? What did you think when you read this?

2. In this chapter, you read that "in animal-based societies, wealth and name follow the male side of the family, male gods are worshipped, women are solely responsible for childcare, and women do more work than men, although their work is valued less." Does this describe your culture? If not, in which ways does it differ? Can you think of a culture with social traits completely opposite to those listed above?

3. Do you anthropomorphize anything that is not human? What is it, and why do you think you do so?

4. Can you identify any overt examples of hyper-masculine behaviors in your culture? What makes them hyper-masculine instead of simply masculine?

Recommended Viewing
- *The Ascent of Woman*
- *Joseph Campbell and the Power of Myth*: Episode 5: "Love and the Goddess"

Chapter 7—The Smith and the Devil

Questions for Discussion

1. Chapter 7 states that "The Smith and the Devil" "describes how humans learned to fashion metal tools for both good and evil." Can you see a bigger picture that this story points to?

2. The story of the Smith and the Devil implies a hierarchy of types of work. Which jobs, or types of jobs, are suggested as being better or worse than others? Why?

3. Can you think of stories that have similar themes to those of "The Smith and the Devil"? What are those stories, and what morals do they teach? Why?

Recommended Viewing
- *Why We Fight*
- *American Factory*

Chapter 8—Masculine Landscapes

Questions for Discussion

1. Mental content that many Americans share includes things like the flag, apple pie, and baseball. Some social scientists call these things mentifacts, or centripetal cultural forces. What are some mentifacts that comprise your mental content and are emotionally significant to you?

2. Take a minute to look at a popular magazine. What images do the retailers use to sell their goods? How are the goods expected to be associated with the images that sell them? From where might those associations have originated?

3. This chapter states, "Human physiology typically prefers a diet comprised of 60–80 percent carbohydrates, 10–20 percent fats, and 10–20 percent proteins." Let's say the ratio is 70:15:15. Does your diet follow this ratio or not? What might different ratios, such as 20:10:70 or 20:40:40, represent socially? Where have you learned about what types and amounts of foods to eat?

4. What did you think when you read that people at one time did not know about paternity? Did that notion seem unimaginable? How much do we value paternity today, and how much do we value maternity? Are they balanced, or is one more important than the other? If so, which one, and why?

5. What are your own masculine and feminine behavioral traits? When are they expressed, and where do they come from?

Recommended Viewing

- *Cowspiracy: The Sustainability Secret*
- *What the Health?*

Chapter 9—The Hyper-Masculine Devolution:
Gods, Patriarchy, and Death

Questions for Discussion

1. Can you think of other common phrases and idioms that use metals to convey a certain message? What are they, and how might they have developed? Do they imply a hierarchy of importance?

2. This chapter connects masculinism and hyper-masculinism to certain religions. If you agree with the arguments made, can you find exceptions whereby feminine cultural traits are lauded and shown to be most important? And if you disagree with the arguments made, can you find evidence that corroborates the chapter's premise?

3. Aryans were warlike tribespeople who were part of the Kurgan invasions between 2,000 and 5,000 BCE. The swastika is a

symbol that represents their supreme sky-god. Can you think of other symbols that represent hyper-masculinity? Where did those symbols come from originally? How about religious symbols? Do they have meanings that predate their commonly known usage?

4. This chapter also touches on environmental destruction, the keeping of livestock, and zoonotic diseases. According to the text, how do gendered landscapes and attitudes toward the natural world produce beneficial or harmful effects?

Recommended Viewing

- *One of Us*
- *Believer*
- *A Girl in the River: The Price of Forgiveness*

Chapter 10—The Lorax

Questions for Discussion

1. This chapter calls attention to the Vietnam War Era, when many forms of inequity were challenged and recast in American society. How do classism, sexism, racism, and environmental decline relate to one another, and why might all have been confronted in the 1960s and 1970s?

2. Inequality takes many different forms. Is one form more consequential than others? Why or why not?

3. Can you think of some organizations that are committed to working toward solutions to the crimes committed against the natural environment, animals, women, people of color, and the poor? Are you or is someone you know associated with those groups? Why or why not?

Recommended Reading and Viewing

- *The Lorax*
- *Breaking Boundaries: The Science of Our Planet*

- *Bending the Arc*
- *Food, Inc.*
- *The True Cost*

Chapter 11—Transformed Landscapes

Questions for Discussion

1. What are some reasons that women still face challenges in the job market today?
2. Given the social construction of gender, why might gay men experience disproportionate employment discrimination?
3. How are impoverished people represented in neighborhoods and other geographical spaces?
4. What are your earliest memories of race and racial differences?
5. Based on the readings, what are three reasons that racial discrimination is so persistent and pervasive?
6. Why do some ethnic groups, compared to others, have superior economic outcomes?
7. Even when a member of a racial minority is economically successful, what challenges might they continue to face?
8. Maybe you've heard of DEI, which stands for Diversity, Equity, and Inclusion. These terms are used in reference to the intersection of gender, race, class, and other categories of socially constructed difference. *Inclusion* means striving to make use of *diversity* to help give minorities and oppressed communities opportunities to overcome obstacles and achieve *equity* and equality. What are some ways in which you can become more inclusive of others at school, in the workplace, or in society in general?

Recommended Viewing

- *Hidden Figures*
- *13th*
- *I Am Not Your Negro*

- *Who We Are: A Chronicle of Racism in America*
- *Reel Injun*
- *Why We Fight*
- *The Invisible War*
- *Class Divide*
- "My Mother's Strange Definition of Empowerment" (TED Talk by Khadija Gbla)
- "Black Doll, White Doll" (YouTube short, https://www. youtube.com/watch?v=ybDa0gSuAcg), in which high-school student Kiri Davis explores the self-image of Black children in the US by repeating Dr. Kenneth Clark's historic "doll test," which led to school desegregation.

Chapter 12—The Consciousness Revolution: Rebirth

Questions for Discussion

1. What are two strategies that the US might adopt to reduce inequality?
2. Imagine you had to design a policy to reduce income inequality in the US. What type of program would you design?
3. What challenges might American politicians face if they proposed some of the strategies you suggested in the previous two questions?
4. What are the causes of growing inequality in the US?
5. In your opinion, which cause(s) has (have) been most consequential to the rapid growth of inequality since 1970?
6. Imagine a scenario wherein America achieved both high national economic growth and low income inequality. What factors would need to change in order to facilitate this kind of transformation?

Recommended Viewing
- *I Am Greta*
- *He Named Me Malala*
- *Seeing Allred*
- *The Big Scary "S" Word*
- *Imagining the Indian: The Fight against Native American Mascoting*
- *The Last Tourist*

ACKNOWLEDGMENTS

During a recent Christmas holiday, my wife Kim and I visited my mom in the Midwest. My mom is still active and healthy, though she's getting up there in age, and so we helped her out around the house, doing odd jobs that she really shouldn't do anymore by herself. She's a truly good person with a heart of gold, and like most parents everywhere, she preserves her children's history in knickknacks and portraits sprinkled around the house.

Feeling nostalgic, I pulled an old album down from a closet to leaf through memories so far removed from me now that they almost seem like they're from someone else's life. But I paused over one photo. I'd seen it countless times before, but this time I noticed something different. In the photo, I'm about four years old, standing outside in the sunshine in front of the iconic castle at the entrance to Walt Disney World, Florida. It must have been when the park was still brand new.* The day looks hot, and I'm wearing shorts, a blue t-shirt, and a floppy white hat. I'm the only one I recognized in the photo, yet there are many people in the background, immersed in their own agendas: a woman in a yellow skirt and cat-eye sunglasses; a man in a striped t-shirt, smoking a cigar; others studying maps or taking their own photos; and loads of kids running

---

* In recent decades, the Walt Disney Company has been scrutinized for the sexist, racist, and homophobic portrayals in its motion pictures based on fairy tales—such as *Aladdin, Dumbo, Peter Pan, Maleficent, Beauty and the Beast, The Little Mermaid, Cinderella,* and many others—as well as its socially biased park rides and employee policies. The Walt Disney Company is attempting to address these inequities.

around, eating, looking surprised or confused, or crying. I don't know any of these people, and my four-year-old self likely populates many of their old photos from this moment too.

I can't help but wonder where all the people in this photograph are today, what lives they've lived, what careers, families, and grandchildren they might now have. No doubt some in that photo, certainly many of the adults, have passed on. I wonder if any of those still living ever looks at photos that captured a little boy wearing a floppy hat—me—and asks, "What happened to him?"

To me, the scene in that old photograph is a clear reminder that all of us are always involved in each other's lives in ways we are scarcely aware of. And so I tell this little story to acknowledge how this book is, to some degree or another, inspired by *everyone's* story, which we all perpetually share and co-create.

Of course, a few people have been more directly involved in the story of the publication of this book, and to them I offer my deepest gratitude. Foremost, I thank my wife, Kim, for her undying patience and advice as I plodded through the years of research and writing, and through the publication phases of this book. She is forever my best friend.

Lantern Publishing & Media has now guided me through the editing and publication process for my books since 2011. The kind and generous people at Lantern are professional, dedicated, and mission-driven, and they expect no less from their authors. Special thanks to Lantern President and Publisher Brian Normoyle for his unwavering patience and guidance. Brian managed to somehow keep an eye on the big picture of publishing, while at the same time encouraging me to move at my own speed and with my own vision. It's a tricky line to walk, and he did so with seeming grace and ease. Also, huge kudos to Lantern Associate Editor Hanh Nguyen for their exceptional attention to detail in copyediting, and Lantern Director of Publishing Emily Lavieri-Scull for their discriminating eye in typesetting and final design. Their efforts ensured that the final shape of this book achieved the level of elegance and professionalism that its subject matter deserves.

Finally, I am deeply indebted to the essayists who contributed their expertise—and not a little corrective guidance—to the book's final form. Many thanks to Dr. Jennifer Fluri, professor of geography and Chair of the Department of Geography at the University of Colorado at Boulder, whose observations in the foreword are both perceptive and elegant. My respect for her, the books that she has authored and coauthored, and her dedication to humanity's most salient causes in social justice cannot be overstated. Also, huge thanks to Dr. Jean Alger, professor of English literature, for her eloquent and penetrating commentaries on gender as a social construct and on the toxic residues of heteronormativity that saturate our broadly conservative culture. Dr. Alger is a true scholar, yet also a peaceful nonconformist, the sort we could use more of in the world. Finally, I extend my sincerest thanks to Dr. Kimberly Munro, professor of Archaeology and Anthropology, whose vast experiences in South America illuminated the gendered lifeways of the Andean cultures, past and present, for the purposes of this book.

BIBLIOGRAPHY

Adams, Carol J. *The Sexual Politics of Meat: A Feminist-Vegetarian Critical Theory.* New York: Continuum International Publishing Group, 1990, pp. 59, 242.

Ahmed, Kaamil. "Ending Hunger by 2030 Would Cost $330 Bn, Study Finds." *The Guardian.* 13 Oct. 2020, accessed 27 Dec. 2020, https://www.theguardian.com/global-development/2020/oct/13/ending-world-hunger-by-2030-would-cost-330bn-study-finds.

Aiken, Richard. "Recruitment and Retention of Hunters and Anglers: 2000–2015." *National Survey Addendum.* USFWS National Digital Library. Report 2016-01, published Apr. 2019, https://digitalmedia.fws.gov/digital/collection/document/id/2249/.

Al-Bukhari, Imam. *Sahih Al-Bukhari.* Published by Mohammad Mohee Uddari, 2020.

Anthony, David W. *The Horse, the Wheel, and Language: How Bronze-Age Riders from the Eurasian Steppes Shaped the Modern World.* Princeton, NJ: Princeton University Press, 2007, p. 360.

Atran, Scott. *In Gods We Trust: The Evolutionary Landscape of Religion.* New York: Oxford University Press, 2002, p. 267.

Ardrey, Robert. *African Genesis: A Personal Investigation into the Animal Origins and Nature of Man.* New York: Atheneum, 1961.

Bachofen, Johann Jacob. *Myth, Religion, and Mother Right.* Stuttgart, Germany: Alfred Kröner Verlag Publishing, 1926 (reprinted by Princeton: Princeton University Press, 1967, 1973, and 1992).

Bagg, Robert, and James Scully. *The Complete Plays of Sophocles: A New Translation.* New York: HarperCollins, 2011.

Barrett, Justin L. *Why Would Anyone Believe in God?* Lanham, Maryland: AltaMira, 2004.

Barry, Herbert, III, Irvine L. Child, and Margaret K. Bacon. "Relation of Child Training to Subsistence Economy." *American Anthropologist* vol. 61, no. 1, 1959, pp. 51–63, doi:10.1525/aa.1959.61.1.02a00080.

Bartlett, Harriet, and Mark A. Holmes, Silviu O. Petrovan, David R. Williams, James L. N. Wood, and Andrew Balmford. "Understanding the Relative Risks of Zoonosis Emergence under Contrasting Approaches to Meeting Livestock Product Demand." *Royal Society Open Science.* 22 June 2022, accessed 10 Oct. 2022, doi:10.1098/rsos.211573.

Beatson, R. M., and M. J. Halloran. "Humans Rule! The Effects of Creatureless Reminders, Mortality Salience and Self-esteem on Attitudes towards Animals." *British Journal of Social Psychology* vol. 46, 2007, pp. 619–32.

Becker, Ernest. *The Denial of Death.* New York: Free Press, 1973.

Bekoff, Marc. "The Psychology and Thrill of Trophy Hunting: Is It Criminal?" *Psychology Today.* 18 Oct. 2015, accessed 30 Oct. 2021, https://www.psychologytoday.com/us/blog/animal-emotions/201510/the-psychology-and-thrill-trophy-hunting-is-it-criminal.

Berndt, Catherine H., and Frances Dahlberg, eds. "Interpretations and Facts in Aboriginal Australia." *Woman the Gatherer.* New Haven: Yale University Press, 1981.

Berndt, Catherine H. "Digging Sticks and Spears, or, the Two-Sex Model." *Woman, Sacred and Profane.* London: Routledge, 1939.

Bell, Diane. *Daughters of the Dreaming.* North Sydney: Allen & Unwin, 1990.

Bellos, Alex. "'Seven' Triumphs in Poll to Discover World's Favorite Number." *The Guardian.* 8 Apr. 2014, accessed 17 June 2021, https://www.theguardian.com/science/alexs-adventures-in-numberland/2014/apr/08/seven-worlds-favourite-number-online-survey.

Bernfeld, Jeremy, and Heath Druzin. "Gun Sales Continue to Boom During the Pandemic." *Guns and America.* 1 June 2020, accessed 19 Feb. 2021, https://gunsandamerica.org/story/20/06/01/gun-sales-continue-to-boom-during-the-pandemic/.

Binford, Lewis R. "Mobility, Housing, and Environment: A Comparative Study." *Journal of Anthropological Research* vol. 46, no. 2, 1990, pp. 119–52, accessed 24 Mar. 2021, doi:10.1086/jar.46.2.3630069.

Black Lives Matter. Accessed 7 Sep. 2021, https://blacklivesmatter.com/about/.

Boccia, M. L., P. Petrusz, K. Suzuki, L. Marson, and C. A. Pedersen. "Immunohistochemical Location of Oxytocin Receptors in Human Brain." *Neuroscience* vol. 253, 2013, pp. 155–64.

Boulding, Elise. *The Underside of History: A View of Women through Time.* Boulder, Colorado: Westview Press, 1976, p. 106.

Boyer, P. "Are Ghost Concepts 'Intuitive,' 'Endemic,' and 'Innate?'" *Journal of Cognition and Culture* vol. 3, 2003.

Bunzel, Peter. "The Wacky World of Dr. Seuss Delights the Child—and Adult— Readers of His Books." *Life.* Chicago: Time, Inc., 1959.

Callaway, Ellen. "Genetic Adam and Eve Did Not Live Too Far Apart in Time: Studies Re-Date 'Y-Chromosome' Adam and 'Mitochondrial Eve.'" *Nature.* 6 Aug. 2013, https://www.nature.com/news/ genetic-adam-and-eve-did-not-live-too-far-apart-in-time-1.13478.

Campbell, Joseph. *The Masks of God, Volume 1: Primitive Mythology.* New York: Penguin Books, 1978, pp. 77, 129.

Centers for Disease Control and Prevention. *Zoonotic Diseases.* 14 July 2017, accessed 13 Nov. 2020, https://www.cdc.gov/onehealth/basics/zoonotic-diseases.html.

Chambers, John W., ed. *The Oxford Guide to American Military History.* Oxford, UK: Oxford University Press, 1999.

Charbonnier, Georges. *Conversations with Claude Levi-Strauss.* New York: Grossman, 1969, pp. 29–30.

Child, Greg, foreword by Jon Krakauer. *Mixed Emotions: Mountaineering Writings of Greg Child.* Seattle: The Mountaineers, 1993.

Cirlot, Juan Eduardo. *A Dictionary of Symbols.* 2nd ed. Dorset Press, 1971.

Clark, Kenneth, and Mamie Clark. "The Development of Consciousness of Self and the Emergence of Racial Identification in Negro Preschool Children." *Journal of Social Psychology* vol. 10, no. 4, 1939, pp. 591–99.

———. "Racial Identification and Preference among Negro Children." *Readings in Social Psychology.* New York: Henry Holt and Company, 1947.

Cookson, John. "The Neurological Origins of Religious Belief." *Big Think.* 10 Sep. 2010, accessed 9 Nov. 2011, https://bigthink.com/surprising-science/ the-neurological-origins-of-religious-belief/.

Corea, Gena. *The Mother Machine: Reproductive Technologies from Artificial Insemination Artificial Wombs.* New York: Harper & Row, 1985, pp. 12–13.

Cotterell, Arthur. *A Dictionary of World Mythology.* Oxford: Oxford University Press, 1997, p. 257.

"Critical Race Theory." *Britannica.* 21 Sept. 2021, https://www.britannica.com/ topic/critical-race-theory.

Crowe, D. *War Crimes, Genocide, and Justice: A Global History*. New York: Springer, 2014.

Crown, Patricia L., et al. *Women & Men in the Prehispanic Southwest: Labor, Power, & Prestige*. Santa Fe, New Mexico: School of American Research Press, 2000, pp. 232–36.

Cumming, R. G., and R. J. Kleinberg. "Consumption of Dairy Products, Particularly at Age 20 Years, Was Associated with an Increased Risk of Hip Fracture in Old Age (Case-Control Study of Risk Factors for Hip Fractures in the Elderly)." *American Journal of Epidemiology* vol. 139, no. 5, 1994.

Da Silva, Sara Graça, and Jamshid J. Tehrani. "Comparative Phylogenetic Analyses Uncover the Ancient Roots of Indo-European Folktales." *The Royal Society*. 1 Jan. 2016, accessed 3 Jan. 2020, doi:10.1098/rsos.150645.

Daggett, Cara. "Petro-Masculinity and Authoritarian Desire." Sage Journals. 20 June 2018, accessed 5 Mar. 2021, doi:10.1177/0305829818775817.

Darwin, Charles. *Descent of Man, and Selection in Relation to Sex*. New ed. Princeton, New Jersey: Princeton University Press, 1981. (Photocopy of original, London: Murray Publishing, 1871.)

———. *On the Origin of Species by Means of Natural Selection, or The Preservation of Favored Races in the Struggle for Life*. London: John Murray Publishing, 1859.

Davis, Elizabeth Gould. *The First Sex*. Baltimore, MD: Penguin Books, 1972.

Davis, Kiri. "Black Doll, White Doll." 13 Aug. 2017, https://www.youtube.com/watch?v=ybDa0gSuAcg.

De Dreu, C. K. "Oxytocin Modulates Cooperation within and Competition between Groups: An Integrative Review and Research Agenda." *Hormones and Behavior* 61, 2012, pp. 419–28.

Dexter, Miriam Robbins. "Proto-Indo-European Sun Maidens and Gods of the Moon." *Mankind Quarterly* vol. 25, no. 1&2, 1984, pp. 137–44, accessed 10 July 2020, https://www.academia.edu/39229885/PROTO_INDO_EUROPEAN_SUN_MAIDENS_AND_GODS_OF_THE_MOON.

Dhont, K., G. Hodson, K. Costelly, and C. C. MacInnes. "Social Dominance Orientation Connects Prejudicial Human–Human and Human–Animal Relations." *Personality and Individual Difference* vol. 61, 2014, pp. 105–108, accessed 2 Dec. 2020, https://www.researchgate.net/publication/260296264_Social_dominance_orientation_connects_prejudicial_human-human_and_human-animal_relations.

Diamond, Jared. *Guns, Germs, and Steel: The Fates of Human Societies*. New York: W. W. Norton & Company, Inc., 1997.

Diop, Cheikh Anta. *The Cultural Unity of Negro Africa: The Domains of Patriarchy and of Matriarchy in Classical Antiquity.* Paris: Présence Africaine Editions, 1962, pp. 34, 75.

Ehnmark, Erland. *Anthropomorphism and Miracle.* Uppsala Universitets Årsskrift. Uppsala: Amqvist & Wiksels Boktyckeri-A.-B., 1939 (Recueil de Travaux Publié par l'Université d'Uppsala).

Eisler, Riane. *The Chalice & the Blade: Our History, Our Future.* New York: HarperCollins, 1987, pp. 67–69, 89.

Ember, Carol R. "Hunter-Gatherers (Foragers)." *Human Area Relations Files (HRAF).* July 2014.

———. "Residential Variation among Hunter-Gatherers." *Behavior Science Research* vol. 10, no. 3, 1975, pp. 199–277, doi:10.1177/106939717501000302.

Ember, Carol R., and Melvin Ember. "Violence in the Ethnographic Record: Results of Cross-Cultural Research on War and Aggressions." *Troubled Times: Violence and Warfare in the Past*, Debra L. Martin and David W. Frayer, eds. New York: Routledge, 1997, pp. 1–20.

FAOSTAT. Archived from the original on 8 Dec. 2021. Accessed 13 Jan. 2022, https://www.fao.org/.

Florida, Richard. *The New Urban Crisis: How Our Cities Are Increasing Inequality, Deepening Segregation, and Failing the Middle Class, and What We Can Do about It.* UK: Hachette, 2017.

Formann, R. T. T. "The Urban Region: Natural Systems in Our Place, Our Nourishment, Our Home Range, Our Future." *Landscape Ecology* vol. 23, 2008.

Forsyth, Kate. *The Rebirth of Rapunzel: A Mythic Biography of the Maiden in the Tower.* Mawson, Australia: FableCroft Publishing, 2016.

Frodi, Ann M., and Michael E. Lamb. "Sex Differences in Responsiveness to Infants: A Developmental Study of Psychophysiological and Behavioral Responses." *Child Development* vol. 49, no. 4, 1978, pp. 1182–88.

Fromm, Erich. *The Anatomy of Human Destructiveness.* New York: Picador, 1973, pp. 152, 190.

Freud, Sigmund. *The Future of Illusion.* 1927. New York: Norton, 1989.

———. *The Interpretation of Dreams: The Basic Writings of Sigmund Freud.* New York: Random House, 1938, pp. 336–67.

Fuetes, Agustín. *The Creative Spark: How Imagination Made Humans Exceptional.* New York: Penguin-Random House, 2017.

Garcia, Hector A. *Alpha God: The Psychology of Religious Violence and Oppression.* New York: Prometheus Books, 2015.

Ghose, Tia. "Battered Skulls Reveal Violence among Stone Age Women." *LiveScience.* 12 Feb. 2013, accessed 3 June 2021, https://www.livescience.com/27055-neolithic-skulls-show-violence.html.

Gibbons, Ann. "The Evolution of Diet." *National Geographic.* Sep. 2014, p. 40.

———. "Neanderthals Carb Loaded, Helping Grow Their Big Brains." *Science.* 10 May 2021, accessed 19 Feb. 2018, https://www.sciencemag.org/news/2021/05/neanderthals-carb-loaded-helping-grow-their-big-brains?fbclid=IwAR3XefUCPrv3PDSRfFwmr31EUvtPZ88AgHm06eeBtojAC-77f_kZwybcf9w.

Gimbutas, Marija. *The Language of the Goddess.* New York: Thames & Hudson, 1989.

———. *The Living Goddesses.* Berkeley: University of California Press, 1999.

Goblet d'Alviella, Count Eugène. *Symbols: Their Migration and Universality.* New York: Dover Publications, 2000.

Goodall, Jane. "The Chimpanzee." *The Quest for Man.* New York: Praeger, 1971. 131–70.

Guthrie, Stewart Elliott. *Faces in the Clouds: A New Theory of Religion.* New York: Oxford University Press, Inc., 1993, p. 88.

Haak, W., I. Lazaridis, N. Patterson, et al. "Massive Migration from the Steppe Was a Source for Indo-European Languages in Europe." *Nature* vol. 522, 2015, pp. 207–11, doi:10.1038/nature14317.

Hamblin, William, J. *Warfare in the Ancient Near East to 1600 BC: Holy Warriors at the Dawn of History.* New York: Routledge, 2006.

Hamer, Dean. *The God Gene: How Faith Is Hardwired into Our Genes.* New York: Anchor Books, 2005, p. 16.

Hammer, Tonya R. "Social Learning Theory." *Encyclopedia of Child Behavior and Development.* San Francisco: Springer, 2011, accessed 21 Sep. 2022, doi:10.1007/978-0-387-79061-9_2695.

Harari, Yuval Noah. *Sapiens: A Brief History of Humankind.* New York: HarperCollins Publishers, 2015.

Harding, M. Esther. *Woman's Mysteries, Ancient and Modern: A Psychological Interpretation of the Feminine Principle as Portrayed in Myth, Story, and Dream.* New York: Bantam, 1973, pp. 64, 103–105.

Hardy, Karen, Jennie Brand-Miller, Katherine D. Brown, Mark G. Thomas, and Les Copeland. Daniel E. Dykhuizen, ed. "The Importance of Dietary Carbohydrates in Human Evolution." *The Quarterly Review of Biology* vol. 90, no. 3, 2015, pp. 251–68, accessed 23 Oct. 2021, doi:10.1086/682587.

Hare, Brian. "Survival of the Friendliest: *Homo sapiens* Evolved via Selection for Prosociality." *Annual Review of Psychology* vol. 68, 2017, pp. 155–86.

Hare, Brian, and Vanessa Woods. *Survival of the Friendliest: Understanding Our Origins and Rediscovering Our Common Humanity.* New York: Random House, 2020.

Harris, Marvin. *Cows, Pigs, Wars, and Witches: The Riddles of Culture.* New York: Random House, 1974.

Hatcher, Bill. *Principles of Flight: Flying Bush Planes through a World of War, Sexism, and Meat.* New York: Lantern Books, Inc., 2018.

———. *Sacred Planes and Axes of Gendered Landscapes in Buhaya, Tanzania.* Graduate thesis, University of Arizona, Tucson, 2004.

Hawkes, Jacquetta. *Dawn of the Gods.* London: Chatto & Windus, 1958.

Hays-Gilpin, Kelly, et al. *Women & Men in the Prehispanic Southwest: Labor, Power, & Prestige.* Santa Fe, New Mexico: School of American Research Press, 2000, p. 111.

Hedges, Chris. *American Fascists: The Christian Right and the War on America.* New York: Free Press, 2006.

Henry, Amanda G., and Benjamin H. Passey. "The Diet of Australopithecus Sediba." *Nature* vol. 487, no. 7405, 2012, pp. 90–93, accessed 6 June 2019, https://www.researchgate.net/publication/228324388_The_Diet_of_Australopithecus_Sediba.

Hodder, Ian. *The Domestication of Europe.* Oxford: Basil Blackwell, 1990.

———. *Towards Reflexive Method in Archaeology: The Example of Çatalhöyük.* McDonald Institute: Cambridge, 2000.

Horrobin, David F. *The Madness of Adam and Eve: How Schizophrenia Shaped Humanity.* London: Transworld Publishers, Ltd., 2002.

Husted, B.W. "Culture and Ecology: A Cross-National Study of the Determinants of Environmental Sustainability." *Management International Review* vol. 45, no. 3, 2005.

Igielnik, Ruth, and Anna Brown. "Key Takeaways on American Guns and Gun Ownership." *Pew Research Center.* 22 June 2017, accessed 27 Apr. 2021, https://www.pewresearch.org/fact-tank/2017/06/22/key-takeaways-on-americans-views-of-guns-and-gun-ownership/.

Isaacson, Andy. "A Visual Dispatch from One of the World's Most Remote Islands." *The New York Times.* 20 May 2020, accessed 25 Oct. 2020, https://www.nytimes.com/2020/05/20/travel/tristan-da-cunha.html.

Institute for Economics & Peace. *Global Peace Index 2022: Measuring Peace in a Complex World,* Sydney, June 2022. http://visionofhumanity.org/resources, accessed 10 May 2023, https://www.visionofhumanity.org/maps/#/

Ishizuka, Katie, and Ramón Stephens. "The Cat is Out of the Bag: Orientalism, Anti-Blackness, and White Supremacy in Dr. Seuss's Children's Books." *Research on Diversity in Youth Literature,* 2019.

Jacobs, Jane. *The Death and Life of Great American Cities.* New York: Vintage, 2016.

Johnson, D. and J. Bering. "Hand of God, Mind of Man: Punishment and Cognition in the Evolution of Cooperation." *Evolutionary Psychology* vol. 4, 2006.

Johnson, Wendy. "Genetic and Environmental Influences on Behavior: Capturing All the Interplay." *Psychological Review,* vol. 114, no. 2, Apr. 2007, pp. 423–40, doi:10.1037/0033-295X.114.2.423. PMID: 17500633.

Jones, Keithly, and Mildred Haley. "Per Capita Red Meat and Poultry Disappearance: Insights Into Its Steady Growth." *USDA Economic Research Service: United States Department of Agriculture.* 4 June 2018, accessed 30 June 2021, https://www.ers.usda.gov/amber-waves/2018/june/per-capita-red-meat-and-poultry-disappearance-insights-into-its-steady-growth/.

Joseph Campbell Foundation. *Goddesses: Mysteries of the Feminine Divine.* Novato, California: New World Library, 2013, pp. 29–34.

Jung, Carl Gustav. *The Archetypes of the Collective Unconscious.* Princeton, NJ: Princeton University Press, 1969.

——. *The Collected Works of C. G. Jung, Volume 7: Two Essays on Analytical Psychology.* 2nd ed. Princeton, NJ: Princeton University Press, 1966.

——. *The Psychology of the Transference.* New York: Bollingen Foundation, 1954.

Kaleta, C., L. F. de Figueiredo, and S. Schuster. "Against the Stream: Relevance of Gluconeogenesis from Fatty Acids for Natives of the Arctic Regions." *International Journal of Circumpolar Health* vol. 71, no. 1–2, 2012, pp. 256–57, accessed 14 Feb. 2019, doi:10.3402/ijch.v71i0.18436.

Kaufman, Alexander C. "A Former Trump Advisor May Have Revealed What the Fossil Fuel Bonanza Was Really About." *HUFFPOST.* 4 Feb. 2021, accessed 7 Feb. 2021, https://www.huffpost.com/entry/trump-fossil-fuels_n_601c626fc5b68e068fbccba6.

Kelly, Raymond C. *Warless Societies and the Origin of War.* Ann Arbor, MI: The University of Michigan Press, 2000.

Kennett, Douglass J., et al. "Shock-Synthesized Hexagonal Diamonds in Younger Dryas Boundary Sediments." *Proceedings of the National Academy of Sciences of the United States America*, vol. 106, no. 31, 2009, pp. 12623–28, accessed 27 May 2021, doi:10.1073/pnas.0906374106.

Keysar, Ariela, and Juhem Navarro-Rivera. "A World of Atheism: Global Demographics." Stephen Bullivant and Michael Ruse, eds. *The Oxford Handbook of Atheism*. Oxford, UK: Oxford University Press, 2016.

Kittay, Eva F. "Woman as Metaphor." *Hypatia* vol. 3, no. 4, 1988, p. 1.

Kradin, Nikolai. "Ancient Steppe Nomad Societies." *Asian History*. 24 May 2018, accessed 19 Aug. 2020, doi:10.1093/acrefore/9780190277727.013.3.

Kucukemre, Banu Aydin, et al. "Frequency of Ambiguous Genitalia in 14,177 Newborns in Turkey." *Oxford Academic: Journal of Endocrine Society* vol. 3, no. 6, 2019, pp. 1185–95, accessed 10 July 2021, doi:10.1210/js.2018-00408.

Kuhnleini, H. V., and R. Soueida. "Use and Nutrient Composition of Traditional Baffin Inuit Foods," *Journal of Food Composition and Analysis* vol. 5, no. 2, 1992, pp. 112–26, accessed 15 Aug. 2020, doi:10.1016/0889-1575(92)90026-G.

Lane, Belden. *The Solace of Fierce Landscapes: Exploring Desert and Mountain Spirituality*. New York: Oxford University Press, 1998, pp. 39–40.

Lange, David. "Number of Participants in Hunting in the United States 2006 to 2019." *Statista: Sports & Recreation, Parks & Outdoors*. 30 Nov. 2020, accessed 30 Oct. 2021, https://www.statista.com/statistics/191244/participants-in-hunting-in-the-us-since-2006/.

Lantz, Paula M. "The Tenets of Critical Race Theory Have a Long-Standing and Important Role in Population Health Science." *Milbank Quarterly Opinion*. 15 July 2021, accessed 21 Sep. 2021, doi:10.1599/mqop.2021.0714.

Larsen, Clark Spencer. *Essentials of Biological Anthropology*. 4th ed. New York: W. W. Norton & Company, Inc., 2019.

MacCullouch, Jan Arnot, and John Arnott. *The Mythology of All Races, Volume 3: Celtic/Slavic*. New York: Cooper Square Publishers, 1964.

Maisels, Charles Keith. *Early Civilizations of the Old World: The Formative Histories of Egypt, the Levant, Mesopotamia, India and China*. New York: Routledge, 2001.

Malinowski, Bronislaw. *The Sexual Life of Savages*. New York: Halcyon House, 1929, pp. 3–7.

Marlow, Frank W. "Hunter-Gatherers and Human Evolution." *Evolutionary Anthropology: Issues, News, and Reviews* vol. 14, no. 2, 2005, pp. 56–67, doi:10.1002/evan.20046.

Martin, Kay M., and Barbara Voorhies. *The Female of the Species*. New York and London: Columbia University Press, 1975.

McClintock, Martha K. "Menstrual Synchrony and Suppression." *Nature* vol. 229, 1971, pp. 171–79.

McCright, Aaron M., and Riley E. Dunlap. "Cool Dudes: The Denial of Climate Change among Conservative White Males in the United States." *Global Environmental Change*. 28 June 2011, accessed 7 Feb. 2021, https://sciencepolicy.colorado.edu/students/envs_5000/mccright_2011.pdf.

McIntosh, Jane. *Ancient Mesopotamia: New Perspectives*. Santa Barbara, California: ABC-CLIO Publishing, 2005.

McDonald, Charlotte. "How Many Earths Do We Need?" *BBC News*. 15 June 2015, accessed 10 July 2021, https://www.bbc.com/news/magazine-33133712.

McNeill, William. *Plagues and Peoples*. New York: Anchor, 1976.

Mekonnen, Mesfin M., and Arjen Y. Hoekstra. "A Global Assessment of the Water Footprint of Farm Animal Products." *Ecosystems* vol. 15, 2012, pp. 401–15.

Mellaart, James. *Earliest Civilizations of the Near East*. London: Thames and Hudson, 1965.

Merritt, D. L. "Sacred Landscapes, Sacred Seasons: A Jungian Ecopsychological Perspective." *BAR International Series 1833*. Oxford, England: Archaeopress, 2008.

"Milk and the Modern Man: The Rise of Adult Milk Drinking." *Stanford at the Tech: Understanding Genetics*. The Tech Interactive. 2019, accessed 28 Sep. 2021, https://genetics.thetech.org/original_news/news45.

Miller, Barbara. *Cultural Anthropology in a Globalizing World*. 4th ed. Boston: Pearson Education, Inc., 2017, pp. 77–80.

Miller, Scot M., et al. "Anthropogenic Emissions of Methane in the United States." *Proceedings of the National Academy of Sciences* vol. 110, no. 50, 18 Oct. 2013, accessed 17 June 2021, doi:10.1073/pnas.1314392110.

Milton, Katherine. "Hunter-Gatherer Diets—A Different Perspective." *The American Journal of Clinical Nutrition* vol. 71, no. 3, 2000, pp. 665–67, accessed 30 Oct. 2019, doi:10.1093/ajcn/71.3.665.

Moore, Robert, and Douglass Gillette. *King, Warrior, Magician, Lover*. Revised ed. San Francisco: HarperOne, 1991.

Morris, Chris. "Here Are the Best-Selling Video Games of the Past 25 Years." *Fortune*. 17 Jan. 2020, https://fortune.com/2020/01/17/best-selling-video-games-past-25-years/.

Muller, Martin N., Richard Wrangham, and David Pilbeam. *Chimpanzees and Human Evolution*. Cambridge, MA: Harvard University Press, 2017.

Nanda, Serena, and Richard L. Warms. *Cultural Anthropology*. 12th ed. Los Angeles: Sage Publications, Inc., 2020, p. 57.

Napier, John Russell. *The Roots of Mankind*. Washington, DC: Smithsonian Institute, 1970.

Nash, George, and Christopher Chippindale. *European Landscapes of Rock-Art*. Oxfordshire, UK: Routledge, 2001.

Nash, Roderick. *The Rights of Nature: A History of Environmental Ethics*. Madison, WI: The University of Wisconsin Press, 1989, pp. 5–7.

———. *Wilderness and the American Mind*. 3rd ed. New Haven, CT: Yale University Press, 1982, pp. 387–88.

Nemet-Nejat, Karen Rhea. *Daily Life in Ancient Mesopotamia*. Westport, CT: Greenwood Publishing Group, 1998.

Nickelsburg, George W. E. "Apocalyptic and Myth in 1 Enoch 6–11." *Journal of Biblical Literature* vol. 96, no. 3, 1977, pp. 383–405.

Nolan, Michael. "Opinion: The Myth of Soulless Women." *First Things*. University College Dublin. Apr. 1997, accessed 7 Apr. 2021, https://www.firstthings.com/article/1997/04/the-myth-of-soulless-women.

———. "Do Women Have Souls? The Story of Three Myths." *New Blackfriars* vol. 74, no. 876, Nov. 1993.

Norgaard, Kari Marie. "Moon Phases, Menstrual Cycles, and Mother Earth: The Construction of a Special Relationship between Women and Nature." *Ethics and the Environment* vol. 4, no. 2, 1999, accessed 29 July 2021, https://www.jstor.org/stable/40338978.

Oppenlander, Richard. "Biodiversity and Food Choice: A Clarification." *Comfortably Unaware: Global Depletion and Food Choice Responsibility*. 9 June 2012, accessed 3 June 2021, http://comfortablyunaware.com/blog/biodiversity-and-food-choice-a-clarification/.

Ortner, S. B. *Anthropology and Social Theory: Culture, Power, and the Acting Subject*. Durham, NC: Duke University Press, 2006.

Oxfam International. "Just 8 Men Own the Same Wealth as Half the World." 16 Jan. 2017, accessed 5 Nov. 2021, https://www.oxfam.org/en/press-releases/just-8-men-own-same-wealth-half-world.

Pagels, Elaine. *The Gnostic Gospels*. New York: Vintage Books, 1989, pp. 64–67.

Park, H., C. Russell, and J. Lee. "National Culture and Environmental Sustainability: A Cross-National Analysis." *Journal of Economics and Finance* vol. 31, no. 1, 2007, pp. 113–14.

Parker-Pope, T. "Writing Your Way to Happiness." *The New York Times.* 19 Jan. 2015, accessed 12 July 2021, http://well.blogs.nytimes.com/2015/01/19/writing-your-way-to-happiness/?_r=4.

Patou-Mathis, Marylène. "The Origins of Violence." *The UNESCO Courier: Many Voices, One World* vol. 1, 2020, accessed 16 May 2021, https://en.unesco.org/courier/2020-1/origins-violence.

Pearce, J., E. Richardson, R. Mitchell, and N. Short. "Environmental Justice and Health: The Implications of the Socio-Spatial Distribution of Multiple Environmental Deprivation for Health Inequalities in the United Kingdom." *Transactions of the Institute of British Geographers* vol. 35, no. 4, 2010, pp. 522–39.

Pendick, Daniel. "How Much Protein Do You Need Every Day?" *Harvard Health Publishing, Harvard Medical School.* 21 June 2019, accessed 27 June 2021. https://www.health.harvard.edu/blog/how-much-protein-do-you-need-every-day-201506188096.

Pew Research Center. "Chapter 1: Importance of Religion and Religious Beliefs." 3 Nov. 2015, accessed 8 June 2021, https://www.pewresearch.org/religion/2015/11/03/chapter-1-importance-of-religion-and-religious-beliefs/.

———. "Religious Landscape Study: Belief in God." Accessed 8 June 2021, https://www.pewresearch.org/religion/religious-landscape-study/belief-in-god/.

———. "The Global Religious Landscape." 12 Dec. 2012, accessed 8 June 2021, https://www.pewresearch.org/religion/2012/12/18/global-religious-landscape-exec/.

Pimentel, David, et al. "Summary of Estimated Water Use in the United States in 2005." *United States Geological Service.* 2005.

———. "Water Resources: Agricultural and Environmental Issues." *BioScience* vol. 54, no. 10, 2004, pp. 909–18, accessed 4 June 2021, doi:10.1641/0006-3568(2004)054[0909:WRAAEI]2.0.CO;2.

Rampino, Michael R., and Stephen Self. "Climate–Volcanism Feedback and the Toba Eruption of ~74,000 Years Ago." *Quaternary Research* vol. 40, no. 3, 1993, pp. 269–80.

Rao, Sailesh. "Animal Agriculture Is the Leading Cause of Climate Change—A Position Paper." *Journal of Ecological Society* vol. 32–33, 2020–2021, pp. 155–67, accessed 30 Oct. 2021, https://3209a1b2-3bad-4874-bf51-8fc2702ffa6c.filesusr.com/ugd/8654c5_5bdb63b57c6b4abaa7f7b9041f7b8487.pdf.

Rappaport, Roy A. *Ritual and Religion in the Making of Humanity.* Cambridge, UK: Cambridge University Press, 1999.

Reed, Evelyn. *Women's Evolution: From Matriarchal Clan to Patriarchal Family.* New York: Pathfinder Press, Inc., 1975.

Rosane, Olivia. "Humans and Big Ag Livestock Now Account for 96 Percent of Mammal Biomass." *Ecowatch: Environmental News for a Healthier Planet and Life.* 23 May 2018, accessed 7 July 2021, https://www.ecowatch.com/biomass-humans-animals-2571413930.html.

Rozell, Ned. "The Most Remote Place in U.S." *UAF News and Information.* University of Alaska, Fairbanks. 3 Jan. 2018, accessed 2 Dec. 2019, https://news.uaf.edu/remote-place-u-s-2/.

Rubenstein, James. M. *The Cultural Landscape: An Introduction to Human Geography.* Hoboken, NJ: Pearson Education, Inc., 2020, p. 317.

Sahlins, M. "Notes on the Original Affluent Society." *Man the Hunter.* R. B. Lee and I. DeVore, eds. New York: Aldine Publishing Company, 1968, pp. 85–89.

Savell, Stephanie, and 5W Infographics. "This Map Shows Where in the World the U.S. Military Is Combatting Terrorism." *America at War: A Smithsonian Magazine Special Report.* Jan. 2019, accessed 5 Apr. 2022, https://www.smithsonianmag.com/history/map-shows-places-world-where-us-military-operates-180970997/.

Sanday, Peggy Reeves. *Female Power and Male Dominance: On the Origins of Sexual Inequality.* Cambridge, UK: Cambridge University Press, 1981, pp. 65–66.

Schembri, Frankie. "Is This Monkey the Inspiration for Dr. Seuss's Lorax?" *Science.* 23 July 2018, accessed 4 Apr. 2021, https://www.sciencemag.org/news/2018/07/monkey-inspiration-dr-seuss-s-lorax.

Schmidt, Peter R. *Iron Technology in East Africa.* Bloomington: Indiana University Press, 1997.

Semple, Ellen Churchill. *Influences of the Geographic Environment, On the Basis of Ratzel's System of Anthropo-geography.* New York: Henry Holt and Company, 1911.

Seuss, Dr. *The Lorax.* New York: Random House, 1971.

Shaw, Robert. *Social Geographies: In Introduction.* London: Rowman & Littlefield, 2021, pp. 32–33.

Shlain, Leonard. *The Alphabet Versus the Goddess: The Conflict between Word and Image.* New York: Viking-Penguin, 1998, p. 1.

Simon, David Robinson. *Meatonomics: How the Rigged Economics of Meat and Dairy Make You Consume Too Much—and How to Eat Better, Live Longer, and Spend Smarter.* Newburyport, MA: Conari Press, 2013.

Sjöö, Monica, and Barbara Mor. *The Great Cosmic Mother: Rediscovering the Religion of the Earth*. San Francisco: Harper & Row, 1987, pp. 106, 170.

Smith, D., P. Schlaepfer, K. Major, et al. "Cooperation and the Evolution of Hunter-Gatherer Storytelling." *Nature Communications* vol. 8, 2017, p. 1853, accessed 1 Oct. 2021, doi:10.1038/s41467-017-02036-8.

Snowden, Scott. "300-Mile Swim through the Great Garbage Patch Will Collect Data on Plastic Pollution." *Forbes*. 30 May 2019, accessed 5 Nov. 2019, https://www.forbes.com/sites/scottsnowden/2019/05/30/300-mile-swim-through-the-great-pacific-garbage-patch-will-collect-data-on-plastic-pollution/?sh=23e956a4489f.

"Space Debris by the Numbers." *The European Space Agency*. Jan. 2019, accessed 5 Mar. 2019, https://www.esa.int/Safety_Security/Space_Debris/Space_debris_by_the_numbers.

Spencer, Alison, and Cary Funk. "Electric Vehicles Get Mixed Reception from American Consumers." Pew Research Center. 3 June 2021, accessed 4 Sep. 2022, https://www.pewresearch.org/fact-tank/2021/06/03/electric-vehicles-get-mixed-reception-from-american-consumers/.

Speth, J. D. "Middle Paleolithic Subsistence in the Near East." *Before Farming*, 2012, pp. 1–45, accessed 17 June 2021, https://lsa.umich.edu/ummaa/people/emeriti-curators/jdspeth/Middle-Paleolithic-Subsistence-in-the-Near-East-Zooarchaeological-Perspectives-Past-Present-and-Future.html.

Starr, Michelle. "Space Debris Has Hit and Damaged the International Space Station." *Science Alert*. 31 May 2021, accessed 13 June 2021, https://www.sciencealert.com/space-debris-has-damaged-the-international-space-station.

Stein, Howard F. *Developmental Time, Cultural Space: Studies in Psychogeography*. University of Oklahoma: University of Oklahoma Press, 1987, p. 15.

Stein, Rebecca L., and Philip L. Stein. *The Anthropology of Religion, Magic, and Witchcraft*. 4th ed. Oxford, England: Routledge, 2017, pp. 72–73, 86, 217.

Stone, Merlin. *When God Was a Woman*. New York: Harvest/Harcourt Brace, in arrangement with The Dial Press, 1976, pp. 2–3, 94–95.

Storl, Wolf D. *A Curious History of Vegetables: Aphrodisiacal and Healing Properties, Folk Tales, Garden Tips, and Recipes*. Berkeley, CA: North Atlantic Books, 2016, p. 360.

Tanner, Nancy Makepeace. *On Becoming Human*. Cambridge, England: Cambridge University Press, 1981, p. 190.

Tatar, Maria. *The Hard Facts of the Grimms' Fairy Tales*. Princeton: Princeton University Press, 1987, p. 277.

Tellier, Luc-Normand. *Urban World History: An Economic and Geographical Perspective*. New York: Springer International Publishing, 2019.

The Cambridge Encyclopedia of Human Evolution. Steve Jones, Robert Martin, and David Pilbeam, eds. Cambridge, UK: Cambridge University Press, 1992.

"The Geena Davis Institute in Media and J. Walter Thompson Present Revealing Findings about Women's Representation in Advertising at Cannes Lions." *Geena Davis Institute on Gender in Media*. 21 June 2017, accessed 22 Aug. 2020, https://seejane.org/gender-in-media-news-release/geena-davis-institute-gender-media-j-walter-thompson-present-revealing-findings-womens-representation-advertising-cannes-lions/.

The Holy Qur'an: With English Translation and Commentary. Maulana Muhammad Ali, ed. Dublin, OH: Ahmadiyya Anjuman Isha'at Islam Lahore, Inc., 2002.

Thompson, William Irwin. *The Time Falling Bodies Take to Light: Mythology, Sexuality & the Origins of Culture*. New York: St. Martin's Press, 1996.

Timmermann, A., and T. Friedrich. "Late Pleistocene Climate Drivers of Early Human Migration." *Nature* vol. 538, 2016, pp. 92–95, accessed 8 Aug. 2020, doi:10.1038/nature19365.

Tolle, Eckhart. *A New Earth: Awakening to Your Life's Purpose*. New York: Plume, 2005.

Trauger, Amy, and Jennifer L. Fluri. *Engendering Development: Capitalism and Inequality in the Global Economy*. Oxford, England: Routledge, 2019.

Tuan, Yi-Fu. *Topophilia: A Study of Environmental Perception, Attitudes, and Values*. Englewood Cliffs, NJ: Prentice-Hall, Inc., 1974.

Tucker, Spencer C. *U.S. Conflicts in the 21st Century: Afghanistan War, Iraq War, and the War on Terror*. Santa Barbara, CA: ABC-CLIO Publishing, 2015.

Tuttle, Will. *The World Peace Diet: Eating for Spiritual Health and Social Harmony*. New York: Lantern Books, 2005.

United Nations Department of Economic and Social Affairs. *International Migration 2020 Highlights*. 15 Jan. 2021, accessed 16 Aug. 2021, https://www.un.org/en/desa/international-migration-2020-highlights.

———. "68% of the World's Population Projected to Live in Urban Areas, UN says." 16 May 2018, accessed 1 Aug. 2021, https://population.un.org/wup/Publications/Files/WUP2018-PressRelease.pdf.

United Nations Development Programme, Human Development Reports. *Gender Inequality Index (GII)* (2020 statistical annex table 5). Accessed 18 June 2021, http://hdr.undp.org/en/content/gender-inequality-index-gii.

United Nations Environment Programme. "Leading International Organizations Commit to Climate Action." 12 Dec. 2018, accessed 12 Sep. 2021, https://www.unenvironment.org/news-and-stories/press-release/leading-international-organizations-commit-climate-action.

United Nations News Centre. "UN Launches International Year of Deserts and Desertification." 1 Jan. 2006, accessed 7 June 2021, https://news.un.org/en/story/2006/01/165052-un-launches-international-year-deserts-and-desertification.

United Nations Sustainable Development Goals. "Rapid Urbanization and Population Growth Are Outpacing the Construction of Adequate and Affordable Housing." 2019, accessed 3 July 2020, https://unstats.un.org/sdgs/report/2019/goal-11/.

USDA Economic Research Service. *Food Access.* 2017, accessed 17 Oct. 2020, https://www.ers.usda.gov/data-products/food-access-research-atlas/documentation/.

United States Environmental Protection Agency. *Understand Global Warming Potentials.* Accessed 1 July 2021, https://www.epa.gov/ghgemissions/understanding-global-warming-potentials.

Van der Toorn, K., Bob Becking, and Pieter Willem van der Horst, eds. *Dictionary of Deities and Demons in the Bible.* Grand Rapids, MI: Wm. B. Eerdmans Publishing, 1999, pp. 512–14.

Vasmer, Max. *Russisches etymologisches Wörterbuch.* Heidelberg, Germany: C. Winter Heidelberg, 1955, pp. 2, 424.

Vescio, Theresa K., and Nathaniel E. C. Schermerhorn. "Hegemonic Masculinity Predicts 2016 and 2020 Voting and Candidate Evaluations." *Proceedings of the National Academy of Sciences of the United States of America.* 12 Jan. 2021, accessed 13 Aug. 2021, https://www.pnas.org/content/118/2/e2020589118.

Von Franz, Marie-Louise. *Creation Myths.* Revised ed. Boston: Shambhala, 2001.

Wang, X., T. Yao, Z. Cong, et al. "Concentration Level and Distribution of Polycyclic Aromatic Hydrocarbons in Soil and Grass around Mt. Qomolangma, China." *Chinese Sci Bull* vol. 52, 2007, pp. 1405–13, accessed 29 Dec. 2019, doi:10.1007/s11434-007-0184-2.

Weiner, Eric. "Are We Born to Wander?" *National Geographic Magazine* vol. 238, no. 2, Feb. 2021, pp. 15–18.

Weisner-Hanks, Merry E. *Gender in History: Global Perspectives.* 2nd ed. West Sussex, UK: Wiley-Blackwell, 2011.

Weiss, Brad. *Sacred Trees, Bitter Harvests: Globalizing Coffee in Northwestern Tanzania.* Portsmouth, NH: Heinemann, 2003.

Wells, Spencer. *Pandora's Seed: The Unforeseen Cost of Civilization.* New York: Random House, Inc., 2010.

Whitley, David S. *Cave Paintings and the Human Spirit: The Origin of Creativity and Belief.* Amherst, NY: Prometheus Books, 2009, pp. 169, 253.

Williams, Terry Tempest. *The Hour of Land: A Personal Topography of American's National Parks.* New York: Picador, 2016.

Wolff, Edward N. "Household Wealth Trends in the United States, 1962 to 2016: Has Middle Class Wealth Recovered?" National Bureau of Economic Research. Nov. 2017, accessed 10 Mar. 2022, https://www.nber.org/system/files/working_papers/w24085/w24085.pdf.

World Bank. *GDP per Capita, PPP (Current International $).* 2019, accessed 14 Aug. 2021, https://data.worldbank.org/indicator/NY.GDP.PCAP.PP.CD.

World Economic Forum. *Global Gender Gap Report: 2021.* Accessed 31 Mar. 2021, http://www3.weforum.org/docs/WEF_GGGR_2021.pdf.

World Health Organization. *WHO-Convened Global Study of Origins of SARS-CoV-2: China Part.* COVID-19: Animal–Human Interface and Food Safety. 30 Mar. 2021, https://www.who.int/publications/i/item/who-convened-global-study-of-origins-of-sars-cov-2-china-part.

Wrangham, Richard W. *The Goodness Paradox: The Strange Relationship between Virtue and Violence in Human Evolution.* New York: Pantheon, 2019.

Wrangham, Richard W., and Dale Peterson. *Demonic Males: Apes and the Origins of Human Violence.* New York: Houghton Mifflin Harcourt, 1996.

Wright, Quincy. *A Study of War, Volume 1.* Chicago: University of Chicago Press, 1942, p. 134.

Yong, Ed. "Neanderthal Dental Plaque Shows What a Paleo Diet Really Looked Like: Some Ate Wooly Rhinos; Some Were Vegetarians." *Science.* 9 Mar. 2017, accessed 15 Mar. 2018, https://www.theatlantic.com/science/archive/2017/03/neanderthal-dental-plaque-shows-what-a-paleo-diet-really-looks-like/518949/.

Zielinski, G. A., P. A. Mayewski, L. D. Meeker, S. Whitlow, M. S. Twickler, and K. Taylor. "Potential Atmospheric Impact of the Toba Mega—Eruption ~71,000 Years Ago." *Geophysical Research Letters* vol. 23, no. 8, 1996, pp. 837–40.

Zondervan New International Version Bible. Grand Rapids, MI: Zondervan Corporation, 1984.

NOTES

Introduction

1. D. Smith, P. Schlaepfer, K. Major, et al., "Cooperation and the Evolution of Hunter-Gatherer Storytelling," *Nature Communications* 8 (2017): 1853, accessed 1 Oct. 2021, doi:10.1038/s41467-017-02036-8. This article explores the impact of storytelling on hunter-gatherer cooperative behavior and the individual-level fitness benefits to being a skilled storyteller. It concludes that one of the adaptive functions of storytelling among hunter-gatherers may have been to organize cooperation.

2. Miriam Robbins Dexter, "Proto-Indo-European Sun Maidens and Gods of the Moon," *Mankind Quarterly* 25(1&2) (1984): 137–44, accessed 10 July 2020, https://www.academia.edu/39229885/PROTO_INDO_EUROPEAN_SUN_MAIDENS_AND_GODS_OF_THE_MOON. The PIE-speaking peoples who migrated from the Pontic Steppes worshipped few goddesses. However, this article reveals that the myths of earlier proto-PIE–speaking peoples show remnants of sun-goddess and moon-god worship.

3. Wolf D. Storl, *A Curious History of Vegetables: Aphrodisiacal and Healing Properties, Folk Tales, Garden Tips, and Recipes* (Berkeley, CA: North Atlantic Books, 2016) 360. Correlations are drawn between medicinal use of herbs and evidence for matrilineal (and possible matriarchal) social structures in Neolithic Europe.

4. Sherry B. Ortner, *Anthropology and Social Theory: Culture, Power, and the Acting Subject* (Durham, NC: Duke University Press, 2006). Fables and fairy tales from Europe and the Middle East share sexist tropes that portray strong-willed, masculine women as witches and passive, feminine women as beautiful damsels in distress—the ideal.

5. Kate Forsyth, *The Rebirth of Rapunzel: A Mythic Biography of the Maiden in the Tower* (Mawson, Australia: FableCroft Publishing, 2016).

6. Maria Tatar, *The Hard Facts of the Grimms' Fairy Tales* (Princeton: Princeton University Press, 1987) 277.

7. Yuval Noah Harari, *Sapiens: A Brief History of Humankind* (New York: HarperCollins Publishers, 2015) 153–54.

8. Ibid., 157–58.

9. David W. Anthony, *The Horse, the Wheel, and Language: How Bronze-Age Riders from the Eurasian Steppes Shaped the Modern World* (Princeton, NJ: Princeton University Press, 2007) 5. When the climate changed between 3500 and 3000 BCE, the Eurasian steppes became drier and cooler. This encouraged Balkan cultures to domesticate the horse and invent the wheel, becoming mobilized. Combined with the introduction of bronze technology, these changes gave an advantage to PIE-speaking peoples.

10. D. L. Merritt, "Sacred Landscapes, Sacred Seasons: A Jungian Ecopsychological Perspective," *BAR International Series 1833* (Oxford, England: Archaeopress, 2008).

11. Ellen Churchill Semple, *Influences of the Geographic Environment on the Basis of Ratzel's System of Anthropo-Geography* (New York: Henry Holt and Company, 1911).

Chapter 1—The Genesis Tree

1. Arthur Cotterell, *A Dictionary of World Mythology* (Oxford: Oxford University Press, 1997) 257.

2. Marie-Louise von Franz, *Creation Myths*, rev. ed. (Boston: Shambhala, 2001).

3. C. G. Jung, *The Archetypes of the Collective Unconscious* (Princeton University Press, 1969). The emergence of our self-awareness first expressed itself in symbolic stories, songs, and art. Much later, people would recast it in creation myths as the point at which the world itself came into being.

4. Rebecca L. Stein and Philip L. Stein, *The Anthropology of Religion, Magic, and Witchcraft*. 4th ed. (Oxford, England: Routledge, 2017) 72. "The religious systems of the Australian Aborigines are focused on expressions of religious time and space. . . . These creatures then traveled over the landscape, creating the world as we see it today—the physical world, the plants, the animals, the people . . . [and] turned themselves into some objects of the landscape, such as a boulder or a hill. The places that are associated with particular mythological beings are today sacred spaces."

5. Merlin Stone, *When God Was a Woman* (New York: Harvest/Harcourt Brace, in arrangement with The Dial Press, 1976) 68. Stone spent ten years researching the material for her book, which shows how Neolithic matriarchies were benevolent and egalitarian, though overthrown by masculine empires in the Bronze Age. Older myths were rewritten to show males as ascendant and females as weak and corrupt.

6. K. van der Toorn, *Dictionary of Deities and Demons in the Bible*, ed. Bob Becking and Pieter Willem van der Horst (Grand Rapids, Michigan: Wm. B. Eerdmans Publishing, 1999) 512–14.

7. Monica Sjöö and Barbara Mor, *The Great Cosmic Mother: Rediscovering the Religion of the Earth* (San Francisco: Harper & Row, 1987) 268.

8. Juan Eduardo Cirlot, *A Dictionary of Symbols*, 2nd ed. (Dorset Press, 1971) 186.

9. Kelly Hays-Gilpin, et al., *Women & Men in the Prehispanic Southwest: Labor, Power, & Prestige* (Santa Fe, NM: School of American Research Press, 2000) 111. The author refers to stories of Puebloan secret societies of men, whose circumcision ceremony for boys initiated them into adulthood.

Chapter 2—Pangendered Landscapes: The Deep Backstory

1. Nancy Makepeace Tanner, *On Becoming Human* (Cambridge, England: Cambridge University Press, 1981) 190.

2. Clark Spencer Larsen, *Essentials of Biological Anthropology*, 4th ed. (New York: W. W. Norton & Company, Inc., 2019) 376. Invaluable undergraduate textbook that spans genetics, taphonomy (fossils), primatology, plate tectonics, human evolution, paleoanthropology, paleoclimatology, stone tool technologies, early agriculture, and forensics.

3. Ellen Callaway, "Genetic Adam and Eve Did Not Live Too Far apart in Time: Studies Re-Date "Y-Chromosome" Adam and "Mitochondrial Eve,"" *Nature* 6 Aug. 2013, accessed 10 Aug. 2020, https://www.nature.com/news/genetic-adam-and-eve-did-not-live-too-far-apart-in-time-1.13478.

4. M. Sahlins, "Notes on the Original Affluent Society," *Man the Hunter*, R. B. Lee and I. DeVore (New York: Aldine Publishing Company, 1968) 85–89. Landmark research on the lifestyles of modern foraging peoples of Africa, in particular comparing the amount of time they spend finding food with the amount of time they have in leisure.

5. Katherine Milton, "Hunter-Gatherer Diets—A Different Perspective," *The American Journal of Clinical Nutrition* 71(3) (2000): 665–67, accessed 30 Oct. 2019, doi:10.1093/ajcn/71.3.665.

6. George Nash and Christopher Chippindale, *European Landscapes of Rock-Art* (Oxfordshire, UK: Routledge, 2001).

7. Brad Weiss, *Sacred Trees, Bitter Harvests: Globalizing Coffee in Northwestern Tanzania*, Social History of Africa Series (Portsmouth, NH: Heinemann, 2003).

8. Peter Schmidt, *Iron Technology in East Africa* (Bloomington: Indiana University Press, 1997). Compiles data from several years of field research on ancient methods of iron smelting technologies of the Haya of Northwestern Tanzania.

9. Monica Sjöö and Barbara Mor, *The Great Cosmic Mother: Rediscovering the Religion of the Earth* (San Francisco: Harper & Row, 1987) 106. Fascinating compendium of research into the symbolism and lifeways of ancient matrilineal and, possibly, matriarchal cultures.

10. Ed Yong, "Neanderthal Dental Plaque Shows What a Paleo Diet Really Looked Like: Some Ate Wooly Rhinos; Some Were Vegetarians," *Science* 9 Mar. 2017, accessed 15 Mar. 2018, https://www.theatlantic.com/science/archive/2017/03/neanderthal-dental-plaque-shows-what-a-paleo-diet-really-looks-like/518949/. Research on Neandertal remains at El Sidron Cave in Spain reveals that some Neandertals ate only plants.

11. Ann Gibbons, "Neanderthals Carb Loaded, Helping Grow Their Big Brains," *Science* 10 May 2021, accessed 19 Feb. 2018, https://www.sciencemag.org/news/2021/05/neanderthals-carb-loaded-helping-grow-their-big-brains?fbclid=IwAR3XefUCPrv3PDSRfFwmr31EUvtPZ88AgHm06eeBtojAC-77f_kZwybcf9w.

12. David S. Whitley, *Cave Paintings and the Human Spirit: The Origin of Creativity and Belief* (Amherst, New York: Prometheus Books, 2009) 169.

13. Ibid., 29–30.

14. Barbara Miller, *Cultural Anthropology in a Globalizing World*, 4th ed. (Boston: Pearson Education, Inc., 2017) 77–80.

15. Ann M. Frodi and Michael E. Lamb, "Sex Differences in Responsiveness to Infants: A Developmental Study of Psychophysiological and Behavioral Responses," *Child Development* 49(4) (1978): 1182–88.

16. Ibid., 79.

17. Tonya R. Hammer, "Social Learning Theory," *Encyclopedia of Child Behavior and Development* (San Francisco: Springer, 2011), accessed 21 Sep. 2022, doi:10.1007/978-0-387-79061-9_2695.

18. Wendy Johnson. "Genetic and Environmental Influences on Behavior: Capturing All the Interplay," *Psychological Review* 114(2) (Apr. 2007): 423–40, doi:10.1037/0033-295X.114.2.423. PMID: 17500633.

19. Serena Nanda and Richard L. Warms, *Cultural Anthropology*, 12th ed. (Los Angeles: Sage Publications, Inc., 2020) 57. Comprehensive undergraduate textbook that give general descriptions of language, religion, sex and sexuality, gender, race and ethnicity, kinship patterns, art, etc., and also specific case studies.

20. Kenneth B. Clark and Mamie P. Clark, "Racial Identification and Preference among Negro Children," *Readings in Social Psychology*, ed. E. L. Hartley (New York: Holt, Rinehart, and Winston, 1947). Indicates that racism is socially internalized before the age of five.

21. Kenneth B. Clark and Mamie P. Clark. "The Development of Consciousness of Self and the Emergence of Racial Identification in Negro Preschool Children," *Journal of Social Psychology* 10(4) (1939): 591–99.

22. "Black Doll, White Doll," 13 Aug. 2017, accessed 7 Apr. 2020, https://www.youtube.com/watch?v=ybDa0gSuAcg.

23. Robert Ardrey, *African Genesis: A Personal Investigation into the Animal Origins and Nature of Man* (New York: Atheneum, 1961).

24. Amanda G. Henry and Benjamin H. Passey, "The Diet of Australopithecus Sediba," *Nature* 487(7405) (2012): 90–93, accessed 6 June 2019, https://www.research-gate.net/publication/228324388_The_Diet_of_Australopithecus_Sediba.

25. Charles Darwin, *On the Origin of Species by Means of Natural Selection, or The Preservation of Favored Races in the Struggle for Life*, 1st ed. (London: John Murray Publishing, 1859).

26. Charles Darwin, *Descent of Man, and Selection in Relation to Sex*, new ed. (Princeton, NJ: Princeton University Press, 1981). (Photocopy of original, London: Murray Publishing, 1871.)

27. Brian Hare, "Survival of the Friendliest: *Homo Sapiens* Evolved via Selection for Prosociality," *Annual Review of Psychology* 68 (2017): 155–86.

28. Brian Hare and Vanessa Woods, *Survival of the Friendliest: Understanding Our Origins and Rediscovering Our Humanity* (New York: Penguin Random House, 2020).

29. Ibid., 28.

30. Richard W. Wrangham and Dale Peterson, *Demonic Males: Apes and the Origins of Human Violence* (New York: Houghton Mifflin Harcourt, 1996).

31. Richard W. Wrangham, *The Goodness Paradox: The Strange Relationship between Virtue and Violence in Human Evolution* (New York: Pantheon, 2019).

32. John Russell Napier, *The Roots of Mankind* (Washington, DC: Smithsonian Institute, 1970).

33. Erich Fromm, *The Anatomy of Human Destructiveness* (New York: Picador, 1973) 152.

34. Agustín Fuetes, *The Creative Spark: How Imagination Made Humans Exceptional* (New York: Penguin-Random House, 2017).

35. Karen Hardy, Jennie Brand-Miller, Katherine D. Brown, Mark G. Thomas, and Les Copeland, "The Importance of Dietary Carbohydrates in Human Evolution," *The Quarterly Review of Biology* 90(3) (2015): 251–68, accessed 23 Oct. 2021, doi:10.1086/682587.

36. Ibid.

37. Martin N. Muller, Richard Wrangham, and David Pilbeam, *Chimpanzees and Human Evolution* (Cambridge, MA: Harvard University Press, 2017).

38. Carol R. Ember and Melvin Ember, "Violence in the Ethnographic Record: Results of Cross-Cultural Research on War and Aggressions," *Troubled Times: Violence and Warfare in the Past* (New York: Routledge, 1997) 1–20.

39. Carol R. Ember, "Hunter-Gatherers (Foragers)," *Human Area Relations Files (HRAF)* (July 2014).

40. Kay M. Martin and Barbara Voorhies, *The Female of the Species* (New York and London: Columbia University Press, 1975).

41. Peggy Reeves Sanday, *Female Power and Male Dominance: On the Origins of Sexual Inequality* (New York: Cambridge University Press, 1981).

42. Ibid.

43. Merry E. Weisner-Hanks, *Gender in History: Global Perspectives*, 2nd ed. (West Sussex, UK: Wiley-Blackwell, 2011) 16.

Chapter 3—The Irrational Revolution: Spirits, Art, and Life

1. Stewart Guthrie, *Faces in the Clouds: A New Theory of Religion* (New York: Oxford University Press, 1993) 88.

2. Erland Ehnmark, *Anthropomorphism and Miracle*, Uppsala Universitets Årsskrift (Uppsala: Amqvist & Wiksels Boktyckeri-A.-B., 1939) (Recueil de Travaux Publié par L'Université D'Uppsala).

3. Jane Goodall, "The Chimpanzee," *The Quest for Man* (New York: Praeger, 1971) 131–70.

4. Michael R. Rampino and Stephen Self, "Climate–Volcanism Feedback and the Toba Eruption of ~74,000 Years Ago," *Quaternary Research* 40(3) (1993): 269–80.

5. G. A. Zielinski, P. A. Mayewski, L. D. Meeker, S. Whitlow, M. S. Twickler, and K. Taylor, "Potential Atmospheric Impact of the Toba Mega—Eruption ~71,000 Years Ago," *Geophysical Research Letters* 23(8) (1996): 837–40.

6. A. Timmermann and T. Friedrich, "Late Pleistocene Climate Drivers of Early Human Migration," *Nature* 538 (2016): 92–95, accessed 8 Aug. 2020, doi:10.1038/nature19365.

7. United Nations Department of Economic and Social Affairs, *International Migration 2020 Highlights*, 15 Jan. 2021, accessed 16 Aug. 2021, https://www.un.org/en/desa/international-migration-2020-highlights.

8. David S. Whitley, *Cave Paintings and the Human Spirit: The Origin of Creativity and Belief* (Amherst, NY: Prometheus Books, 2009) 169.

9. Joseph Campbell Foundation, *Goddesses: Mysteries of the Feminine Divine* (Novato, CA: New World Library, 2013).

10. Jared Diamond, *Guns, Germs, and Steel: The Fates of Human Societies* (New York: W. W. Norton & Company, Inc., 1997).

11. David F. Horrobin, *The Madness of Adam and Eve: How Schizophrenia Shaped Humanity* (London: Transworld Publishers, Ltd., 2002).

12. Dean Hamer, *The God Gene: How Faith Is Hardwired into Our Genes* (Anchor Books, 2005) 16.

13. John Cookson, "The Neurological Origins of Religious Belief," *Big Think*, 10 Sep. 2010, accessed 9 Nov. 2011, https://bigthink.com/surprising-science/the-neurological-origins-of-religious-belief/.

14. David S. Whitley, *Cave Paintings and the Human Spirit: The Origin of Creativity and Belief* (Amherst, NY: Prometheus Books, 2009) 253.

15. Greg Child, *Mixed Emotions: Mountaineering Writings of Greg Child* (Seattle: The Mountaineers, 1993).

16. Stewart Elliott Guthrie, *Faces in the Clouds: A New Theory of Religion* (New York: Oxford University Press, Inc., 1993).

17. Eric Weiner, "Are We Born to Wander?" *National Geographic Magazine* 238(2) (2021): 15–18.

18. Brian Hare, "Survival of the Friendliest: *Homo Sapiens* Evolved via Selection for Prosociality," *Annual Review of Psychology* 68 (2017): 155–86.

19. M. L. Boccia, P. Petrusz, K. Suzuki, L. Marson, and C. A. Pedersen, "Immunohistochemical Location of Oxytocin Receptors in Human Brain," *Neuroscience* 253 (2013): 155–64.

20. C. K. De Dreu, "Oxytocin Modulates Cooperation within and Competition between Groups: An Integrative Review and Research Agenda," *Hormones and Behavior* 61 (2012): 419–28.

21. Justin L. Barrett, *Why Would Anyone Believe in God?* (Lanham, MD: AltaMira, 2004).

22. David S. Whitley, *Cave Paintings and the Human Spirit: The Origin of Creativity and Belief* (Amherst, NY: Prometheus Books, 2009).

23. Scott Atran, *In Gods We Trust: The Evolutionary Landscape of Religion* (New York: Oxford University Press, 2002) 267.

24. D. Johnson and J. Bering, "Hand of God, Mind of Man: Punishment and Cognition in the Evolution of Cooperation," *Evolutionary Psychology* 4 (2006).

25. P. Boyer, "Are Ghost Concepts 'Intuitive,' 'Endemic,' and 'Innate?'" *Journal of Cognition and Culture* 3 (2003).

26. Ernest Becker, *The Denial of Death* (New York: Free Press, 1973).

27. Roy A. Rappaport, *Ritual and Religion in the Making of Humanity* (Cambridge, UK: Cambridge University Press, 1999).

28. Robert Shaw, *Social Geographies: An Introduction* (London: Rowman & Littlefield, 2021) 32–33.

29. Howard F. Stein, *Developmental Time, Cultural Space: Studies in Psychogeography* (Norman, OK: University of Oklahoma Press, 1987) 15.

Chapter 4—Pandora's Box

1. George W. E. Nickelsburg, "Apocalyptic and Myth in 1 Enoch 6–11," *Journal of Biblical Literature* 96(3) (1977): 383–405.

2. Sigmund Freud, *The Interpretation of Dreams: The Basic Writings of Sigmund Freud* (New York: Random House, 1938) 336–67.

Chapter 5—Feminine Landscapes

1. Yi-Fu Tuan, *Topophilia: A Study of Environmental Perception, Attitudes, and Values* (Englewood Cliffs, NJ: Prentice-Hall, Inc., 1974).

2. Kelly Hays-Gilpin, et al., *Women & Men in the Prehispanic Southwest: Labor, Power, & Prestige* (Santa Fe, NM: School of American Research Press, 2000) 93–95.

3. Ibid.

4. Alex Bellos, "'Seven' Triumphs in Poll to Discover World's Favorite Number," *The Guardian*, 8 Apr. 2014, accessed 17 June 2021, https://www.theguardian.com/science/alexs-adventures-in-numberland/2014/apr/08/seven-worlds-favourite-number-online-survey.

5. Ibid.

6. Eckhart Tolle, *A New Earth: Awakening Your Life's Purpose* (New York: Plume Penguin Group, 2005).

7. Carl G. Jung, *The Psychology of the Transference* (New York: Bollingen Foundation, Inc., 1954).

8. Monica Sjöö and Barbara Mor, *The Great Cosmic Mother: Rediscovering the Religion of the Earth* (San Francisco: Harper & Row, 1987) 170.

9. Bill Hatcher, "Sacred Planes and Axes of Gendered Landscapes in Buhaya, Tanzania," graduate thesis, University of Arizona, Tucson, 2004. Text is taken directly from the author's own work and modified for use here.

10. Ibid.

11. C. G. Jung, *The Collected Works of C. G. Jung, Volume 7: Two Essays on Analytical Psychology*, 2nd ed. (Princeton, NJ: Princeton University Press, 1966).

12. Merlin Stone, *When God Was a Woman* (New York: Harvest/Harcourt Brace, in arrangement with The Dial Press, 1976) 2–3.

13. Joseph Campbell Foundation, *Goddesses: Mysteries of the Feminine Divine* (Novato, CA: New World Library, 2013) 52.

14. M. Esther Harding, *Woman's Mysteries, Ancient and Modern: A Psychological Interpretation of the Feminine Principle as Portrayed in Myth, Story, and Dream* (New York: Bantam, 1973) 64, 103–105.

15. Cheikh Anta Diop, *The Cultural Unity of Negro Africa: The Domains of Patriarchy and of Matriarchy in Classical Antiquity* (Paris: Présence Africaine Editions, 1962) 75.

16. Luc-Normand Tellier, *Urban World History: An Economic and Geographical Perspective* (New York: Springer International Publishing, 2019).

Chapter 6—The Horticultural Revolution:
Goddesses, Matriarchy, and Birth

1. Douglass J. Kennett, et al., "Shock-Synthesized Hexagonal Diamonds in Younger Dryas Boundary Sediments," *Proceedings of the National Academy of Sciences of the United States America* 106(31) (2009): 12623–28, accessed 27 May 2021, doi:10.1073/pnas.0906374106.

2. Julian Murton, et al., "Identification of Younger Dryas Outburst Flood Path from Lake Agassiz to the Arctic Ocean," *Nature* 464(7289) (Apr. 2010): 740–43, doi:10.1038/nature08954.

3. Riane Eisler, *The Chalice & the Blade: Our History, Our Future* (New York: HarperCollins Publishers, Inc., 1987) 67–69.

4. Spencer Wells, *Pandora's Seed: The Unforeseen Cost of Civilization* (New York: Random House, Inc., 2010).

5. *The Cambridge Encyclopedia of Human Evolution*, ed. Steve Jones, Robert Martin, and David Pilbeam (Cambridge, UK: Cambridge University Press, 1992).

6. Patricia L. Crown, et al., *Women & Men in the Prehispanic Southwest: Labor, Power, & Prestige* (Santa Fe, NM: School of American Research Press, 2000) 232–36.

7. William McNeill, *Plagues and Peoples* (New York: Anchor, 1976).

8. Jared Diamond, *Guns, Germs, and Steel: The Fates of Human Societies* (New York: W. W. Norton, Inc., 1997).

9. Peggy Sanday, *Female Power and Male Dominance: On the Origins of Sexual Inequality* (Cambridge, UK: Cambridge University Press, 1981) 65-66.

10. Carol J. Adams, *The Sexual Politics of Meat: A Feminist-Vegetarian Critical Theory* (New York: Continuum International Publishing Group, 1990) 59.

11. "Milk and the Modern Man: The Rise of Adult Milk Drinking," Stanford at the Tech: Understanding Genetics, *The Tech Interactive*, 2019, accessed 28 Sep. 2021, https://genetics.thetech.org/original_news/news45.

12. R. G. Cumming and R. J. Kleinberg, "Consumption of Dairy Products, Particularly at Age 20 Years, Was Associated with an Increased Risk of Hip Fracture in Old Age (Case-Control Study of Risk Factors for Hip Fractures in the Elderly," *American Journal of Epidemiology* 139(5) (1994).

13. Martha K. McCintock, "Menstrual Synchrony and Suppression," *Nature* 229 (1971): 171–79.

14. Elise Boulding, *The Underside of History: A View of Women through Time* (Boulder, CO: Westview Press, 1976) 106.

15. Kari Marie Norgaard, "Moon Phases, Menstrual Cycles, and Mother Earth: The Construction of a Special Relationship between Women and Nature," *Ethics and the Environment* 4(2) (1999): 197–209, accessed 29 July 2021, https://www.jstor.org/stable/40338978.

16. Joseph Campbell Foundation, *Goddesses: Mysteries of the Feminine Divine* (Novato, CA: New World Library, 2013).

17. Ibid.

18. William Irwin Thompson, *The Time Falling Bodies Take to Light: Mythology, Sexuality & the Origins of Culture* (New York: St. Martin's Press, 1996).

19. Sigmund Freud, *The Future of Illusion*, reissue ed. (New York: Norton, 1989 [1927]).

20. Rebecca L. Stein and Philip L. Stein, *The Anthropology of Religion, Magic, and Witchcraft*, 4th ed. (Oxford, England: Routledge, 2017) 217.

21. Joseph Campbell Foundation, *Goddesses: Mysteries of the Feminine Divine* (Novato, CA: New World Library, 2013) 29–34.

22. Riane Eisler, *The Chalice & the Blade: Our History, Our Future* (New York: HarperCollins Publishers, Inc., 1988) 89.

23. Ian Hodder, *Towards Reflexive Method in Archaeology: The Example of Çatalhöyük* (Cambridge: McDonald Institute, 2000).

24. James Mellaart, *Earliest Civilizations of the Near East* (London: Thames and Hudson, 1965).

25. Elizabeth Gould Davis, *The First Sex* (Baltimore, MD: Penguin Books, 1972).

26. Evelyn Reed, *Women's Evolution: From Matriarchal Clan to Patriarchal Family* (New York: Pathfinder Press, Inc., 1975).

27. David W. Anthony, *The Horse, the Wheel, and Language: How Bronze-Age Riders from the Eurasian Steppes Shaped the Modern World* (Princeton, NJ: Princeton University Press, 2007) 360.

28. Ibid.

29. Max Vasmer, *Russisches etymologisches Wörterbuch* (Heidelberg, Germany: C. Winter Heidelberg, 1955) 2, 424.

30. Jacquetta Hawkes, *Dawn of the Gods* (London: Chatto & Windus, 1958).

31. W. Haak, I. Lazaridis, N. Patterson, et al., "Massive Migration from the Steppe Was a Source for Indo-European Languages in Europe," *Nature* 522 (2015): 207–11, doi:10.1038/nature14317.

32. Where Yahweh is characterized as husband and lover in the Old Testament, his "spouse" is described as the community of Israel (e.g., Isaiah 50:1, 54:1–8; Jeremiah 2:2–3, 2:20–25, 3:1–20; Hosea 1–4, 14) or as the land of Israel (e.g., 62:1–5).

Chapter 7—The Smith and the Devil

1. Sara Graça da Silva and Jamshid J. Tehrani, "Comparative Phylogenetic Analyses Uncover the Ancient Roots of Indo-European Folktales," *The Royal Society*, 1 Jan. 2016, accessed 3 Jan. 2020, doi:10.1098/rsos.150645.

2. Marylène Patou-Mathis, "The Origins of Violence," *The UNESCO Courier: Many Voices, One World* 1 (2020), accessed 16 May 2021, https://en.unesco.org/courier/2020-1/origins-violence.

3. Ian Hodder, *The Domestication of Europe* (Oxford: Basil Blackwell, 1990).

4. Tia Ghose, "Battered Skulls Reveal Violence among Stone Age Women," *LiveScience*, 12 Feb. 2013, accessed 3 June 2021, https://www.livescience.com/27055-neolithic-skulls-show-violence.html.

Chapter 8—Masculine Landscapes

1. Eckhart Tolle, *A New Earth: Awakening to Your Life's Purpose* (New York: Plume, 2005).

2. Ibid.

3. "The Geena Davis Institute in Media and J. Walter Thompson Present Revealing Findings about Women's Representation in Advertising at Cannes Lions," *Geena Davis Institute on Gender in Media*, 21 June 2017, accessed 22 Aug. 2020, https://seejane.org/gender-in-media-news-release/geena-davis-institute-gender-media-j-walter-thompson-present-revealing-findings-womens-representation-advertising-cannes-lions/.

4. Belden Lane, *The Solace of Fierce Landscapes: Exploring Desert and Mountain Spirituality* (New York: Oxford University Press, 1998) 39–40.

5. Marija Gimbutas, *The Language of the Goddess* (New York: Thames & Hudson, 1989).

6. Catherine H. Berndt and Frances Dahlberg, eds, "Interpretations and Facts in Aboriginal Australia," *Woman the Gatherer* (New Haven: Yale University Press, 1981).

7. Catherine H. Berndt, "Digging Sticks and Spears, or, The Two-Sex Model," *Aboriginal Woman, Sacred and Profane* (London: Routledge, 1939).

8. Carol R. Ember, "Residential Variation among Hunter-Gatherers," *Behavior Science Research* 10(3) (1975): 199–277, accessed 16 July 2019, doi:10.1177/106939717501000302.

9. Lewis R. Binford, "Mobility, Housing, and Environment: A Comparative Study," *Journal of Anthropological Research* 46(2) (1990): 119–52, accessed 24 Mar. 2021, doi:10.1086/jar.46.2.3630069.

10. Raymond C. Kelly, *Warless Societies and the Origin of War* (Ann Arbor, MI: The University of Michigan Press, 2000).

11. Frank W. Marlow, "Hunter-Gatherers and Human Evolution," *Evolutionary Anthropology: Issues, News, and Reviews* 14(2) (2005): 56–67, accessed 30 Apr. 2021, doi:10.1002/evan.20046.

12. Daniel Pendick, "How Much Protein Do You Need Every Day?" *Harvard Health Publishing*, Harvard Medical School, 21 June 2019, accessed 27

June 2021, https://www.health.harvard.edu/blog/how-much-protein-do-you-need-every-day-201506188096. The US Food and Drug Administration, which calculates the RDA (Recommended Daily Allowances) used on all food packaging in the US, holds to the upper safe limit for protein ingestion of 35 percent, or alternatively, the full range of 10–35 percent. Interestingly, according to Pendick, the author of the article cited here, the 2019 "Protein Summit," held in Washington DC, "was organized and sponsored by beef, egg, and other animal-based food industry groups." The summit generated a number of reports published in the *American Journal of Clinical Nutrition.*

13. H. V. Kuhnleini and R. Soueida, "Use and Nutrient Composition of Traditional Baffin Inuit Foods," *Journal of Food Composition and Analysis* 5(2) (1992): 112–26, accessed 15 Aug. 2020, doi:10.1016/0889-1575(92)90026-G.

14. J. D. Speth, "Middle Paleolithic Subsistence in the Near East," *Before Farming* (2012) 1–45, accessed 17 June 2021, https://lsa.umich.edu/ummaa/people/emeriti-curators/jdspeth/Middle-Paleolithic-Subsistence-in-the-Near-East-Zooarchaeological-Perspectives-Past-Present-and-Future.html.

15. C. Kaleta, L. F. de Figueiredo, and S. Schuster, "Against the Stream: Relevance of Gluconeogenesis from Fatty Acids for Natives of the Arctic Regions," *International Journal of Circumpolar Health* 71(1–2) (2012): 256–57, accessed 14 Feb. 2019, doi:10.3402/ijch.v71i0.18436.

16. Ibid.

17. Rebecca L. Stein and Philip L. Stein, *The Anthropology of Religion, Magic, and Witchcraft,* 4th ed. (Oxford, England: Routledge, 2017) 86.

18. Cheikh Anta Diop, *The Cultural Unity of Negro Africa: The Domains of Patriarchy and of Matriarchy in Classical Antiquity* (Paris: Présence Africaine Editions, 1962) 34.

19. Ibid.

20. Monica Sjöö and Barbara Mor, *The Great Cosmic Mother: Rediscovering the Religion of the Earth* (San Francisco: Harper & Row, 1987) 106, 170.

21. Marija Gimbutas, *The Language of the Goddess* (New York: Thames & Hudson, 1989).

22. James Mellaart, *Earliest Civilizations of the Near East* (London: Thames and Hudson, 1965).

23. Banu Aydin Kucukemre, et al., "Frequency of Ambiguous Genitalia in 14,177 Newborns in Turkey," *Oxford Academic: Journal of Endocrine Society* 3(6) (2019): 1185–95, accessed 10 July 2021, doi:10.1210/js.2018-00408.

24. Barbara Miller, *Cultural Anthropology in a Globalizing World*, 4th ed. (Boston: Pearson Education, Inc., 2017) 77–80.

25. Rebecca L. Stein and Philip L. Stein, *The Anthropology of Religion, Magic, and Witchcraft*, 4th ed. (Oxford, England: Routledge, 2017) 73.

26. Bronislaw Malinowski, *The Sexual Life of Savages* (New York: Halcyon House, 1929) 3–7.

27. Johann Jacob Bachofen, *Myth, Religion, and Mother Right* (Stuttgart, Germany: Alfred Kröner Verlag Publishing, 1926). (Reprint, Princeton: Princeton University Press, 1967, 1973, and 1992.)

28. Nikolai Kradin, "Ancient Steppe Nomad Societies," *Asian History*, 24 May 2018, accessed 19 Aug. 2020, doi:10.1093/acrefore/9780190277727.013.3.

29. Marija Gimbutus, *The Living Goddesses* (Berkeley: University of California Press, 1999).

30. Yi-Fu Tuan, *Topophilia: A Study of Environmental Perception, Attitudes, and Values* (Englewood Cliffs, NJ: Prentice-Hall, Inc., 1974).

31. Hector A. Garcia, *Alpha God: The Psychology of Religious Violence and Oppression* (New York: Prometheus Books, 2015).

Chapter 9—The Hyper-Masculine Devolution:
Gods, Patriarchy, and Death

1. Charles Keith Maisels, *Early Civilizations of the Old World: The Formative Histories of Egypt, the Levant, Mesopotamia, India and China* (New York: Routledge, 2001).

2. William J. Hamblin, *Warfare in the Ancient Near East to 1600 BC: Holy Warriors at the Dawn of History* (New York: Routledge, 2006).

3. Jane McIntosh, *Ancient Mesopotamia: New Perspectives* (Santa Barbara, CA: ABC-CLIO, 2005).

4. Karen Rhea Nemet-Nejat, *Daily Life in Ancient Mesopotamia* (Westport, CT: Greenwood Press, 1998).

5. Robert Bagg and James Scully, *The Complete Plays of Sophocles: A New Translation* (New York: HarperCollins, 2011).

6. Georges Charbonnier, *Conversations with Claude Levi-Strauss* (New York: Grossman, 1969) 29–30.

7. Leonard Shlain, *The Alphabet Versus the Goddess: The Conflict between Word and Image* (New York: Viking-Penguin, 1998) 1.

8. Joseph Campbell Foundation, *Goddesses: Mysteries of the Feminine Divine* (Novato, CA: New World Library, 2013) 29–34.

9. Erich Fromm, *The Anatomy of Human Destructiveness* (New York: Picador, 1973) 190. This reference to the Babylonian epic *Enuma Elish* is quoted from a translation authored by Alexander Heidel, *The Babylonian Genesis: Enuma Elish* (Chicago: University of Chicago Press, 1942).

10. Ibid.

11. Merline Stone, *When God Was a Woman* (New York: Harvest/Harcourt Brace, in arrangement with The Dial Press, 1976) 2–3, 94–95.

12. Ibid., 72.

13. Marija Gimbutas, *The Language of the Goddess* (New York: Thames & Hudson, 1989).

14. Riane Eisler, *The Chalice & the Blade: Our History, Our Future* (New York: HarperCollins, 1987) 67–69, 89.

15. Count Eugène Goblet d'Alviella, *Symbols: Their Migration and Universality* (New York: Dover Publications, 2000).

16. Ibid.

17. Peter R. Schmidt, *Iron Technology in East Africa* (Bloomington: Indiana University Press, 1997).

18. Elaine Pagels, *The Gnostic Gospels* (New York: Vintage Books, 1989) 64–67.

19. Riane Eisler, *The Chalice & the Blade: Our History, Our Future* (San Francisco, CA: HarperCollins, 1989) 126.

20. *Zondervan New International Version Bible* (Grand Rapids, MI: Zondervan Corporation, 1984).

21. Bill Hatcher, *Principles of Flight: Flying Bush Planes through a World of War, Sexism, and Meat* (New York: Lantern Books, Inc., 2018). Text is taken directly from the author's own work and modified for use here.

22. Michael Nolan, "Opinion: The Myth of Soulless Women," *First Things*, University College Dublin, Apr. 1997, accessed 7 Apr. 2021, https://www.firstthings.com/article/1997/04/the-myth-of-soulless-women.

23. *The Holy Qur'an: With English Translation and Commentary*, ed. Maulana Muhammad Ali (Dublin, OH: Ahmadiyya Anjuman Isha'at Islam Lahore, Inc., 2002).

24. Imam Al-Bukhari, *Sahih Al-Bukhari* (Mohammad Mohee Uddari, 2020).

25. D. Crowe, *War Crimes, Genocide, and Justice: A Global History* (New York: Springer, 2014).

26. Jan Arnot MacCullouch and John Arnott, *The Mythology of All Races, Volume 3: Celtic/Slavic* (New York: Cooper Square Publishers, 1964).

27. Ibid.

28. Roderick Nash, *Wilderness and the American Mind*, 3rd ed. (New Haven, CT: Yale University Press, 1982) 387–89.

29. Eckhart Tolle, *A New Earth: Awakening to Your Life's Purpose* (New York: Plume Publishing, 2005).

30. Robert Moore and Douglass Gillette, *King, Warrior, Magician, Lover*, rev. ed. (San Francisco: HarperOne, 1991).

31. Centers for Disease Control and Prevention, *Zoonotic Diseases*, 14 July 2017, accessed 13 Nov. 2020, https://www.cdc.gov/onehealth/basics/zoonotic-diseases.html.

32. World Health Organization, *WHO-Convened Global Study of Origins of SARS-CoV-2: China Part*, COVID-19: Animal-human interface and food safety, accessed 30 Mar. 2021, https://www.who.int/publications/i/item/who-convened-global-study-of-origins-of-sars-cov-2-china-part.

33. Harriet Bartlett, Mark A. Holmes, Silviu O. Petrovan, David R. Williams, James L. N. Wood, and Andrew Balmford, "Understanding the Relative Risks of Zoonosis Emergence under Contrasting Approaches to Meeting Livestock Product Demand," *Royal Society Open Science*, 22 June 2022, accessed 10 Oct. 2022, doi:10.1098/rsos.211573. "One approach proposed to reduce emerging infectious diseases is to dramatically reduce meat consumption. In the extreme, this could allow widespread restoration of natural habitats, increasing the health of wild populations while also greatly reducing opportunities for transmission to livestock and people—hence reducing the risks of disease emergence."

34. B. W. Husted, "Culture and Ecology: A Cross-National Study of the Determinants of Environmental Sustainability," *Management International Review* 45(3) (2005).

35. H. Park, C. Russell, and J. Lee, "National Culture and Environmental Sustainability: A Cross-National Analysis," *Journal of Economics and Finance* 31(1) (2007).

36. Ibid., 113–14.

37. Carl Gustav Jung, *The Archetypes of the Collective Unconscious* (Princeton, NJ: Princeton University Press, 1969).

38. Eva F. Kittay, "Woman as Metaphor," *Hypatia* 3(4) (1988): 1.

39. Bill Hatcher, *Principles of Flight: Flying Bush Planes through a World of War, Sexism, and Meat* (New York: Lantern Books, Inc., 2018). Text is taken directly from the author's own work and modified for use here.

Chapter 10—The Lorax

1. Dr. Seuss, *The Lorax* (New York: Random House, 1971).
2. Peter Bunzel, "The Wacky World of Dr. Seuss Delights the Child—and Adult—Readers of His Books," *Life* 6 Apr. 1959. "Most of Geisel's books point a moral, though he insists that he never starts with one. 'Kids,' he says, 'can see a moral coming a mile off and they gag at it. But there's an inherent moral in any story.'"
3. Ibid.
4. Katie Ishizuka and Ramón Stephens, "The Cat Is Out of the Bag: Orientalism, Anti-Blackness, and White Supremacy in Dr. Seuss's Children's Books," *Research on Diversity in Youth Literature* (2019).
5. Frankie Schembri, "Is This Monkey the Inspiration for Dr. Seuss's Lorax?" *Science*, 23 July 2018, accessed 4 Apr. 2021, https://www.sciencemag.org/news/2018/07/monkey-inspiration-dr-seuss-s-lorax.
6. Ibid.

Chapter 11—Transformed Landscapes

1. Ned Rozell, "The Most Remote Place in U.S.," *UAF News and Information*, University of Alaska, Fairbanks, 3 Jan. 2018, accessed 2 Dec. 2019, https://news.uaf.edu/remote-place-u-s-2/.
2. Andy Isaacson, "A Visual Dispatch from One of the World's Most Remote Islands," *The New York Times*, 20 May 2020, accessed 25 Oct. 2020, https://www.nytimes.com/2020/05/20/travel/tristan-da-cunha.html.
3. Scott Snowden, "300-Mile Swim through the Great Garbage Patch Will Collect Data on Plastic Pollution," *Forbes*, 30 May 2019, accessed 5 Nov. 2019, https://www.forbes.com/sites/scottsnowden/2019/05/30/300-mile-swim-through-the-great-pacific-garbage-patch-will-collect-data-on-plastic-pollution/?sh=23e956a4489f.
4. X. Wang, T. Yao, Z. Cong, et al., "Concentration Level and Distribution of Polycyclic Aromatic Hydrocarbons in Soil and Grass around Mt. Qomolangma, China," *Chinese Sci Bull.* 52 (2007): 1405–13, accessed 29 Dec. 2019, doi:10.1007/s11434-007-0184-2.

5. Michelle Starr, "Space Debris Has Hit and Damaged the International Space Station," *Science Alert*, 31 May 2021, accessed 13 June 2021, https://www.sciencealert.com/space-debris-has-damaged-the-international-space-station.

6. "Space Debris by the Numbers," *The European Space Agency*, Jan. 2019, accessed 5 Mar. 2019, https://www.esa.int/Safety_Security/Space_Debris/Space_debris_by_the_numbers.

7. James M. Rubenstein, *The Cultural Landscape: An Introduction to Human Geography* (Hoboken, NJ: Pearson Education, Inc., 2020) 31.

8. Edward N. Wolff, "Household Wealth Trends in the United States, 1962 to 2016: Has Middle Class Wealth Recovered?" National Bureau of Economic Research, Nov. 2017, accessed 10 Mar. 2022, https://www.nber.org/system/files/working_papers/w24085/w24085.pdf.

9. "Just 8 Men Own the Same Wealth as Half the World," Oxfam International, 16 Jan. 2017, accessed 5 Nov. 2021, https://www.oxfam.org/en/press-releases/just-8-men-own-same-wealth-half-world.

10. United Nations Department of Economic and Social Affairs, "68% of the World's Population Projected to Live in Urban Areas, UN Says," 16 May 2018, accessed 1 Aug. 2021, https://population.un.org/wup/Publications/Files/WUP2018-PressRelease.pdf.

11. J. Pearce, E. Richardson, R. Mitchell, and N. Short, "Environmental Justice and Health: The Implications of the Socio-Spatial Distribution of Multiple Environmental Deprivation for Health Inequalities in the United Kingdom," *Transactions of the Institute of British Geographers* 35(4) (2010): 522–39.

12. Aaron M. McCright and Riley E. Dunlap, "Cool Dudes: The Denial of Climate Change among Conservative White Males in the United States," *Global Environmental Change*, 28 June 2011, accessed 7 Feb. 2021, https://sciencepolicy.colorado.edu/students/envs_5000/mccright_2011.pdf.

13. Cara Daggett, "Petro-Masculinity and Authoritarian Desire," *Sage Journals*, 20 June 2018, accessed 5 Mar. 2021, doi:10.1177/0305829818775817.

14. Alexander C. Kaufman, "A Former Trump Advisor May Have Revealed What the Fossil Fuel Bonanza Was Really About," *HUFFPOST*, 4 Feb. 2021, accessed 7 Feb. 2021, https://www.huffpost.com/entry/trump-fossil-fuels_n_601c626fc5b68e068fbccba6.

15. Alison Spencer and Cary Funk, "Electric Vehicles Get Mixed Reception from American Consumers," Pew Research Center, 3 June 2021, accessed 4 Sep. 2022, https://www.pewresearch.org/fact-tank/2021/06/03/electric-vehicles-get-mixed-reception-from-american-consumers/.

16. Charlotte McDonald, "How Many Earths Do We Need?" *BBC News*, 15 June 2015, accessed 10 July 2021, https://www.bbc.com/news/magazine-33133712.

17. United Nations Sustainable Development Goals, "Rapid Urbanization and Population Growth Are Outpacing the Construction of Adequate and Affordable Housing," 2019, accessed 3 July 2020, https://unstats.un.org/sdgs/report/2019/goal-11/.

18. Olivia Rosane, "Humans and Big Ag Livestock Now Account for 96 Percent of Mammal Biomass," *Ecowatch: Environmental News for a Healthier Planet and Life*, 23 May 2018, accessed 7 July 2021, https://www.ecowatch.com/biomass-humans-animals-2571413930.html.

19. Ibid.

20. Ibid.

21. USDA Economic Research Service, *Food Access*, 2017, accessed 17 Oct. 2020, https://www.ers.usda.gov/data-products/food-access-research-atlas/documentation/.

22. Keithly Jones and Mildred Haley, "Per Capita Red Meat and Poultry Disappearance: Insights into Its Steady Growth," *USDA Economic Research Service: United States Department of Agriculture*, 4 June 2018, accessed 30 June 2021, https://www.ers.usda.gov/amber-waves/2018/june/per-capita-red-meat-and-poultry-disappearance-insights-into-its-steady-growth/.

23. Ibid.

24. Ann Gibbons, "The Evolution of Diet," *National Geographic* Sep. 2014: 40.

25. David Pimentel, et al., "Water Resources: Agricultural and Environmental Issues," *BioScience* 54(10) (2004): 909–18, doi:10.1641/0006-3568(2004)054[0909:WRAAEI]2.0.CO;2.

26. Mesfin M. Mekonnen and Arjen Y. Hoekstra, "A Global Assessment of the Water Footprint of Farm Animal Products," *Ecosystems* 15 (2012): 401–15.

27. Pimentel et al.

28. FAOSTAT, archived 8 Dec. 2021, accessed 13 Jan. 2022, https://www.fao.org/.

29. David Robinson Simon, *Meatonomics: How the Rigged Economics of Meat and Dairy Make You Consume Too Much—and How to Eat Better, Live Longer, and Spend Smarter* (Newburyport, MA: Conari Press, 2013).

30. Richard Oppenlander, "Biodiversity and Food Choice: A Clarification," *Comfortably Unaware: Global Depletion and Food Choice Responsibility*, 9 June 2012, accessed 3 June 2021, http://comfortablyunaware.com/blog/biodiversity-and-food-choice-a-clarification/.

31. United Nations News Centre, "UN launches International Year of Deserts and Desertification," 1 Jan. 2006, accessed 7 June 2021, https://news.un.org/en/story/2006/01/165052-un-launches-international-year-deserts-and-desertification.

32. Scot M. Miller, et al., "Anthropogenic Emissions of Methane in the United States," *Proceedings of the National Academy of Sciences* 110(50) (18 Oct. 2013), accessed 17 June 2021, doi:10.1073/pnas.1314392110.

33. United States Environmental Protection Agency, *Understand Global Warming Potentials*, accessed 1 July 2021, https://www.epa.gov/ghgemissions/understanding-global-warming-potentials.

34. Boris Worm, "Averting a Global Fisheries Disaster," *The Proceedings of the National Academy of Sciences*, 19 Apr. 2016, accessed 3 July 2022, https://www.pnas.org/doi/10.1073/pnas.1604008113.

35. Sandra Altherr and Nicola Hodgins, "Small Cetaceans, Big Problems: A Global Review on the Impacts of Hunting on Small Whales, Dolphins, and Porpoises," *Food and Agriculture Organization of the United Nations*, 2018, accessed 3 July 2022, https://uk.whales.org/wp-content/uploads/sites/6/2018/08/small-cetaceans-big-problems.pdf.

36. Will Tuttle, *The World Peace Diet: Eating for Spiritual Health and Social Harmony* (New York: Lantern Books, 2005).

37. David Lange, "Number of Participants in Hunting in the United States 2006 to 2019," *Statista: Sports & Recreation, Parks & Outdoors*, 30 Nov. 2020, accessed 30 Oct. 2021, https://www.statista.com/statistics/191244/participants-in-hunting-in-the-us-since-2006/.

38. Bill Hatcher, *Principles of Flight: Flying Bush Planes through a World of War, Sexism, and Meat* (New York: Lantern Books, Inc., 2018). Text is taken directly from the author's own work and modified for use here.

39. K. Dhont, G. Hodson, K. Costelly, and C. C. MacInnes, "Social Dominance Orientation Connects Prejudicial Human–Human and Human–Animal Relations," *Personality and Individual Difference* 61 (2014): 105–108, accessed 2 Dec. 2020, https://www.researchgate.net/publication/260296264_Social_dominance_orientation_connects_prejudicial_human-human_and_human-animal_relations.

40. Brian Hare and Vanessa Woods, *Survival of the Friendliest: Understanding Our Origins and Rediscovering Our Common Humanity* (New York: Random House, 2020).

41. Joseph Campbell, *The Masks of God, Volume 1: Primitive Mythology* (New York: Penguin Books, 1978) 77, 129.

42. Carol J. Adams, *The Sexual Politics of Meat: A Feminist-Vegetarian Critical Theory* (New York: Continuum International Publishing Group, 1990) 59, 242.

43. Richard Aiken, "Recruitment and Retention of Hunters and Anglers: 2000–2015," *National Survey Addendum*, USFWS National Digital Library. Report 2016-01, published 2019-04, https://digitalmedia.fws.gov/digital/collection/document/id/2249/.

44. Marc Bekoff, "The Psychology and Thrill of Trophy Hunting: Is It Criminal?" *Psychology Today*, 18 Oct. 2015, accessed 30 Oct. 2021, https://www.psychologytoday.com/us/blog/animal-emotions/201510/the-psychology-and-thrill-trophy-hunting-is-it-criminal.

45. Ibid.

46. United Nations Development Programme, Human Development Reports, *Gender Inequality Index (GII)* (2020 statistical annex table 5), accessed 18 June 2021, http://hdr.undp.org/en/content/gender-inequality-index-gii.

47. Ibid.

48. World Economic Forum. *Global Gender Gap Report: 2021*, accessed 31 Mar. 2021, http://www3.weforum.org/docs/WEF_GGGR_2021.pdf.

49. Ibid.

50. Ibid.

51. Ibid.

52. Ibid.

53. Ibid.

54. Ibid.

55. Gena Corea, *The Mother Machine: Reproductive Technologies from Artificial Insemination Artificial Wombs* (New York: Harper & Row, 1985) 12–13.

56. Chris Morris, "Here Are the Best-Selling Video Games of the Past 25 Years," *Fortune*, 17 Jan. 2020, accessed 13 July 2021, https://fortune.com/2020/01/17/best-selling-video-games-past-25-years/.

57. Ruth Igielnik and Anna Brown, "Key Takeaways on American Guns and Gun Ownership," *Pew Research Center*, 22 June 2017, accessed 27 Apr. 2021, https://www.pewresearch.org/fact-tank/2017/06/22/key-takeaways-on-americans-views-of-guns-and-gun-ownership/.

58. Ibid.

59. Jeremy Bernfeld and Heath Druzin, "Gun Sales Continue to Boom during the Pandemic," *Guns and America*, 1 June 2020, accessed 19 Feb. 2021, https://gunsandamerica.org/story/20/06/01/gun-sales-continue-to-boom-during-the-pandemic/.

60. Theresa K. Vescio and Nathaniel E. C. Schermerhorn, "Hegemonic Masculinity Predicts 2016 and 2020 Voting and Candidate Evaluations," *Proceedings of the National Academy of Sciences of the United States of America*, 12 Jan. 2021, accessed 13 Aug. 2021, https://www.pnas.org/content/118/2/e2020589118.

61. Stephanie Savell and 5W Infographics, "This Map Shows Where in the World the U.S. Military Is Combatting Terrorism," *America at War: A Smithsonian Magazine Special Report*, Jan. 2019, accessed 5 Apr. 2022, https://www.smithsonianmag.com/history/map-shows-places-world-where-us-military-operates-180970997/.

62. "Budget of the United States Government," *GovInfo*, accessed 13 Feb. 2022, https://www.govinfo.gov/app/collection/budget/2022.

63. Ryan Browne, "With a Signature, Trump Brings Space Force into Being," *CNN*, 21 Dec. 2019, retrieved 3 Feb. 2021.

64. Joseph Biden, "Statement by the President on S. 1605, the National Defense Authorization Act for Fiscal Year 2022" (press release), White House, retrieved 28 Dec. 2021.

65. Kaamil Ahmed, "Ending Hunger by 2030 Would Cost $330 Bn, Study Finds," *The Guardian*, 13 Oct. 2020, accessed 27 Dec. 2020, https://www.theguardian.com/global-development/2020/oct/13/ending-world-hunger-by-2030-would-cost-330bn-study-finds.

66. John W. Chambers, ed., *The Oxford Guide to American Military History* (Oxford, UK: Oxford University Press, 1999).

67. Spencer C. Tucker, *U.S. Conflicts in the 21st Century: Afghanistan War, Iraq War, and the War on Terror* (Santa Barbara, CA: ABC-CLIO Publishing, 2015) 97.

68. Ibid., 98.

69. Institute for Economics & Peace. *Global Peace Index 2022: Measuring Peace in a Complex World*, Sydney, June 2022. http://visionofhumanity.org/resources, accessed 10 May 2023, https://www.visionofhumanity.org/maps/#/. Published annually, the Global Peace Index uses 23 indices, qualitative and quantitative, to generate its index. (Data gathered on 163 countries of approximately 200 total sovereign states.)

Chapter 12—The Consciousness Revolution: Rebirth

1. Yuval Noah Harari, *Sapiens: A Brief History of Humankind* (New York: HarperCollins Publishers, 2015) 153–54.

2. Terry Tempest Williams, *The Hour of Land: A Personal Topography of American's National Parks* (New York: Picador, 2016) 220.

3. United Nations Environment Programme, "Leading International Organizations Commit to Climate Action," 12 Dec. 2018, accessed 12 Sep. 2021, https://www.unenvironment.org/news-and-stories/press-release/leading-international-organizations-commit-climate-action.

4. Sailesh Rao, "Animal Agriculture Is the Leading Cause of Climate Change—A Position Paper," *Journal of Ecological Society* 32–33 (2020–2021): 155–67, accessed 30 Oct. 2021, https://3209a1b2-3bad-4874-bf51-8fc2702ffa6c.filesusr.com/ugd/8654c5_5bdb63b57c6b4abaa7f7b9041f7b8487.pdf.

5. "La Via Campesina (LVC): International Peasants' Movement," accessed 5 May 2022, https://viacampesina.org/en/international-peasants-voice/.

6. Roderick Nash, *The Rights of Nature: A History of Environmental Ethics* (Madison, WI: The University of Wisconsin Press, 1989) 5–7.

7. Roderick Nash, *Wilderness and the American Mind*, 3rd ed. (New Haven, CT: Yale University Press, 1982) 387–88.

8. "Black Lives Matter," accessed 7 Sep. 2021, https://blacklivesmatter.com/about/.

9. Paula M. Lantz, "The Tenets of Critical Race Theory Have a Long-Standing and Important Role in Population Health Science," *Milbank Quarterly Opinion*, 15 July 2021, accessed 21 Sep. 2021, doi:10.1599/mqop.2021.0714.

10. World Bank, "GDP per Capita, PPP (Current International $)," 2019, accessed 14 Aug. 2021, https://data.worldbank.org/indicator/NY.GDP.PCAP.PP.CD.

11. Amy Trauger and Jennifer L. Fluri, *Engendering Development: Capitalism and Inequality in the Global Economy* (Oxford, England: Routledge, 2019) 39–40.

12. Ariela Keysar and Juhem Navarro-Rivera, "A World of Atheism: Global Demographics," *The Oxford Handbook of Atheism*, ed. Stephen Bullivant and Michael Ruse (Oxford, UK: Oxford University Press, 2016).

13. Pew Research Center, "Religious Landscape Study: Belief in God," accessed 8 June 2021, https://www.pewresearch.org/religion/religious-landscape-study/belief-in-god/.

14. Pew Research Center, "Chapter 1: Importance of Religion and Religious Beliefs," 3 Nov. 2015, accessed 8 June 2021, https://www.pewresearch.org/religion/2015/11/03/chapter-1-importance-of-religion-and-religious-beliefs/.

15. Ibid.

16. Pew Research Center. "The Global Religious Landscape," 12 Dec. 2012, accessed 8 June 2021, https://www.pewresearch.org/religion/2012/12/18/global-religious-landscape-exec/.

17. Amy Trauger and Jennifer L. Fluri, *Engendering Development: Capitalism and Inequality in the Global Economy* (Oxford, England: Routledge, 2019) 148.

18. T. Parker-Pope, "Writing Your Way to Happiness," *The New York Times*, 19 Jan. 2015, accessed 12 July 2021, http://well.blogs.nytimes.com/2015/01/19/writing-your-way-to-happiness/?_r=4.

GLOSSARY

Altered States of Consciousness (ASC): Any experience of reality that is outside of a normal waking state, including conditions induced by psychoactive substances (drugs), fasting, repetitive music/drumming/dancing, brain damage, daydreaming, hyperventilation, sleep deprivation, etc.

Anthropogenic: Relating to, or resulting from, the influence of human beings on nature.

Anthropomorphic: The human tendency to view anything that is not essentially human as having human form or attributes.

BP, or years Before Present: Refers to when an event or time period occurred in terms of the approximate number of years before the "present day," which scholars generally accept should be set as AD 1950. This is due to the discovery of carbon-14 (radiocarbon) dating by American chemist Willard Libby in 1949. This year also predates large-scale atmospheric testing of nuclear weapons, which altered the global ratio of carbon-14 to carbon-12 and made radiocarbon dating of events that occurred afterwards less accurate.

Critical Race Theory (CRT): In brief, CRT holds that white people benefit from racism ingrained in US institutions, and further that the concept of race is a social construction, that racism is institutional, structural, and prevalent and creates numerous inequities in measures of health, education, and quality of life.

Egalitarianism: Social systems that provide equitable roles and resources to all members of society.

Environmental determinism: Similar to social Darwinism (which implied white supremacy), environmental determinism suggested that physical characteristics of the environment such as landforms and climate determine patterns of human cultural and societal development. Developed in the nineteenth century, it had a premise based on the theory of natural selection and biological evolution. It was replaced by possibilism in the mid-twentieth century.

Equality: Each person has, or is given, the same resources or opportunities.

Equity: Each person has different circumstances *but is allocated* the resources and opportunities needed to reach an equal outcome.

GLT, or Gendered Landscapes Theory: Asserts that geography shaped our minds and in turn shaped our cultures.

Hyper-Masculine Devolution: Indicates the era when the Hyper-Masculine Paradigm rose to power in western Asia, beginning roughly 6,000 BP, before expanding across the globe and extending into the present day.

HMP, or Hyper-Masculine Paradigm: Exaggerates masculinity and masculine pursuits to the exclusion of feminine and intermediary gendered traits. It includes general violence, racism, gender disparities, capitalism, social exclusion, ethnocentrism, environmental degradation, and animal exploitation, among many other elements.

Horticultural Revolution: The experimental garden-farming cultivation of cereal grasses between 11,000 and 12,000 BP, which became the dominant food-production strategy between 10,000 and 6,000 BP for most human populations.

Hypersensitive Egoic Agency Detection Structure (HEADS): A cognitive mutation in the human genome that emerged approximately 60,000 BP and may have marked the flowering of the human imagination and ego—the ability to conceptualize past and future, and distance.

Inequality: Each person has, or is given, different resources and opportunities and is treated differently.

Inequity: Each person has different circumstances; *some people are therefore discouraged or prevented* from attaining the same outcome as others. Inequities cause inequality.

Irrational Revolution: A profound genetic shift in human cognition that began to occur by 60,000 to 70,000 BP. It gave birth to humans' curiosity, imagination, and ability to represent reality in symbolic terms, including language and art, and the social constructions of gender and religion.

Matriarchy: A social system in which women hold primary economic, social, and political power.

Matriliny: The practice of tracing descent through the mother's line. Wealth and family name follow the mother's side of the family.

Matrilocal: When newly wedded couples live with the wife's side of the family.

Misogyny: Animosity shown toward women that often results in sexual harassment, violence, and institutional oppression.

Pangendered: Having or representing all genders at once, or certain genders at certain times under certain circumstances. This may refer to a person's perception of themself or of any environmental situation, including the natural environment. It may also refer to degrees of environmental quality that indicate both feminine and masculine characteristics of climate and biodiversity.

Paradigm: A mental framework of the world that's based on a central, unifying theme.

Patriarchy: A society that is politically, economically, socially, and institutionally dominated by men and masculine values.

Patriliny: The practice of tracing descent through the father's line. Wealth and family name follow the father's side of the family.

Patrilocal: When newly wedded couples live with the husband's side of the family.

Proto-Indo-European (PIE) languages: A language, or collection of related languages, that linguists theorize existed in Western Asia and Eastern Europe approximately 7500 BP. Many languages of Europe and South Asia developed from the PIE languages, including the Romance, Germanic, Balto-Slavic, Indo-Iranian, and other language families.

Social Darwinism: Various theories of the nineteenth century that claimed human cultures respond to the same forces as does biological evolution (in accordance with "survival of the fittest"). Therefore, certain people—and by extension, races of people—become powerful because they are innately better; a racial group that holds power is superior to those that do not. This theory implicitly supported racism, imperialism, and fascism. It was largely discredited after World War II due to its use in Nazi racial propaganda and eugenics. It was further discredited by Richard Lewontin's genetics research in the 1970s.

Socialization: The process by which the people, things, and events one experiences in one's earliest childhood shape how they view the world as an adult.

Therianthropic (art): Drawings or paintings of part-animal, part-human creatures, generally considered to be spirit beings.

Zoomorphic (art): Drawings or paintings of animal creatures, generally considered to be spirit beings.

Zoonoses: Diseases that are, or can be, transmitted from animals to humans.

INDEX

2001: A Space Odyssey, 49

Abram, (Abraham), in *Genesis,* 119
Abrams, Stacey, 161
absent referent, 145
Adam, in *Genesis,* 32, 33–35, 61, 131
Adams, Carol J., 145
Afghanistan, 144, 148
Africa
    East, 51, 66
    North, 141, 144
    West, 43, 80, 84, 110
    South Africa (country), 21, 28, 41,
        48, 60, 136
    sub-Saharan, 30, 65, 119
African Genesis: A Personal Investigation
    into the Animal Origins and Nature
    of Man, 49
agency detection device, 63–64
    See also Hypersensitive Egoic
        Agency Detection Structure
        (HEADS)
agnostics, 158
agriculture, 67, 72, 87, 101, 154
Agricultural Revolution, 72
    See also Horticultural Revolution

Ajna (Hindu), 75
    See also liminal qualities
Akkad, Akkadian, 115–117
Alaska, 56, 80, 136
The Alphabet Versus The Goddess
    (Shlain), 115
altered states of consciousness (ASC),
    62
Amazon Rainforest, 141
America
    Americas, 124
    Central, 84
    North, 83–84, 96, 124, 141
    South, 84, 96, 124
    United States of, 143, 146,
    See also Mesoamerica
Amnesty International, 157
Anatolia, 85, 113, 117
    See also Asia Minor; Turkey; and
        Turkic
animal(s)
    bones and animal-based societies,
        84–86
    carnivores, 50, 52–54, 84
    cruelty, 93, 112
    exploitation, 15, 21, 123

figurines, 60–61

as food, 44, 48, 50, 55–60

mythologically in *The Garden of Eden* and *The Genesis Tree*, 27–32

in pictographs and petroglyphs, 45–46

protein, 79, 109–110, 141, 145

rights, 159

slaughter, 91

social and cultural, 47–50

as having tools and language, 57–59

welfare, 154

See also rock art; therianthropic

Antarctica, 136

antelope, 91

Anthony, David, 92–93

anthropogenic, 136, 142, 153

anthropomorphic, anthropomorphism, anthropomorphized 45–46, 89–90, 106, 131

anti-racism, 159

Arab(s), 22, 118–119

Arabian Peninsula, 93, 110, 118

Aranda, 21

Arapesh, 21

archetype(s), archetypal

feminine, 32–35, 42, 76–77, 125, 129

in general, 5, 18, 23, 112, 151–152

Maiden in the Tower, 17

masculine, 42, 71–72, 76–77, 112, 120

Theft of Fire, 71–72

warrior, 123, 129

wise old man, 131

yin and yang, 76

Arctic National Wildlife Refuge, 136

Ardipithecus ramidus, Ardipithecus kadabba, 38

Ardrey, Robert, 49

armor, 93, 98, 101, 114, 117

art, 30, 32, 44, 45–46, 58–61, 63, 66, 98–99, 101, 152, 158

See also rock art; symbols

Aryan(s), 117–118

Asia

central, 21, 91, 93, 106–108, 110, 117

eastern, 39, 96

in general, 49, 65, 84, 124

south, 51, 93, 108

southwest, 84–85, 91, 95, 118, 144

west, 17, 100

Asia Minor, 90

Assyria(s), 118, 122

atheists, 158

Austrian Tyrol, 122

Atran, Scott, 64

Aurochs, 45, 91

Australia, 21, 65, 80, 108

Aboriginal, Aborigines, Indigenous, 82, 110–111

Aranda, 21

australopithecine(s), 38–39, 48–49

Australopithecus africanus, 48

axis mundi, 33, 88

Bachofen, J.J., 55, 111

Bactrian camels, 91

Baha'i, 119
Balkans, 113–114
Barrett, Justin, 63–64
Basque, 100
Bathonga, 21
Bavarian Alps, 122
Becker, Ernest, 64
    See also Terror Management
        Theory (TMT)
Bedouins, 118
Beyond The Hashtag,
    #BeyondTheHashtag, 156
Bible, biblical, 2, 18, 32–35, 76,
    117–121
Biden, Joe, 147
Black
    as in color, 13, 99–100
    as in people, 130, 153–156
Black Lives Matter, #BlackLivesMatter,
    16
blacksmith, blacksmithing, 98–101, 112
    See also metalworking; metallurgy
biocultural, bioculturally, 73–74, 137,
    149, 152
bipolar disorder, 61–62
    See also mood disorders
Black Girl Environmentalist, 153–154
Black Power movements, 130
Black Sea, 66
Bland, Sandra, 156
boar(s), 91, 98, 100–101
bonobos, 51–52, 63, 160,
Breuil, Abbé, 44–45
Britain, British Isles, 42, 93, 99, 112, 136
brass, 113
    See also metals
Brazil, 136

Brazilian Institute of Environment
    and Renewable Natural Resources
    (IBAMA), 153
bronze, 93, 113–114, 117, 119
    Bronze Age, 32, 80, 101–102, 113,
        118, 126, 160
    See also metals
brown bears, 91, 132
Brown, Michael, 156
Buhaya, 43
    See also Haya
bulls, 91, 113
Burke, Tarana, 156
Bush, George W., 147
Bushmen, 30
    See also Khoisan

calculus (tartar), 49
calories, 25, 84, 140
capitalism, capitalist, 95, 123, 131,
    137–139, 159
    anti-capitalism, 159
carbon, 113
carbon dioxide, 142, 153–154
CARE International, 157
caribou, 56, 109
carnivores, carnivorous, 43, 50–54,
    84
caste system, 93
Çatalhöyük, 90–92, 114
caves
    Blombos, 60
    in general, 28, 31, 44–46, 60, 63,
        79
    Kalyabagole, or The Cave That Ate
        The Bride, 79
    Lascaux, 45

Lwemboijole, or The Cave of God, 79
Skhul, 50
The Centers for Disease Control and
    Prevention, 124
Chalcolithic, 101
    See also Copper Age
chariots, 98, 101
Chauvin, Derek, 156
chauvinism, 112
chickens, 85
chimpanzees, 39, 51–52, 58–59, 160
China, 80, 106, 119, 141
Christ, Christian, Christianity,
    2, 32–33, 42, 71, 76, 89, 100,
    118–124, 158
    Catholicism, 123
    Orthodoxy, 123
    See also Jesus of Nazareth;
        monotheism
Chukchi, 55
civilization, civilized, 6, 71, 114, 131,
    135, 148
class, class struggle, 1, 7, 137–139,
    147, 152
climate change, 4, 56, 59–60, 83–85,
    114, 123, 153–154
Cognitive Revolution, 61
    See also Irrational Revolution;
        Great Leap Forward; Upper
        Paleolithic Revolution
colonial, colonialism, 12, 121–124
Colonial Era, Euro-American, 123
decolonization, 159
Colorado, 135–136
Leadville, 136
    See also wilderness
Colossians, Book of, 120

Columbus, Christopher, 124
commoditize, commodity, 117, 124, 145
continental drift, 159
cook food, 39, 82
copper, 101, 113–114
    Copper Age, Chalcolithic, 101
    See also metals
Corinthians, Book of, 120–121
corn (maize), 84, 86, 140
coronavirus (*See* COVID-19)
Cousteau, Jacques, 133
COVID-19, 124, 135, 147
cowboy, 104–105
cows, cattle, 21, 85, 91, 101, 108, 111, 141
creativity genes, 61–62
Critical Race Theory (CRT), 156–157
    See also race
Crusades, Christian, 122–123
cuneiform, 114–117
Czech, 45, 122

Daggett, Cara, 139
Dahl, Ophelia, 157–158
dairy, 86, 140–141, 154
Dart, Raymond, 48–49
Darwin, Charles, 49
Dead Sea, 93
dental caries (teeth cavities), 86
desertification, 141
Devil, 76, 91, 97–102, 111, 161
    See also Lucifer; Satan
discrimination, 123, 154–156
diet (human), 44, 53–54, 84–86, 109,
    140–141
    carbohydrates, 53, 109
    fats, 109
    proteins, 79, 109, 140–141, 145

diseases(s)
    in general, 44, 70, 85, 124, 158
    measles, 85, 124
    smallpox, 124
    typhoid, 124
    See also zoonoses
DNA (deoxyribonucleic acid), 19, 40,
    51, 62
    See also genetic
Doctors Without Borders (*Médecins
    Sans Frontières*), 157
Doctrine of Discovery, 124
Dogon, 43
domesticated (crops, animals), 84–85,
    91–92, 141
dopamine, 63
Dr. Seuss, 129–131
    See also The Lorax
Duke University, 160
Dum Diversas, papal bull, 124

Earth, 9–10, 18, 27, 30, 32–33, 41, 43, 59,
    69, 75, 77, 80, 93, 99–100, 102, 106,
    120, 125, 136, 139, 141, 153, 159
Ebola, 85
Ecumenical Council, 121
egalitarian, 19, 25, 54, 85, 90, 96, 108
Einstein, Albert, 126
ego, 20, 32, 48, 64, 72, 77, 80, 107,
    112, 123, 125, 151
    hypermasculine, 101, 120, 123, 126
    masculine, 111, 112
Egypt, 80, 106, 117, 122, 148,
ekwa root (*vigna frutescens*), 81
Ember, Carol, 54
emmer wheat, 90
Engels, Friedrich, 55

Epimetheus, 69–70, 72, 85
Enuma Elish, 116
environment
    human built, 80, 112
    human social surroundings, 23,
      56, 125
    natural, 2, 4, 15, 18, 23, 38,
      40–41, 49, 52, 67, 80, 90,
      108, 112, 125, 133, 136, 149,
      152, 153–154
environmental
    determinism, 22–23
    health, 140
    injustice (crises, destruction,
      racism), 4, 20–21, 95
    justice (health, sustainability,
      protections), 125, 131,
      139–140, 154, 159
    policies, 125, 157
    quality, 20, 25, 52, 54–55, 78, 85,
      114, 151
Equator, 40, 87, 135
Erasmus, 71
*Errementari: The Blacksmith and the
    Devil,* 100
Euphrates, 82, 114–115
    See also landscapes; rivers
Eurasia, 39, 83, 101, 152
Europe, 17, 21, 60, 65, 84, 91, 106,
    117, 119, 123
    eastern, 106
    northern, 39, 59
    southeastern, 111
Eve, in *Genesis,* 18, 32, 34–35, 61, 71,
    85, 131
The Everyday Sexism Project, 156
Ezekiel, Book of, 120

Far East, 86

fall of man, 86

Farmer, Paul, 157

female, 3, 9, 17, 21, 33, 50–52, 54–55,
    65, 71, 73–75, 77, 79, 81, 87, 93,
    104, 110, 112, 116–117, 119, 125,
    131–132, 143–145

female genital mutilation (FGM), 144

feminine, 3, 9–10, 12, 18, 21–22, 32–35,
    40–43, 47, 55–56, 65, 71–72, 73–77,
    79–80, 82, 85, 87–88, 91, 93,
    101–102, 104–105, 110–112, 115,
    116–117, 119–120, 122, 124–127,
    131–132, 143, 145–146, 152
    divine, sacred, 18, 72, 88, 101, 119
    See also gender

feminist, 3, 125, 145

fire, 29, 34, 44, 69, 71–72, 76–78,
    106, 112

firearm(s), 147
    See also weapons

fish, 1, 4, 58, 65

Floyd, George, 156

foragers, 21, 25, 30, 40, 54, 56, 81–82,
    84, 87, 109, 137, 143

Ford, John, 104

fossil fuels, 136, 137, 139, 153
    coal, 137, 153
    oil, petroleum, 137, 153
    natural gas, 137, 153
    nonrenewable energy, fuels, 137,
        139

foxes, 91

France, 44, 89
    Brittany, 112

Freud, Sigmund, 71, 89

frog, 91

Gabriel, the angel, 118

gammadion, 118
    See also swastika

Gandhi, Mohandas K. (Mahatma),
    142, 148

Ganges, Gangetic Plains, 66, 93, 117

The Garden of Eden, 31–34, 59, 65, 72,
    86, 99, 131, 161

Gatheru, Wanjiku "Wawa," 153–154

gazelles, 91

gender, gendered, 1–4, 12, 17, 20–22, 48,
    66, 74, 80, 87, 89, 95, 112, 120–121,
    123–124, 131, 133, 139, 144
    equality, 3, 154, 156
    feminine, 21, 34, 47, 65, 79, 124,
        132, 143, 145, 152, 157
    inequality (binaries, discrimination,
        etc.), 3, 7, 19–21, 47, 67, 72,
        120, 136, 143, 147, 156
    LGBTQIA+, 131
    masculine, 21, 47, 65, 87, 79, 106,
        116, 124, 143
    pangender (fluidity), 3, 22, 75
    pay-gap, 143
    transgender, 3, 75

gendered landscapes, spaces, 18, 20,
    22, 34, 41, 64–65, 76, 78–79, 80,
    106, 152

Gendered Landscapes Theory (GLT),
    10, 20, 23, 46, 56, 76, 80, 106,
    111, 133, 152

Genesis, Book of, 31–32, 34
    See also The Garden of Eden

The Genesis Tree, 27, 30–31, 33–34, 42,
    65, 71–72, 88, 99, 131, 161

genetic, 20, 30, 39, 47, 50–51, 62, 93,
    138, 151, 158

German, Germanic, Germany, 93, 99, 101, 148, 159

Gimbutas, Marija, 55, 91–92

Global Environmental Change, 139

Global War on Terror, 147

globalization, 159

goats, 85, 93, 111, 118, 135

Göbekli Tepe, 91

The God Gene, vesicular monoamine transporter 2 (VMAT2), 62

gods, male deities

    Allah, 119, 121

    El, El Shaddai, Elohim, 119

    Hephaestus, 69

    Marduk, 116–117

    Surya, 118

    trickster, 99

    Vishnu, 93

    Yahweh, 32–33, 35, 80, 117, 119–120

    Zeus, 69–71

goddesses, female deities

    Aphrodite, 96

    Athena, 69

    Mother, 10, 34, 38, 43, 80–81, 88, 91–92

    Tiamat, 116

gold, 81, 114

    See also metals

Goliath, 119

Goodall, Dr. Jane, 58

gorillas, 39, 51–52

gray wolves, 53, 91

Great Pacific Garbage Patch, 136

Great Leap Forward, 61

    See also Cognitive Revolution; Irrational Revolution; Upper Paleolithic Revolution

Great Plains, 141

Greece, 71, 99, 106, 117, 142

Green Man, 42, 131

greenhouse gases, 141–142, 153–154

    See also carbon dioxide; methane; nitrous oxide

Grimm's fairy tales, 5, 17

groundwater, 84, 141

The Guardian, 148

gun(s), 47–48, 142, 146–147

    See also weapons

Guthrie, Stewart, 63

Hacilar, 91

Hadith, 121–122

Hadza, 54

Hamer, Dean, 62

Hammurabi, King, 116

    See also Akkad

Harari, Yuval, 19, 151

Haya, 43, 79

healthcare, 154, 157–158

Heaven, 33, 75–76, 97, 99, 122, 158

Hebrew(s), Hebraic, 31, 118–119

Heifer International, 157

Hell, 75, 97, 99–100

herbivore(s), 52–53, 84

Herodotus, 111

Hesiod, 71

hierarchy, hierarchies, hierarchical, 3, 6, 19, 55, 67, 87, 93, 115, 117, 122, 138, 147, 157

hieros gamos, 17

Hindu Trimurti, 76

Hinduism, 33, 93

Hittites, 117, 119

Hodder, Ian, 101

Holy Trinity, 76

Homo erectus, 39

Homo naledi, 65

Homo sapiens, 25, 39, 41, 44–45, 60

Homo sapiens neandertalensis
    See Neandertals

hominid, 39

hominin(s), 38, 44, 48–49, 53

honor killings, 144

Hopi, 21

Horrobin, David, 61

horses, 45, 84, 91, 93, 98, 108

horticulture, horticultural, 72, 84–85,
    91, 111, 137

Horticultural Revolution, 35, 83, 101,
    137, 152
    See also Neolithic Revolution

Huang He, 82
    See also landscapes; rivers

human rights, 122, 159

human exceptionalism, 57
    See also speciesism

The Human Rights Campaign (HRC),
    154–155

The Humane Society of the United
    States (HSUS), 155

humors (as in physical elements,
    materials), 76, 106

Hungary, 101

hunter-gatherers, 25, 54
    See also foragers

hunt, hunter, hunting, 25, 43–45,
    48–49, 52, 54–56, 85, 87, 91, 104,
    108–109, 111, 142–143, 147, 152
    See also kill, killing

Husted, Bryan, 124–125

hydrocarbons, 153

    See also fossil fuels

Hyksos, 118

hyper-masculine
    behaviors (e.g., violence, control,
        domination), 114, 120, 125,
        137, 143
    ego, 101, 120, 123, 126
    empires, 21, 93
    gods, deities, 116
    immature, irresponsible, 72
    religions(s), 121
    social traits, 102
    See also Hyper-Masculine
        Paradigm (HMP); masculine

Hyper-Masculine Devolution, 75, 113,
    139, 155

Hyper-Masculine Paradigm (HMP),
    21, 46, 57, 72, 93, 95, 112, 120,
    127, 131, 132, 133, 138, 139, 147,
    152, 156, 161

Hyperactive Agency Detection Device
    (HADD), 63–64
    See also Hypersensitive Egoic
        Agency Detection Structure
        (HEADS)

Hypersensitive Egoic Agency
    Detection Structure (HEADS), 64,
    71, 73, 80, 89, 151

hysteria, 71

Ice Age, 20, 25, 59, 65, 82, 83, 137,
    151

India, 21, 93, 99, 106, 117

Indigenous, 10, 12, 30–31, 46, 80, 86,
    93, 96, 108–109, 124, 131, 153,
    158

Indo-European languages, 17, 93, 117

Germanic, 93
  Indo-Iranian, 93
  Proto-Indo-European, 93
  Romance, 93
  Slavic, 92–93
  See also PIE languages
industrialism, 132, 137
Industrial Revolution, 137
inequality, 16, 19, 21, 46, 70, 86, 95, 143
inequity, 138
influenza, 85
Ingenuity (NASA drone helicopter), 159
Inuit, 55, 109–110
Inupiat, 56
Inter Caetera, papal bull, 124
International Rescue Committee
  (IRC), 157
intersex, 75, 110
  See also liminal qualities; sex;
    third term(s)
iron, 43, 113, 117, 119
Iron Age, 80, 113, 119
See also metals
Irrational Revolution, 35, 57, 61, 80, 151
  See also Cognitive Revolution;
    Great Leap Forward; Upper
    Paleolithic Revolution
Islam, 2, 33, 119, 121
Israel, Israelite, 50, 119, 122
Ituri Rainforest, 56

Jack and the Beanstalk, 18
Jerusalem, 123
Jesus of Nazareth, 89, 120, 121
  See also Christ
jihads, radical Islamic, 123
Joshua, Book of, 119

Ju/'Hoansi, 54
Judaism, Jewish, Jews, 2, 32, 33, 71,
  119, 121, 123
Judges, Book of, 119
Jung, Carl, 32, 76, 80

Kaang, 27–29, 31, 33–34
Kalahari Desert, 30, 40, 56
Kenya, 131, 148
Khoisan, 21, 30–31, 34–35
Kilianstädten, Germany, 101
kill, killing
  biblical mandate, 119
  diseases, 124
  god killing goddess, 116
  humans killing humans or
    nonhuman animals, 45,
    48–50, 87, 91, 93, 109–110,
    142–144, 147, 149
  influence of masculine
    landscapes, 108
  nonhuman animals killing
    nonhuman animals, 38, 49,
    51–52, 58
  pollutions effects on animals
    (example in The Lorax), 132
  racial, 156
  See also push-pull factors
Kim, Jim Yong, 157
Kish, 116
  King of, 116
Kittay, Eva, 125
knife, knives, 105, 114, 145
  See also weapons
Köppen, Wladimir, 107–108, 159
  Köppen Climate Classification
    System, 107

Kubric, Stanley, 49

Kurgan(s), 92–93, 99, 108, 117, 118
    See also Scythians; Turks/Turkic
        Peoples; Yamnaya

La Via Campesina (LVC), 154

Lane, Belden, 106

landscapes
    arctic, 108
    circumpolar areas, 79, 106
    coast, coastlines, coastal areas, 11,
        65, 66, 67, 75, 79, 118
    desert(s), 40, 66, 74, 77, 79, 93,
        95, 104, 106, 107, 112, 114,
        118, 141, 152
    grassland(s), 42, 106, 141
    hill(s), 15, 37, 63, 100
    lake(s), 30, 37, 40, 65, 79, 83
    mountain(s), mount, 9, 37, 41,
        59, 66, 71–72, 74–75, 78, 79,
        80, 81, 90, 95, 104, 106–107,
        108, 112, 120, 125, 135, 136,
        138, 148
    ocean(s), 16, 65, 83, 79, 106, 136
    plains, 66, 67, 75, 79, 91, 93, 95,
        104, 106, 107, 112, 141
    polar, 107
    rainforest(s), 40, 56, 77, 141, 153
    river(s), 11, 40, 52, 56, 65, 66, 67,
        77, 79, 80, 82, 84, 105, 108,
        114, 116, 117
    savanna(s), 25, 38, 41, 75, 141
    steppes, 79, 91, 93, 106, 107
    subarctic, 108
    valley(s), 12, 25, 41, 67, 74, 75, 77,
        78, 79, 82, 84, 108, 112

language(s), language families,
    language groups, 17, 30, 58, 61,
    93, 99, 100, 118, 145
    See also symbols; writing; written
        languages

Lantz, Paula M., 157

lead, 114
    See also metals

Leroi-Gourhan, Andre, 89

Levant, 119

Levi-Strauss, Claude, 73, 115
    See also structuralism

LGBTQIA+, 131, 154
    See also gender

Lilith, 32, 120

liminal
    spaces, conditions, or qualities, 75,
        76, 79, 80, 100–101, 131, 152
    Hindu *Ajna*, 75
    See also third term(s)

livestock, 15, 72, 85, 86, 100–101,
    108, 111, 118, 124, 140–141, 154

Loess Plateau, 141

The Lorax, 76, 129–133, 161
    Once-ler, 76, 129–130, 132, 133
    Thneeds, 129
    Truffula, 129–133
    See also Seuss; trees

Lucifer, 122
    See also Devil; Satan

Lycians, 111

Maathai, Wangari, 161

magic, 14, 17, 18, 81
    hunting magic, 44–45
    magico-religious, 76

maloccluded teeth, malocclusions, 39, 86

Malwa, 21, 51

Maiden in the Tower, 17

   See also archetypes

male, as in human biological sex, 7, 21, 50, 55, 74, 85, 86, 111, 116–117, 122, 143, 145

   as allies, 155

   anthropomorphized landscapes, 65, 75

   behemoth, 33

   bonobos, 51

   chimpanzees, 51–52

   dualities, 33, 73–74, 110

   film actors, 104

   as gender, 3

   genitalia, 46

   gibbons, 51

   gods, deities, 34, 77, 80, 86, 93, 116–117

   gorillas, 50–51

   orangutan, 51

   power, dominance, violence, 2, 143, 145–146

   symbols, 78, 112

Malinowski, Bronislaw, 111

man, 13, 19, 27, 29, 31, 53, 61, 85, 97, 100, 110, 111, 117, 144

   archetypes, 131

   Black, 156

   conqueror, dominator, 125

   as Iron Man, 113

   as Man of Steel, 113

   as Man the Hunter, 45, 48, 49

   manly man, 104, 145

   as Marlboro Man, 104

   scriptural references, 119–122

manganese, 113

   See also metals

manic depression, 62

   See also mood disorders

Marduk, 116–117

   See also gods

Marlboro Man, 104

Mars

   god of war, 117

   planet, 159

Martin, Trayvon, 156

Mary Magdalene, 120

masculine

   archetypes, 42, 71–72, 75, 76, 78, 106, 112

   binaries, dualities, 3, 74, 75, 79, 124, 152

   constructive behaviors (e.g., initiative, order, strength), 9, 18, 20, 34, 42, 115

   destructive behaviors, (e.g., aggression, conquest, power, violence), 10, 72, 87, 112, 114, 117, 125, 152

   ego, 111, 112

   gods, deities, 33, 34, 77, 78, 80, 85, 93, 112

   insecurity, 18, 143

   landscapes, 10, 18, 20, 22, 32, 40–42, 54, 56, 65, 78–79, 80, 85, 103–105, 106, 108, 120, 126, 127, 152

   materials, 74

   religion(s), 33, 80, 112

   territorial, 12

   See also gender

mass murder, shootings, 101, 125

matriarchy, matriarchal, 55, 83, 87,
    91, 108
matrilineal, 21, 54, 85, 111
matrilocal, 21, 54
Mbuti, 56
McCormack, Todd, 157
measles, 85, 124
    See also diseases; zoonoses
meat
    as animals killed by nonhuman
        animals, 52
    as animals killed for food, 43, 48,
        53, 140–141
    as animals inferior to humans, 142
    as symbolic patricide, 142
    as symbolic matricide, male
        dominance, 143
    as symbolic misogyny, rape,
        commoditization, 145
    See also speciesism
Meatonomics, 141
Mediterranean Sea, region, 65, 66,
    110, 117, 118
megaliths, 112
Mellaart, James, 90, 91
menstrual, menstruation, 34, 43, 77,
    87, 89
mental, mind
    abstract, symbolic, 117
    afflictions, 62
    binary opposites, dualities, 73
    conditioned, 145
    content, 74, 103, 104
    ego, 77, 80
    and geography, 23
    perceptions, 56

    socialized patterns, 48
    structure, framework, 20, 103
    See also Theory of Mind
mentifact, 46
Merritt, D.L., 22
Mesoamerica, 96, 112
Mesopotamia, Mesopotamian(s), 32,
    114, 117
metal(s), 56, 74, 98, 113
    plows, 100
    tools, 97, 98, 99
    See also brass; bronze; copper;
        gold; iron; lead; manganese;
        molybdenum; silver; steel; tin;
        zinc
metalworking, 98
    metallurgy, 111
    metallurgical, 100, 118
    metallurgist, 113
    See also blacksmithing; tools
methane, 142, 154
MeToo, #MeToo, 156
Middle East, 22, 65, 108
Milano, Alyssa, 156
military
    budget, spending, 138, 147
    drones, 148
    campaigns, engagement, 114, 123,
        148
    violent video games, 146, 147
milk
    butterfly (from The Lorax), 131
    cow, 86, 131, 141
    dental caries (teeth cavities), 86
    as feminized protein, 145
    goat, 86

and osteoporosis, 86

water input, 141

Minangkabau, 21

misogyny, misogynistic, 21, 34, 112, 120–122, 158

Mitochondrial Eve, 40

molybdenum, 113

See also metals

monkeys

De Brazza'a, 131

patas, 131

monotheism(s), monotheistic, 2, 22, 100, 118, 119, 122

See also Baha'i; Christianity; Islam; Judaism; Parsi; Zoroastrianism

mood disorders, 61, 62

See also bipolar disorder; manic depression; unipolar depression; schizophrenia

moon

as Earth's satellite, 76, 77

as a god, 80

as a goddess, 77, 80, 88–89

in stories, myths, rituals, 13, 79, 80

symbolic of life, agriculture, 80, 89

symbolic of women and menstrual cycle, 77, 86, 87, 91

Moses, 116

Mount Everest, 80, 136

See also landscapes; mountains

Mount Toba eruption, 59

mountains

as symbols, archetypes, 71–72, 75, 78, 79, 107, 112, 125

as god(s), 80, 90

as goddess(es), 80

masculine, 71–72, 78, 79, 80, 95, 104, 106

physical landforms, 37, 41, 59, 66, 106, 108, 135

See also landscapes

Muhammed, The Prophet, 118–119

mumps, 85

See also diseases; zoonoses

murder, 101

Muslim, 121, 144

NASA, 159

Napier, John, 53

Nash, Roderick, 154

National Academy of Sciences, 147

National Geographic, 63, 140

National Outdoor Leadership School (NOLS), 87

Navajo, 21

Nazi, 22

Neandertals, Homo sapiens neandertalensis, 43, 44, 66

Neolithic, 80, 84, 87, 91, 101, 124

New Stone Age, 72

See also Horticultural Revolution

Neptune (god), 76

New Testament, 33, 118, 120, 121

Newman, Paul, 145

Nile

corridor, 65

river, 82, 116

valley, 112

See also landscapes, rivers

Nin, Anaïs, 103

Noah (biblical), 76

norepinephrine, 63

nuclear, atomic

   See weapons

Oceania, 124

Old Testament, 80, 118, 120

Old World, 113

Olmec, 33, 96

omnivore(s), omnivorous, 53, 84

On the Origin of Species, 49

onagers, 91

Oppenheimer, Robert, 93

orangutans, 52

Orrorin tugenensis, 38

Ortner, Sherry, 17

osteoporosis, 86

ovulate, 87

Oxfam International, 157

oxytocin, 63

Pacific Ocean, 106, 136

paleoanthropologists, 50

paleolithic

   feminine social traits, 127

   foragers, 84

   human populations, 45, 82

   Late Paleolithic, 106

   men, 50

   myths, 32

   religion, 158

   rock art, 44

   Upper Paleolithic Revolution, 61

   See also Cognitive Revolution;

      Irrational Revolution; Old

      Stone Age; rock art

Paltrow, Gwyneth, 156

Pandora's Box, 69–70

   feminine as scapegoat, 72, 85

   hope for future, 126, 132

   number three as liminal element,

      76

   story origins, 71

   thematic origins, 86, 99

Pangaea, 127, 159, 160, 161

pangendered

   human built environments, tools,

      43

   landscapes, 35, 37, 41–42, 67, 159

   liminal qualities, 75, 152

   matrix, 7, 42, 66

   planet, 161

   See also gender; liminal qualities;

      third term(s)

paradigm

   feminine, 127

   Hyper-Feminine Paradigm, 80

   as mental framework, 21

   See also Hyper-Masculine

      Paradigm (HMP)

Partners in Health, 157

pastoral, pastoralism, pastoralist(s),

   40, 54, 55, 72, 85, 100–101, 108,

   111, 118, 137, 152

paternity, 110–111, 152

patriarchal

   control, dominance, 7, 147

   cultures, 92–93, 110

   effects of literacy on brain, 115

   gods, 93, 123

   hunting societies, 142

   invaders, 55

   principles, 85, 117

   religions, 3

social orders, societies, 3, 73, 108, 118
socioeconomic structures, 20, 152
patriarchal gene, 19
patriarchy
    blended forms, 108
    and hierarchy, 2
    Hyper-Masculine Devolution, 113
    Kurgans, 108
    and pastoralism, 111
    as a society, 20
    targeting Critical Race Theory (CRT), 157
patricide, 142
patrilineal, 55, 85
patrilocal, 55
Paul, the apostle, (Saul), 121
people of color, 7, 15, 102, 133, 155, 158
People for the Ethical Treatment of Animals (PETA), 155
Perseverance (NASA rover), 159
Persia, 31, 118, 122
petroglyphs
    See rock art
petro-masculinity, 139
Pew Research Center, 158
phallic, 18, 43, 72, 112, 143
    See also male genitalia
pictographs, 45
    See also rock art
PIE languages, 93, 99, 118
    PIE-speaking peoples, 108
    See also Proto-Indo-European languages
pig(s), 85, 91, 122
pillars, 11, 112

plains
    See landscapes
Plains Indians, 74
plants, 32, 77, 83, 84, 109
    carbohydrates, 53
    as crops, 77, 82, 84
    as foraged foods, 25, 44, 77, 84, 108
    proteins, 109, 140
Polynesians, 82
polytheisms, 118, 119, 121
Pontic-Caspian Steppes, 91
Pope Alexander VI, 124
Pope Nicholas V, 124
Pope Urban II, 123
poor people, 15, 133, 139, 157
    poverty, 70, 138
Promised Land, 119
protein(s)
    deficiency, 140
    effects of animal versus plant sources on environment, 141
    as grasshoppers, 79
    percent from meat in US, 140
    limits, 109
    toxicity, 109
    feminized (eggs and cowmilk), 145
    plant sources, 140
    See also animals; plants
Proto-Indo-European Languages, 93
    See also Indo-European Languages; PIE languages
Puebloan Peoples, 74
    Southwest Native Americans, 21, 90
push-pull factors, 60
pyramid(s), 11, 112

Pyrenees, 100
Pythagoras, 142

Qur'an, 2, 33, 118–119, 121

race
    as categories of people, 123
    as hierarchy, 147, 152
    origins of word, 124
    perceptions of, 1, 2, 4, 156
    race theory, 6
    representations of, 5
    as a social construct, 157
    urban stratification, 139
    See also anti-racism; Critical Race
        Theory (CRT)
racial
    bias, 48
    bigotry, 95
    discrimination, 123
    diversity (or lack), 133
    hierarchy, 6, 22
    inequalities, 137, 156
    inequities, 139
    justice, 154
racism
    environmental, 4
    inequality, 21, 112
    institutional, 157
    origins, 123–124
    systemic, 157
rape
    animals, 125, 145
    humans, 145
    landscapes, 132
rapunzel
    plant, rampion flower, 5, 13, 14, 18

    See also stories, *Rapunzel*
Red Power movements, 130–131
Red Sea, 93
religion(s), 2, 3, 7, 20, 22, 58, 64, 66,
        89, 112, 152, 158
    See also monotheisms and specific
        religions
religious
    aid organizations, 158
    in art, 45, 58
    behaviors in nonhuman animals,
        58
    committees, 121
    conversion, 158
    institutions, 125
    intensification, 110
    law, 121
    specialists, 109
    species, 158
    in storytelling, 3, 5
Rice, Tamir, 156
rock art
    animals, 45–46
    humans, 30, 101
    therianthropic, 60
    tree, 30
Romanus Pontifex, papal bull, 124
Rumpelstiltskin, 18
    See also stories
Russia, 89, 99

Sahel, 141
Sahelanthropus tchadensis, 38
Sahlins, Marshal, 40
San, 28, 54, 56, 71
Sanday, Peggy, 86
Satan, 33, 34, 120

See also Devil; Lucifer

Sapiens: A Brief History of Humankind, 19, 151

Sargon the Great, Sargon of Akkad, 115–116, 118

   See also Akkad

Save the Children, 157

Scandinavia, Scandinavian, 117, 122

schizophrenia, schizoaffective disorder

   See also mood disorders

Scythian, 92

seal(s), the animal, 109, 110

Semite, Semitic, 93, 115, 118

Semple, Ellen Churchill, 22

serotonin, 63

serpent, 18, 32, 33, 34, 35

Seuss, Dr. (Theodore Seuss Geisel), 130, 131, 133

   See also The Lorax

sex

   hormones, 110

   trafficking, 145

sexual

   abuse, 156

   dimorphism, 50–51, 52

   intercourse, 110

The Sexual Politics of Meat: A Feminist-Vegetarian Critical Theory, 145

shamans, 46, 64, 109, 131

Shang, 96

Sharia Law, 121–122

sheep, 85, 93, 118

Shlain, Leonard, 115

silver, 114

   See also metals

Simon, David Robinson, 141

Sinai-Arabian Peninsula, 93, 110, 118

sky-god, 77, 91, 93, 99, 112, 116, 118

   See also god

Slovak, 122

Slovakia, 143

smallpox, 124

   See also diseases; zoonoses

The Smith and the Devil, 97, 99, 161

snake, 91

   See also serpent

social constructs, social construction, 64, 75, 138, 157, 177

   See also gender; race

   See also religion

social justice, 154, 177

   movements, 131

socialization, 46, 48, 144

socialized, 46, 48, 56, 64, 74, 103, 125, 139, 145

Sophocles, 114

sorrel (*oxalis pes-caprae*), 81

Southwest Asia, 84, 91, 144

Spain, 89

Spanish Inquisition, 122–123

spear(s), 58, 114, 119

spearheads, 101

speciesism, 57, 142

spiritual, 3, 33, 35, 75, 91, 112, 123, 143

St. Helena, 136

steeples, 112

Stein, Howard, 65

steppes, 79, 91, 93, 106, 107

   Pontic-Caspian Steppes, 91

   See also landscapes

Stone Age, 32, 72, 160

   See also neolithic; paleolithic

Stonehenge, 112

stories, 1, 16, 60, 83
    binaries, dualities, 18, 76
    creation myths, 31, 32, 34, 86
    egalitarian sociopolitical
        structures, 2–5
    geographic elements, 23
    hierarchical sociopolitical
        structures, 2–3, 7, 66, 122
    morals, 2, 5, 18, 130, 160–161
    self-awareness, 32
    symbolic contents, 76, 89, 122
    The Garden of Eden, 31–32, 33,
        34–35, 59, 65, 71, 72, 86, 99,
        117, 131, 161
    The Genesis Tree, 27, 30, 31, 33, 34,
        42, 71, 72, 88, 99, 131, 161
    Jack and the Beanstalk, 18
    The Lorax, 76, 129–131, 133, 161
    Pandora's Box, 69, 71, 86, 99, 132
    Rapunzel, 5–6, 13, 15, 16, 17, 23
    The Smith and the Devil, 97, 99,
        161
strontium, 84
structuralism, 73
Sumer, Sumerians, 80, 114, 115, 117
Surya, 118
    See also gods
swastika, 118
swords, 101, 114
symbol(s)
    of consciousness, 32
    in creation myths, 7, 31, 32, 66
    female, 77, 43
    feminine, 3234, 72, 77, 91, 101, 125
    gendered, 43, 76, 78
    industrialism, 132
    gods, 78

goddesses, 77
    of landscapes, 32, 41, 73, 76, 78
    liminal, 33
    male, 78, 43
    masculine, 72, 78
    meat as female body, 145
    sun, 117–118
    swastika, 118
    written languages, 114
symbolic behavior(s), 44, 58, 59, 63
    human language, 58, 61, 145

Talmud, 32, 33
Taoism
    yin and yang, 76
    See also archetypes
teeth cavities
    See dental caries
temple(s), 11, 112
Terror Management Theory (TMT), 64
terrorist, terrorism, 50, 101
Theft of Fire, 71
    See also archetypes
Theory of Mind, 63
therianthropic, 35, 60, 131
third term(s), 75
    See also liminal
thneeds, 129
Thurman, Uma, 156
Tigris, 82, 114
    See also landscapes; rivers
Timothy, Book of, 120
tin, 113, 114
    See also metals
titan(s), 69
    Epimetheus, 69–70, 72, 85
    Prometheus, 69, 71, 72

Tolle, Eckhart, 123
tools
    bone, 48, 49
    gendered, 74, 100
    human production of, 57, 58
    metal, 98, 48, 56, 97, 98, 99
    nonhuman animal tools, 51, 58
    olhuabyo, 43
    stone, 72, 38, 48, 56, 60, 74
    as symbolic behavior, 63
    technology as, 159
    as weapons, 48, 49
    wood, 38
Torah, 2, 118
totemic, 110–111
tower(s)
    archetype, 17, 18, 23
    in stories, 14, 129
trance states, 62
    See also altered states of
        consciousness (ASC)
transgender, 3, 75
    See also gender; liminal qualities;
        third term(s)
trees
    anthropomorphized, 89
    Ashwatta Tree of Life, 33
    Bodhi Tree of Enlightenment, 33
    central/sacred tree motifs, 30, 31,
        32, 33, 34, 42, 43, 72
    gendered, 35, 42, 43, 72
    Great/Central Tree, Khoisan, 27,
        28, 29, 30, 31, 34, 42, 65, 71,
        72, 88, 99
    and human evolution, 37, 38, 54
    in landscapes, 42
    as nonhuman animal tools, 58

    in stories, 13, 27, 42, 99
    Tree of Knowledge, 33, 34, 72
    Tree of Life, 33, 34, 72, 88
    Tree of Immortality, 33
    Truffula trees, 129–130, 131, 132,
        133
    Yggdrasil Tree, 33
treeline, 135–136
triangular slave trade, 123
trickle-down economics, 138
trilithons, 112
    See also megaliths, Stonehenge
Trinity Site, NM (nuclear bomb), 93
Tristan de Cunha, 136
Trobriand Islanders, 111
trophies, 143
Trump, Donald, 147
tuberculosis, 85
    See also diseases; zoonoses
Thunberg, Greta, 153
Turkey, 85, 90, 99
    Turkic, 92–93
Tuttle, Will, 142
typhoid, 124
    See also diseases; zoonoses

unipolar depression, 62
    See also mood disorders
United Nations, 139
    United Nations Children's Fund
        (UNICEF), 157
    UN Environmental Programme
        (UNEP), 153
    UN Food and Agricultural
        Organization (FAO), 140
    UN Intergovernmental Panel on
        Climate Change (IPCC), 153

Upper Paleolithic Revolution, 61
  See also Cognitive Revolution;
    Great Leap Forward; Irrational
    Revolution
urban, 37, 38, 135, 138, 154
Utopia, 15–16

valley(s), 12, 25, 41, 67, 74, 75,
    77–79, 82, 84, 108, 112
  See also landscapes
vegan(s), 52, 154
veganism, 154
Vegan Society, 154
vegetarian, 53, 145, 154
Venus of Laussel, 88–89
video game(s), 146–147
Vietnam War, 46, 130
violence
    alleviating violence, 154–156
    against nature, 136–137, 149
    animal cruelty, 112, 136–137
    Bronze Age, 113
    chimpanzees, 52
    genetic cause, human nature, 19,
        49, 101–102, 138, 151, 152
    gods/religions of war, 112, 122
    guns, 146–147
    hypermasculine ego, 3, 21, 101,
        112, 113, 122, 125, 138
    Iron Age, 113
    idioms, 113
    landscapes, 55, 112
    misogyny, 21, 112, 122
    murder, mass shootings, 101, 125
    pastoralism, 101
    neolithic, 19, 101–102
    paleolithic, 44

    racial, 21, 112, 156
    sex or gender differences, 19
    sexual, 3, 21, 156
    warfare, 122, 147–148
    See also hunting; guns; racism;
        sexual abuse; terrorism; video
        games; war
Vishnu, 93
von Franz, Marie-Louise, 32

war, warfare
    as business, 123
    chimpanzees, 52
    Global War on terror, 147
    gods of, 19, 117
    spread in twenty-first century, 147
    tools of, 98
    Vietnam War, 46, 130–131
    World War I, 49
    World War II, 22
water
    archetypal, unconscious, inner
        Self, 77
    binaries, dualities, 74, 75, 76
    caves, 79
    crops, 77, 82
    coasts, liminal areas, 75
    environmental quality, 20
    feminine, 10, 32, 76–77, 78, 82,
        112
    food, 27
    forests, 82
    freshwater availability, use,
        141–142
    goddesses, 10
    livestock, 111, 118, 141-142
    metallurgy, 98

metaphor, 3, 4, 133
oceans, 16, 65, 83, 106, 136
   polluted, 139
   ritual act, 109
   rivers, streams, 15, 77, 27
   safety, 37
   valleys, 77, 78
   waterholes, 42
   water rights, 154
   See also landscapes
weapon(s), weaponry
   bone, 49
   bow (and arrows), 142
   bronze, 93, 114, 117, 119
   firearm(s), 147
   gun(s), 47, 48, 142, 146, 147
   iron, 119
   knife, knives, 105, 114, 145
   metal, 56, 98
   nuclear, atomic, 93, 123, 126
   phallic, sexual symbolism, 143
   stone, 91
   traps, 142
Wegener, Alfred, 159
Weinstein, Harvey, 156
white
   men, 19, 125, 137, 139, 155, 157
   patriarchy, 157
   people, 153, 155–157
   savior complex, 157
   supremacy, 22, 156–157
   women, 7, 132, 139, 155, 156,
      157
White, Tom, 157
wilderness, 6, 18, 38, 87, 104, 106,
   136, 153
   Mount Massive Wilderness, 136

Weminuche Wilderness, 135
wild
   animals, 15, 85, 142
   binary, archetype, 6, 64, 131
   boars, 91, 100
   landscapes, 11, 64, 131, 153
   plants, 81
   woman, 122
   See also wilderness
wildlife, 132, 140
Williams, Terry Tempest, 153
witch(es), 13–15, 17, 18, 123
witchcraft, 100
woman, women
   in art, 46, 89
   divine feminine, 88
   economic contributions, 54, 55,
      109
   female genital mutilation (FGM),
      144
   first woman, 34–35, 119, 120
   gendered divisions of labor,
      horticulture, 43, 74, 81, 84,
      87, 111
   genetic ancestors, 40
   inequalities, 6, 15, 101, 104, 105,
      109, 112, 122, 132, 139,
      143–144, 146
   maturation, 34
   menstruation, 43, 77, 86–87
   metaphors, 6, 34, 89, 125, 145
   misogyny, 21
   movements for equality, 133,
      154–156
   objectification, 19, 104, 105, 117,
      132, 157
   ovulation, 87

portrayed with enmity, as
villainous, 17, 35, 71, 72, 91,
102, 126
in power, 19, 86, 87, 114
pregnancy, life, reproduction,
110–11
in scripture, 120, 121, 122
sexist norms, 7, 43–44, 86, 112,
125, 139, 157
sexual dimorphism, 50
sexually gendered spaces, 21
social protections, 121
societies, 17
in stories, 13, 14, 27, 31, 32, 69,
79, 100, 115, 119, 120, 122
as subservient, inferior, 121, 122,
126, 132, 144, 146
Woodward, Joanne, 145
World Economic Forum, 144
World Meteorological Organization
(WMO), 153
The World Peace Diet, 142
writing, 5, 18, 99, 114–115, 118, 121,
130, 176
See also cuneiform; languages(s);
symbols

Xia, 96
xenophobic, 19, 102

Y-chromosome Adam, 40
Yahweh, 32, 33, 35, 80, 117, 119–120
Yamnaya, 92
See also Kurgans; Scythians; Turkic
Yellowstone National Park, 136
Younger Dryas (*Dryas octopetala*), 83,
84, 91, 152

Zeus, 69, 70, 71
ziggurats, 112
zika, 85
Zimmerman, George, 156
zinc, 113
See also metals
zoomorphic, 35
zoonoses, zoonotic diseases, 85, 124
Zoroaster, Zarathustra, 118
Zoroastrianism, Parsi, 33, 118
See also monotheism

ABOUT THE AUTHOR

 **BILL HATCHER** has instructed geography and anthropology courses since 1994, including: Peace Corps Tanzania, Alaska Pacific University, Matanuska-Susitna College, Blackburn University, National Outdoor Leadership School, Colorado Mountain College, Trinidad State College, and Pikes Peak State College. As an author, he has written for *Colorado Central* magazine, appeared on local radio shows, and has previously written two books published by Lantern: *The Marble Room* investigates religion and racism, and *Principles of Flight* examines the intersections of sexism, animal cruelty, and religious jingoism. (*Principles* was judged a finalist in the 2018 National Indie Excellence Awards in Social and Political Change.) Bill now teaches in southern Colorado, where he lives with his wife, Kim.

ABOUT THE PUBLISHER

LANTERN PUBLISHING & MEDIA was founded in 2020 to follow and expand on the legacy of Lantern Books—a publishing company started in 1999 on the principles of living with a greater depth and commitment to the preservation of the natural world. Like its predecessor, Lantern Publishing & Media produces books on animal advocacy, veganism, religion, social justice, humane education, psychology, family therapy, and recovery. Lantern is dedicated to printing in the United States on recycled paper and saving resources in our day-to-day operations. Our titles are also available as ebooks and audiobooks.

To catch up on Lantern's publishing program, visit us at www.lanternpm.org.

facebook.com/lanternpm
instagram.com/lanternpm
twitter.com/lanternpm